T0314070

BEYOND THE FRUITED PLAIN

Beyond the Fruited Plain

FOOD AND AGRICULTURE IN U.S. LITERATURE, 1850–1905

Kathryn Cornell Dolan

University of Nebraska Press | Lincoln and London

Part of chapter 3 originally appeared in "Thoreau's
'Grossest Groceries': Dietary Reform in *Walden* and *Wild
Fruits*," *ESQ: A Journal of the American Renaissance* 56,
no. 2 (Summer 2010): 162–91. Copyright 1984 by the
Board of Regents of Washington State University. Part
of chapter 5 originally appeared in "A 'Mighty World-
Force': Wheat as a Natural Corrective in Norris," 19, no. 2
(Spring 2012): 295–316, by permission of *Interdisciplinary
Studies in Literature and Environment*. Part of chapter
5 originally appeared in "Sinks to Death in a Grain
Pit," BANC MSSS C-H80, Frank Norris collection
of papers: and related material, circa 1889–1930, the
Bancroft Library, University of California, Berkeley.

Publication of this volume was assisted by The Virginia
Faulkner Fund, established in memory of Virginia Faulkner,
editor in chief of the University of Nebraska Press.

Library of Congress Cataloging-in-Publication Data
Dolan, Kathryn Cornell.
Beyond the fruited plain: food and agriculture in U.S.
literature, 1850–1905 / Kathryn Cornell Dolan.
pages   cm
Includes bibliographical references and index.
ISBN 978-0-8032-4988-2 (hardback: alk. paper)
ISBN 978-0-8032-6944-6 (epub)
ISBN 978-0-8032-6943-9 (pdf)
ISBN 978-0-8032-6945-3 (mobi) 1. American literature—
19th century—History and criticism. 2. Agriculture
in literature. 3. Food in literature. 4. Literature and
globalization. 5. Ecocriticism—United States. I. Title.
PS217.A38D65 2014   810.9'36—dc23
2014013500

Set in Garamond Premier by Renni Johnson.
Designed by N. Putens.

For my parents, Doug and Sandy Dolan, this book is dedicated with love. Thanks for your boundless ability to go with the flow and love me no matter what.

CONTENTS

ACKNOWLEDGMENTS

Beyond the Fruited Plain spans the width and breadth of the expanding United States of the nineteenth century. Fittingly, my own career has traveled widely across the United States as well, from California to Florida and Missouri, with regular visits to New York and Massachusetts. In my writing process, life has followed literature. This breadth of experience has left me with an extensive list of mentors and colleagues to thank.

First, I want to express my gratitude to my professors, advisors, and employers at University of California–Santa Barbara. I owe my largest debts to my dissertation advisor, Stephanie LeMenager, and my employer at the Thoreau Edition, Elizabeth Witherell, for being my tireless champions throughout the PhD and book-writing process. I also want to thank Giles Gunn, Candace Waid, Patricia Fumerton, Alan Liu, Mark Maslan, Chris Newfield, Rita Raley, and Emily Zinn for their support throughout the PhD process.

The Graduate School and English Department at the University of South Florida provided me with an invaluable opportunity for research. The Provost's Postdoctoral Scholars in the Humanities and Social Sciences Program was a wonderful, relatively rare, and therefore much appreciated resource for interdisciplinary work. I had the privilege to work with colleagues in the Departments of Anthropology, Communications, History, Political Science, and Sociology, as well as in English. Thanks to Karen Liller, Hunt Hawkins, Eric Andersen, Eric Hoyer, and especially, Monica Giraldo Hernandez for this opportunity.

My colleagues, students, and friends at Missouri University of Science and Technology have charmed me and made me feel welcome at my new home with their intellectual fellowship. Thanks especially to Kristine Swenson, Linda Sands, Anne Cotterill, Kate Drowne, Kathryn Northcut, Daniel Reardon, and the rest of the department for your encouragement. In the community, thanks to Sundhya Gelles, Dianna Morrison, and Cynthia Riley for showing me around the region.

I am grateful to Kristen Elias Rowley and Kathryn Owens, my editors at University of Nebraska Press, as well as to the anonymous reviewers, copyeditors, and indexers. In addition, I received nothing but kind assistance from the librarians at the Bancroft Library at University of California–Berkeley, both at the Frank Norris Collection and the Mark Twain Papers. In addition, I appreciate the feedback from my colleagues who have heard various parts of this manuscript at conferences.

I have had the wonderful support from all my much-loved friends who have tolerated and welcomed draft reading, dinner dates, movie nights, and general companionship. Thank you Shanna Salinas, Sarah Hirsch, Aimee Woznick, Rachel Mann, Anne Cong-Huygen, Summer Star, Katrina Hanna, Manoucheka Celeste, Deepanwita Dasgupta, Jennifer Gully, Koonyong Kim, John Barnshaw, and Karen Griener. Also, thanks to Jennifer Berkman, Raidis Maypa, and Wendy Norberg for being my homes away from home throughout this process.

I wouldn't have been able to complete this project without the encouragement, trust, and love of my family. Thanks to Doug, Sandy, Kevin, John, Kristi, and Olivia for putting up with me throughout this process. And, finally, like so many academics before me, I want to thank my cat-mascots, Aussie and Missy. Keep sunning yourselves while I write!

BEYOND THE FRUITED PLAIN

INTRODUCTION

Fruits of Expansion

It will not be doubted, that with reference either to individual, or National Welfare, Agriculture is of primary importance. In proportion as Nations advance in population, and other circumstances of maturity, this truth becomes more apparent; and renders the cultivation of the Soil more and more, an object of public patronage.

GEORGE WASHINGTON, "National Board of Agriculture," 41

In his last annual congressional address on December 7, 1796, President George Washington frames the early and lasting connection between agriculture and the United States. He joins the "circumstances of maturity" to the "advance in population" he foretells. Washington continues to discuss the need for developing U.S. agriculture in his personal correspondence. In a letter to Arthur Young, who would become the secretary of the British Board of Agriculture, Washington describes agriculture as "amongst the most favourite amusements of my life."[1] He is therefore understandably worried that the U.S. agricultural system of the era "is as unproductive to the practitioners as it is ruinous to the land-holders. Yet is pertinaciously adhered to"; he further argues, "To pursue a course of husbandry which is altogether different and new to the gazing multitude, ever averse to novelty in matters of this sort, and much attached to their old customs, requires resolution; and without a good practical guide, may be dangerous."[2] As early as the eighteenth century, then, the first U.S. president sought a new form of agriculture at the national level. While Thomas Jefferson would become more widely known for his agrarian focus through his works like *Notes on the State of Virginia*, the issue of agriculture and politics, and even a nascent form of U.S. expansionism, was developed as early as George Washington's presidency.

Thomas Jefferson, on the other hand, contributed to the nation and its agriculture by making one of the largest expansionist transactions of the nation's history during his presidency. The Louisiana Purchase of 1803 added approximately 529 million acres to the nation, doubling its size at that time. These newly incorporated lands were to be used as a buffer against European aggression and a start to the agricultural expansion of the United States. In a July 18, 1804, letter to his Italian friend Philip Mazzei, Jefferson focuses on the larger agrarian potential and military advantage following the nation's growth into the previously French territory. He commends, "The acquisition of Louisiana, besides doubling our extent, and trebling our quantity of fertile country, is of incalculable value, as relieving us from the danger of war."[3] While calling the Louisiana Purchase one of "incalculable value," Jefferson ironically calculates the increase of land in terms of both territorial acquisition and agricultural production. He argues for a significant agricultural focus as well as a militaristic one in order to establish a strong United States. Like Washington, Jefferson joins national politics and agriculture during the course of his presidency. Two of the country's earliest leaders, therefore, set the tone for the nation's development through the nineteenth century, which in turn has had its effects felt into the twenty-first century. U.S. agriculture became—and perhaps always must be—of great cultural and political significance, and it remained so during the nation's most aggressively expansionist period of the second half of the nineteenth century.[4]

The nation's founding fathers discussed a form of agriculture connected to land growth in a way that would be developed more fully throughout the nineteenth century. For much of the century, the United States aggressively expanded west, involving itself in wars and other political maneuverings against nations and peoples so as to obtain greater expanses of territory that were converted into large and productive farms. During this time the United States developed into a global power, able to do so largely on the basis of its agricultural strength. Cultural critics and reformers challenged these changes at the time of their occurrence. In *Beyond the Fruited Plain*, I study the cultural work of five nineteenth-century authors as they suggest reforms to early agricultural expansion—what I call agri-expansion—in their literature. Moreover, the actions and attitudes of the time put into motion developments that have resulted in the industrialized, globalized, and destructive agribusinesses of the early twenty-first century. During this period, globalization and agriculture continue to be recognized in their cultural significance. Writers and activists promote organic farming, farmers' markets, and local farming movements. Such criticisms of modern agriculture are actually the most recent in the history of food and agricultural reforms, having predecessors in the reform literature written during the nineteenth century. As the nation expanded, developments like industrialization, urbanization, and new technologies affected the way people grew food. Policy makers and cultural critics debated the best way to produce food and wealth for an expanding population that filled larger territories. They sought agricultural methods to take advantage of the land recently obtained through expansion, as well as developing technologies that made each acre of farmland increasingly productive. As agriculture intensified, and people left their farms for the cities, the agrarian dream of the founding fathers was largely lost. Indeed, the reform literature of the time worked to counter what its authors regarded as dangerous agricultural policies as the nation expanded and industrialized its food production during the nineteenth century.

In *Beyond the Fruited Plain*, I employ theories of agricultural studies, eco-criticism, and globalization to examine U.S. literature as symbolic of, and resistant to, the national project from the mid-nineteenth century through the aftermath of the Spanish-American War, the era Walter LaFeber names "The New Empire," one that is concurrently the time of a major upheaval in the nation's agriculture. During this era expansionistic politics and agriculture are historically connected. I focus on the issue of food production in the works of Herman Melville, Henry David Thoreau, Harriet Beecher Stowe, Mark Twain, and Frank Norris, as their texts evaluate U.S. agri-expansion and its consequences on the individual and national levels, as well as suggest reforms to this growth. For these authors, literature is a necessary tool to assess various forms of nineteenth-century U.S. expansion, and they often turn to farm-based imagery and praxis in their literary works. I argue that these authors use their literature to imagine alternatives to national policies that prefigure twenty-first-century concerns with issues of globalization, resource depletion, food security, and the relation of industrial agriculture to pollution, disease, and climate change. Literature is a foundational site of cultural production, as a nation defines itself through its literary works. Moreover, a nation's cuisine and food production are similarly important markers of identity. Therefore, the intersection of agriculture and literature becomes a critical place for understanding both nineteenth-century U.S. culture as well as central elements of U.S. culture in the twenty-first century.

In my work I engage with an established tradition of U.S. agrarian literary studies, as works with a focus on husbandry inform discussions of nineteenth-century literature following the tradition of Leo Marx and Raymond Williams. In more recent criticism, much work is being done in literary channels that refer to the writings of Wendell Berry and Aldo Leopold. Discussions of agriculture often focus on the issues of industrialization and modernization and their impact on farmers. The agrarian style of agriculture is one of the markers of U.S. culture: the wide-open spaces of the prairies and the middle ground of the individual garden are foundational national images. As opposed to an agrarian study, though, I discuss agriculture more broadly, using a less idyllic and more industrial, extractive, and speculative model. This reading of U.S. agriculture parallels and is in many ways causal for the further expansion of the nation in terms of land and population growth. I apply the term "agriculture" to indicate any aspect of the production of food and other basic consumables, like wheat, dairy products, or sugar. Agriculture incorporates husbandry, harvesting, and other forms of food production; it does not, however, include the processing or marketing of foods after they have been produced. By "expansion" I refer to both the physical and economic forms, as witnessed throughout the mid-to-late nineteenth century. Works on economic and territorial expansion in the nation's history, as well as their representations in literature, are well established in literary criticism. Henry Nash Smith, Annette Kolodny, and Richard Slotkin have provided useful readings of U.S. expansion, for example.[5] The nation is particularly expansionist from roughly the time of "manifest destiny" through the Spanish-American War, after which the nation's boundaries looked much as they would into the twenty-first century. During this period of expansion, the United States turned toward more aggressive—even bloody—methods to acquire new lands that were often developed into large-scale farms. Moreover, historians and critics note the long history of U.S. industry influencing food production, as opposed to an idealized domestic production involving small farms and large kitchens. I argue that nineteenth-century critics warned of potential agricultural consequences of the nation's expansionist and industrializing actions in a similar manner.[6] I expand my focus to the underlying causes of this shift in food production by studying the correlation between nineteenth-century expansion and agriculture, showing that the theme of large-scale food production was used to promote the nation's development into a global power.[7]

Part of the nation's agri-expansionism involved global trade. Therefore, I also apply globalization studies to my discussion of nineteenth-century U.S. agriculture and literature. I study the period following Immanuel Wallerstein's "modern world-systems" and preceding the contemporary, postmodern era; these eras are dependent on and built upon each other. While global patterns in economics and politics existed before the nineteenth century and have exploded in an unprecedented way since World War II, the period I discuss occurs at a critical fulcrum of U.S. development into a global power, largely owing to the nation's focus on agri-expansion. As described by Malcolm Waters, the concept of globalization is centered on trade and culture, as in the case of the United States as it established itself as the breadbasket of the world in the nineteenth century. Furthermore, this globalization implies a corresponding domestic project—often connected to localization movements—seen in the works of the authors discussed herein, who argue against the depersonalizing element of a nineteenth-century form of globalization.[8] In addition, without making an exceptionalist argument about the United States, the version of U.S. economic and territorial expansion during the nineteenth century was noticeably different than the imperialism of contemporary European nations or other American nations of previous centuries. The United States has always been uniquely connected economically to its growth into a global power, according to Michael Hardt and Antonio Negri.[9] While nineteenth-century U.S. imperialism is not the globalism of Hardt and Negri's "Empire" of the late twentieth century, many of the same impulses that guide the later were already present in the earlier period. In the nineteenth century, the United States was engaged in a form of "continuous hybridization" in terms of economics, politics, and agriculture, one that changed the national body into an imperial power by the end of the century.[10] Manfred Steger adds that the United States has always fluctuated between acting as a "soft" and "hard" power over the history of its global expansion.[11] As policy makers tried to move the nation toward an economic form of industrialized agriculture, critics responded by representing the victims of this kind of expansion as well as by presenting agricultural alternatives at the domestic level.

Discussions of agriculture and literature in the nineteenth century often focus on the farm's effects on the environment, its use and potential abuse of natural resources. Issues of environmentalism are embedded within those of agriculture therefore. Lawrence Buell describes the developing theory about environmental criticism as one in which "bioregionalists" argue for greater self-sufficiency and sustainability regarding the use of resources; this argument can be usefully applied to nineteenth-century authors as well.[12] While many modern environmentalists agree that by the end of the twentieth century, we had reached Bill McKibben's "end of nature," Buell observes that a "second nature"—"nature as re-processed by human labor"—had established itself already by the middle of the nineteenth century.[13] In addition, critics like Ulrich Beck, Ursula Heise, and Dana Phillips have contributed to a developing environmental criticism that has been usefully applied to nineteenth-century literature.[14] I agree that the trends dominating U.S. society in the postmodern era had their roots in the period analyzed by Karl Marx and the capitalism he criticized so powerfully. I maintain that cultural critics were not passive observers in the midst of the industrialization that predetermined much of what continues to be of concern in the twenty-first century. They were apprehensive about the consequences of the exploitation of people and land that made up a large part of the national project during that period—and their form of praxis was to write critically of and offer alternatives to that agri-expansion.

Idealized representations of domestic agriculture have been part of the national narrative since early in the nineteenth century, and they became more poignant as a nondomestic form of agriculture increased. In *Recollections of a Lifetime* (1856), Samuel Griswold Goodrich describes the life he remembers in a traditional New England village, before expansionism, industrialization, and general mechanization: "Nearly all the inhabitants of Ridgefield were farmers. . . . Even the persons not professionally devoted to agriculture, had each his farm, or at least his garden and home lot, with his pigs, poultry, and cattle."[15] In this village Goodrich's neighbors are all connected to farming; even those who are not self-described as farmers provide services for the professionals, while depending on their own kitchen-garden plots for much of their subsistence food. In many ways this represents the U.S. agrarian model, and this village farm life could easily be associated with Jefferson's concept of agrarianism. At this point, at least in the literature of the period, the expansionist politics of the midcentury and the second half of the nineteenth century are not yet overriding, and village life dominates the U.S. landscape. Moreover, Goodrich gives a description of a garden farm familiar to New England villages: "To the left was the garden, which in the productive season was a wilderness of onions, squashes, cucumbers, beets, parsnips, and currants, with the never-failing tansey for bitters, horseradish for seasoning, and fennel for keeping old women awake in church time."[16] This domestic description of a cornucopia of vegetables in the average New England farm is nostalgic in tone, contrasted to the changing agricultural model of the midcentury, when western farmers began to challenge this agrarian image.

Another version of the conflict between traditional small farms and the large farms of the U.S. frontier appears in Caroline Kirkland's memoir, *A New Home—Who'll Follow* (1839). In one passage Kirkland observes the resilience and pride of her hostess, who describes her life uncomplainingly: "Many's the day I've worked from sunrise till dark in the fields, gathering brush-heaps and burning stumps. But that's all over now; and we've got four times as much land as we ever should have owned in York state."[17] About this comment Kirkland's narrator thinks,

> I have since had occasion to observe that this forms a prominent and frequent theme of self-gratulation among the settlers in Michigan. The possession of a large number of acres is esteemed a great good, though it makes but little difference in the owner's mode of living. Comforts do not seem to abound in proportion to landed increase, but often, on the contrary, are really diminished for the sake of it; and the habit of selling out so frequently, makes that *home*-feeling which is so large an ingredient in happiness elsewhere, almost a nonentity in Michigan. The man who holds himself ready to accept the first advantageous offer, will not be very solicitous to provide those minor accommodations, which, though essential to domestic comfort, will not add to the moneyed value of his farm, which he considers merely an article of trade, and which he knows his successor will look upon in the same light.[18]

Kirkland's views complement those of Goodrich, privileging the lifestyle of small farmers and challenging pioneer farmers who are associated with growth and capitalism. Kirkland finds much to admire in the West of her experience. However, she wonders openly about the attitudes of western pioneers toward land and agricultural interests as a result of the nation's expansionism during this time.

Agriculture is the primary form of U.S. employment during this early period. U.S. agriculture remained relatively unchanged until industrialization: it was largely based on tradition and habit. The U.S. Industrial

Revolution closely followed the British, and the drastic economic changes involved in this revolution created a correspondingly dramatic shift in the nation's agricultural system. Joseph Schafer notes that the Industrial Revolution provided U.S. citizens with pistols, barbwire, windmills, and new machinery to help reap fields. In each case technical advances in agriculture became part of the narrative of westward expansion.[19] Over the nineteenth century, developments in agriculture expanded at the global level as well. In the second half of the nineteenth century, agricultural products became the nation's primary export, and trade in foodstuffs became a significant source of national wealth. The United States first successfully shipped beef to Britain in 1875 and by 1880 was shipping twelve thousand tons of beef to that nation annually. The United States also shipped 28 million bushels of wheat globally during the 1860s, this number growing to 140 million bushels by the 1880s. Between 1800 and 1913, world trade in foodstuffs grew twenty-five times greater than its original number; of this, three-quarters of that trade was between Europe, North America, and Oceania.[20] In addition, the United States held a strong trading presence in the Atlantic and South Pacific; U.S. Americans acquired foods from farther away more easily than ever before, obtaining "fruit from the Mediterranean, spices from Indonesia, wheat from Australia," according to Waverly Root and Richard de Rochemont.[21] Because of such advances, the United States increased its relative wealth among other nations, once again connecting agriculture, economics, and expansion at the national and global levels. This wealth represented in per capita dollars makes a startling statistic. While in 1820 the world's richest nations were three times richer than the poorest, by the period following the Spanish-American War, the wealth distribution had changed to the extent that the wealthy nations were ten times richer than the poorest, and Europe was no longer the site of the world's richest nation.[22] The average per capita income in 1913 in the United States was $5,300; meanwhile, in Western Europe it was $3,500. With this stronger national economy came more global influence. As territory increased, intensifying the nation's agricultural production, the focus on farm production helped fuel an economic growth that placed the United States among the wealthiest nations in the world.

The nineteenth century was a time of drastic change and development on a national and global scale in terms of technology and communications as well, and this change was especially strong in agriculture.[23] Pivotal nineteenth-century advances in agricultural technologies were the 1846 mass production of the John Deere steel plow, the 1849 establishment of a Baltimore fertilizer factory, and the first usage of refrigerated cars for agricultural transportation in 1875.[24] In addition, the telegraph was invented in 1839, revolutionizing communication for every kind of business—perhaps none more than food production. It internationalized operations, broke down regional barriers, and shrank the world unimaginably for the people of that era.[25] In this way the telegraph created a kind of "global village" precursor to the theories of Marshall McLuhan. Jürgen Osterhammel and Niels Peterson note that the invention of the telegraph ultimately decoupled information and the material object, creating a new market economy in foodstuffs. Industries were no longer limited by the physicality of their goods, and speculation became a symbolic exercise in terms of the food item being transferred. These advances in trade and commerce were largely responsible for the agricultural revolution of the nineteenth century.[26]

The technological innovations and expansion discussed in the literature of *Beyond the Fruited Plain* respond to earlier agricultural movements. The early nineteenth century saw the nation call for a new form of agriculture, one that emphasized intensification, developing technologies, and specific crop selection. Two leading figures of this agricultural reform of the early nineteenth century were Elkanah Watson and Henry Colman; they looked away from traditional farming methods and toward novel ones, motivated by a desire to keep the lands of the Northeast as productive as the "virgin soil" of the developing territories of the expanding West. Watson founded an agricultural society in the Berkshires in 1811. Later, Colman researched farms across Massachusetts and published a comprehensive report on his findings between the years 1838 and 1841. In the first half of the nineteenth century, prices increased for such staples as corn and wheat. As a result, farmers moved to the fertile lands of the western regions newly incorporated into the United States to reap the wealth of the new territories. The lands of the West were able to produce exponentially greater quantities of agricultural products than the tired soils of the Northeast. Watson and Colman made suggestions primarily to northeastern farmers who felt they were working against an economics of scale that they could not maintain. The farming regions of the Northeast were being forced to adapt in order to remain relatively competitive, as Sarah Phillips observes in her historical work on antebellum agricultural reform. She adds that northeastern farmers focused on scientific developments in agriculture, including livestock husbandry, in order to compete with the exploitative mentality of farmers mining the rich soils in the West.[27] The agrarian ideal of the United States was no longer a viable option. Agriculture followed the expansionist politics of the nation in the nineteenth century, and farmers were forced to follow suit.

Writers like Watson and Colman focused exclusively on production and economics, not on maintenance and sustainability of crops or on the laborers themselves. Speaking to the Berkshire Agricultural Society in 1814, Watson argued, "The native vigor of a virgin soil in the early settlements of the Country, answered every temporary purpose.... Our misfortune is—we have too much land—the consequence, generally speaking, is wretched husbandry, and half crops."[28] He looked to the French and the Flemish as models for the United States: "They reduced the quantity of arable land—encreased [sic] their manures—ploughed deeper, and oftener—and kept their tillage ground perfectly clean like gardens. They soon found that ten acres of land well managed, would yield more than forty acres by their previous mode of cultivation."[29] European nations produced more crops on less land through agricultural intensification. Some twenty years later, Henry Colman recommended similar practices in his report: "It has often been a question by many farmers, whether one hundred bushels of shelled corn can be produced on an acre.—The fact, however, of its having been done has been so repeatedly established, that it can no longer be disputed."[30] Colman continued Watson's push for new agricultural methods in the antebellum period. By this era fewer people ran larger, more intensive farms. This freed redundant farm laborers to work in growing urban centers. The industrialization and urbanization of the nation were joined by the nation's expansion, and agriculture once again became part of that conversation. In each case this movement of early agricultural reformers concentrated on the productive capacity of the land. These writers worked to address specific concerns of northeastern U.S. farmers during the initial stages of U.S. agri-expansion.

In the United States, agri-expansion got its start as early as the Louisiana Purchase. However, it was the wars and aggressive growth of the midcentury that created the figurative boom in the nation's agriculture. Food production was involved in some of the most tumultuous events of the nineteenth century. The U.S.-Mexican War of 1848 brought lands from Mexico into the nation, and the aggressive policies of the Indian wars throughout the nineteenth century focused on the plains region of the expanding United States. These lands developed primarily into large-scale farms. By the Civil War, agriculture had become a recognized factor in divisive national politics. Historians like R. Douglas Hurt have observed that one of the most significant issues during the antebellum period was an agricultural battle between the yeoman farmers of the North and Midwest and the gentrified farmers of the South, who ran large-scale operations dependent on slavery. Agriculture around the time of the Civil War thus forced a revolution in southern labor through emancipation, while bringing a technological transformation to the North, as inflation and wartime shortages—specifically in labor—encouraged innovation in order to replace traditional labor requirements.[31] The innovations developed as a result of these shortages, the emancipation of slaves, and advances in transportation are some of the direct causes of the U.S. agricultural revolution of the late nineteenth century. In other words, one of the most dramatic periods of national politics was also a moment of upheaval in terms of U.S. agriculture.

Literary figures were quick to comment on such drastic developments in U.S. agriculture. At an 1858 address to the Middlesex Cattle Society,

Ralph Waldo Emerson presented his most agricultural piece of writing in his essay, "Farming." In this piece, published in 1870 in *Society and Solitude*, Emerson writes, "The glory of the farmer is that, in the division of labors, it is his part to create. All trade rests at last on his primitive activity. He stands close to nature; he obtains from the earth the bread and the meat. The food which was not, he causes to be"; he continues, "And the profession has in all eyes its ancient charm, as standing nearest to God, the first cause."[32] Emerson speaks to the popular agrarian concept of farming in the United States, emphasizing nature, labor, and creation. He shows farmers as close to a sense of divinity; he also shows them as grounded firmly in their status as professionals. The concerns of the nation—expansion and potentially imperialism—remain entwined in such a "creative" form of labor as agriculture. Throughout, though, the farmer is challenged by territorial political practices. Emerson's essay becomes an effort to use transcendental philosophy to a practical application—one as foundational as farming.[33] The authors discussed in *Beyond the Fruited Plain* write about alternative agricultural practices as well, focusing on the local, the domestic, and the small.[34]

Emerson's language, additionally, takes on a comparable tone to the mechanistic jargon of the middle of the nineteenth century: "The earth works for him [the farmer]; the earth is a machine which yields almost gratuitous service to every application of intellect. Every plant is a manufacturer of soil. In the stomach of the plant development begins. The tree can draw on the whole air, the whole earth, on all the rolling main. The plant is all suction-pipe—imbibing from the ground by its root, from the air by its leaves, with all its might."[35] At one time Emerson merges the tone of land stewardship with the industrialized rhetoric of the age. The farmer improves upon nature in some of the same ways that the Industrial Revolution progresses society. The farmer here, though, is not the machinist; rather, nature is in charge of the machinery. The earth "works for" the farmer, yet at the same time, the plants represent the great machines capable of achieving transformations humans cannot. Emerson develops over the course of his lecture from the agrarian to the mechanistic. In this way agriculture becomes part of a system that resembles a factory—producing the food by which the nation is sustained. Emerson continues thematically connecting agriculture and the developing tools of industry. Such mechanical imagery of food production is a product of industrialization and directly connected to westward expansion. The authors of *Beyond the Fruited Plain* engage themselves with Emerson's speech about the "ancient charms" involved in farming as it had become more complicated by industrialization, expansion, and other primary concerns of the nineteenth century. Abraham Lincoln continues this discussion one year after Emerson in his own agricultural speech.

In 1859, while campaigning for the presidency, Lincoln addressed a Wisconsin agricultural fair, describing his concern that agriculture would be directly and irrevocably altered by agri-expansion and national politics. Lincoln notes, "The ambition for broad acres leads to poor farming, even with men of energy. I scarcely ever knew a mammoth farm to sustain itself; much less to return a profit upon the outlay. . . . Mammoth farms are like tools or weapons, which are too heavy to be handled. Ere long they are thrown aside, at a great loss."[36] Lincoln called for a new kind of agricultural reform, challenging the lessons of Watson and Colman and their engagement in forms of agri-expansion through crop intensification and monoculture. Furthermore, Lincoln responded to the state of agriculture in which farmers made up the largest share of the population, but not a representative share of government. Gilbert C. Fite writes that though the trade and exports in foodstuffs was impressive, in key areas like population, farms, jobs, or economics, agriculture as a profession was in a state of decline by the second half of the nineteenth century. If in 1860 farm workers made up 60 percent of labor, by 1890 they made up a smaller 42.7 percent, and their numbers steadily declined after that time.[37] The comparison of farming and frontier policies based on trade and industrialization developed into concerns about agricultural expansion and the need for reform once again.

In answer to the concerns raised by Lincoln, several agricultural reform movements developed in the second half of the nineteenth century. The Civil War had fundamentally altered agriculture; the nation had changed from an agrarianism based largely on slavery to a more mechanized, technologically advanced form. This was to some extent the result of the depleted labor force—soldiers—both during and following the war. Farmers were understandably encouraged to develop new technologies. In this context President Andrew Johnson sent Oliver Hudson Kelley to the South to collect agricultural data in 1867. As a northerner, Kelley was met with suspicion, but he soon realized that his common status as a Freemason helped to break down potentially strong regional barriers. Inspired by this level of connection, he decided to establish an organization like the Freemasons that focused on agriculture. The National Grange of the Order of Patrons of Husbandry was founded in 1867, reached its peak in the 1890s, and remains active in the twenty-first century. In a letter to Anson Bartlett, Kelley writes, "We want to bring in the whole farming community,— get the brains inside the vineyard, then put ideas into the brains,—set them to thinking,—let them feel that they are human beings, and the strength of the nation, their labor honorable, and farming the highest calling on earth."[38] Kelley recognized the potentially degrading elements of farming life as early as the mid-nineteenth century. The national emphasis by this point was already moving away from the farms and to the urban centers, where other careers had become available to challenge husbandry. The Grange operated to help farmers during a time of economic development that made their lives more difficult. Following a similar original cause—keeping agriculture relevant and significant at a time of profound change in U.S. history—Kelley challenged the reformers of the previous generation through the Grange movement. In this way the Grange returned some of the significance to U.S. farmers that they had lost owing to expansion, industrialization, and urbanization in the nineteenth century.

Similarly, the land-grant college system came about as an attempt to democratize higher education in coordination with a democratized West, focusing on agriculture. The Morrill Act of 1862—followed by the Hatch Act of 1887 and the second Morrill Act of 1890—set the organization of land-grant colleges at the national level. The idea of a well-educated society focused on agriculture and a more rural-based lifestyle had been around since the urbanization movement following industrialization. Since their founding, land-grant colleges have been designed to appeal to the agricultural and engineering elements of society, linking expansion, agrarianism, scientific and technological advances, and emerging industrialism to a broad range of the population.[39] The first land-grant colleges were established in Pennsylvania and Michigan in 1855.[40] From there, they increased, eventually numbering seventy-one colleges developed by federal and state governments. More focused on elements of the rural and agricultural life than were the private universities of the Northeast, these institutions focused on research in the sciences as well as agricultural engineering. Indeed, agriculture became the most identified vocation of the land-grant institutions. The nation endeavored to maintain its agrarian identity through its educational system, while demographics were shifting to a more decidedly urban and industrial U.S. society. Meanwhile, the government was also working to reform the issue of agri-expansion through a number of policy changes, with varying levels of success. The effects of reform movements like the Grange movement and the land-grant college system resonated throughout the nineteenth century.

During this time of national restructuring, in the years leading up to and shortly following the Civil War, a surge of writers focused their attention on matters of food production and consumption through more direct routes than the literature of their contemporaries. Domestic manuals, for example, became popular for educating families on household matters at a time when a growing number of people no longer had traditional forms of education available to them. In addition to providing recipes, these manuals taught U.S. women how to use new technologies developed to complement agriculture, such as canning with newly invented Mason jars.[41] Two of the most popular domestic authors of this genre were Lydia Maria Child and Catharine Beecher, sister to Harriet Beecher Stowe. Child wrote *American Frugal Housewife* (1831) for families of modest means, and she was hugely popular with audiences along the nation's western frontier, as six thousand copies of her manual were quickly sold upon publication. Her book went through thirty-three printings by 1870. Families found her collection of maxims, philosophy of practical economy, and convenient recipes helpful as they moved to the Far West of their time, Illinois and Kentucky. Such families leaving the Northeast were forced to look elsewhere for education as to agricultural and domestic procedures. Meanwhile, Beecher focused on the domestic arrangements of the middle-class eastern housewife in *A Treatise on Domestic Economy* (1841), a nearly universally popular work.[42] In it she gave detailed suggestions on several key aspects of domestic life, including particulars such as sketches of plumbing plans and anatomical drawings of a woman's muscular system. Beecher intended for her manual to be practical and as all encompassing as possible. She too engaged in the domestic aspect of a new agri-expansion in the United States. These manual writers complemented the agricultural reform efforts of other nineteenth-century reformers, like Kelley.

Meanwhile, more than a hundred reform communities were established around this time, often focusing on agriculture and diet modification as part of their overall projects.[43] In Massachusetts Brook Farm and Fruitlands were two of the more well-known communities; Nathaniel Hawthorne and Margaret Fuller were notable supporters of Brook Farm, while the Alcott family—including the transcendentalist Bronson Alcott and his daughter, Louisa May—lived at Fruitlands. Emerson, moreover, was a close personal friend of members of both communities. At Fruitlands agriculture was a profoundly ethical activity, and members abstained not only from all consumption of animal foods but also from using cotton owing to its connection to slavery, any products made from animals (like wool) out of concern for their welfare, crops that would require the labor of animals, and finally foods that grew down rather than upward toward the heavens based on their symbolic importance.[44] The severity of Fruitlands drove the families to near starvation before their mission's ultimate failure. Meanwhile, the lack of experience on the part of the poet-farmers at Brook Farm resulted in a decided agricultural failure as well, and the reformers soon abandoned their experiment after having accomplished little more than amusing their neighboring farmers. Though both communities were unsuccessful agriculturally, two literary works by U.S. authors did come from these experiments: Nathaniel Hawthorne wrote *The Blithedale Romance* (1852) about his experiences on Brook Farm, and Louisa May Alcott reminisced about her family's time at Fruitlands in her fictionalized essay "Transcendental Wild Oats" (1873). These examples show the link between nineteenth-century agricultural reform and the literature of the era, making useful models for the authors discussed in *Beyond the Fruited Plain*.

As models, though, both Hawthorne and Alcott show contrasting examples of the earnest projects of the authors described in *Beyond the Fruited Plain*. Neither Hawthorne nor Alcott was involved in successful farming endeavors, and their works to a large degree satirize the reformers of the kind discussed throughout this study. At one point Hawthorne's narrator laments the mercenary aspects of their philosophical goal: "It struck me as rather odd, that one of the first questions raised, after our separation from the greedy, struggling, self-seeking world, should relate to the possibility of getting the advantage over the outside barbarians in their own field of labor."[45] Hawthorne's narrator, Coverdale, finds himself in a somewhat ridiculous situation, one that calls for the entire separation of the farm and the market. Following this logic, farmers who work for money devolve into barbarians. In a similar vein, Alcott mocks the zealous and impractical attitudes of the philosopher-farmers in her own work: "The band of brothers began by spading garden and field; but a few days of it lessened their ardor amazingly. Blistered hands and aching backs suggested the expediency of permitting the use of cattle till the workers were better fitted for noble toil by a summer of the new life."[46] Alcott is somewhat kinder in her description of her family in this sketch, however. She notes that "such farming probably was never seen before since Adam delved" to demonstrate both their naïveté as well as their righteous goals in this mode of farming.[47] In these cases the efforts of reformers were unrealistic in practice, and they inevitably failed. However, this does not change the fact that both writers at one point were earnestly engaged in reform efforts against what they saw as a dangerous development in the nation's agriculture. This impulse can, indeed, be taken further to include the agricultural—even agrarian—goal within their desire for a more wholesome form of producing and consuming food. Not only did people of this time in the United States seek closer human relationships, they were also desirous of a greater connection with the natural world. I study these themes in greater depth in this work.[48]

In *Beyond the Fruited Plain*, I examine some of the nation's most recognized nineteenth-century cultural critics—authors who were influential both during their own time as well as in more recent history. Harriet Beecher Stowe's *Uncle Tom's Cabin* is considered one of the most historically significant novels in U.S. literature. Mark Twain may have been an even more famous author than Stowe, and his fame has never wavered. The 2010 publication of both a new *Autobiography* and a new version of the perennially controversial *Adventures of Huckleberry Finn* demonstrate Twain's relevance as it continues into the twenty-first century.[49] Herman Melville, on the other hand, died in almost complete obscurity. It was only in the twentieth century that his work started receiving a significant amount of critical attention, to the point where he is currently one of the most relevant cultural critics of society in U.S. literature. Henry David Thoreau was not entirely unknown during his life, but his fame was miniscule compared to what it has become after a legacy of translations through Leo Tolstoy, Mahatma Gandhi, and Martin Luther King Jr. Thoreau is now perhaps the nineteenth-century U.S. author studied in the greatest number of disciplines. Frank Norris lies somewhere in between these extremes. Neither obscure nor world renowned, he died too young to establish the lasting reputation of a Twain or Stowe, and his writings are rarely featured in U.S. literature reading lists. However, his thorough work on the development of the U.S. wheat industry is particularly helpful to any discussion of post-Spanish-American-War agri-expansion. The five authors I study are therefore united by their imaginative responses to U.S. culture of the second half of the nineteenth century as well as through their critical reflections on national policies during this period of growth. Studying these responses to developing agri-expansion can give scholars a deeper understanding of their work and of the period—as well as of the cultural and agricultural history of the United States.[50]

Furthermore, I focus on authors engaged specifically in challenging various elements of the nation's course of agri-expansion during the nineteenth century. A pattern runs throughout these texts; issues of intensive agricultural production and a need for a global market for surplus foodstuffs were not, in other words, a new phenomenon for the United States in the twentieth century. They had been as much a part of the cultural and national discourse during the nineteenth century. Writers of that century were actively engaged in debating issues of agriculture and expansion, using literature to challenge and potentially reform what they saw as harmful trends in U.S. culture and politics. These authors primarily discuss reform during periods of political and economic upheaval—the decades, for example, directly preceding and following the Civil War and the Spanish-American War. Moreover, each of the authors I discuss spent time on farms: a farm of their own or one they were researching for their writing. Domestic agriculture is a common theme throughout both their agricultural and literary work. Their writings therefore allow readers to follow nineteenth-century agri-expansion as it relates to class, gender, race, and the environment from the years following the U.S.-Mexican War through the Spanish-American War. For this reason examining works of this period that deal with agri-expansion helps demonstrate new approaches to issues of nineteenth-century U.S. expansion. In other words, *Beyond the Fruited Plain* draws new connections between two formative periods in U.S. expansion by looking at the literature of the second half of the nineteenth century as it resonates with a similar moment in the twenty-first century. I look specifically at the writings and the authors whose questions during the nineteenth century most closely mirror our own. I argue that during this time cultural critics used their writings to identify and challenge what they saw as an exploitative production on an individual and national level. These authors not only understood the ideological nature of agriculture but were alarmed by its role in the justification and propulsion of expansionist national politics. By observing parallels between the two periods, we can bring the issues of the nineteenth century into our modern context, while also applying our current information to the earlier literature. *Beyond the Fruited Plain* suggests that reading key authors of this period through the lens of agri-expansion will prove truly fruitful.

Herman Melville charted the development of U.S. agri-expansion during the mid-nineteenth century through his land-based novels and short stories in "Expanding Agriculture." For Melville, agriculture became a specter over the lives of working families; in every case farmers suffered from an exploitative U.S. economy. Following the theme of agriculture through Melville's land-based works, one can chart the development of a new form of U.S. agriculture—as well as some of Melville's own accounts of such developments. Melville twists the image of the agrarian ideal in *Pierre* (1852). In key scenes in this novel, farmers and their families suffer both in the quasi-feudal villages in which they live under the Glendinnings as well as in the urban cities to which they must turn for work. Farmers like the Millthorpes provide an alternative to the story of Pierre Glendinning's fallen aristocracy during the time of the anti-rent movement in the Northeast. Following this discussion of farm labor, I study two of Melville's poverty-based diptychs, "Poor Man's Pudding and Rich Man's Crumbs" (1854) and "The Paradise of Bachelors and the Tartarus of Maids" (1855), focusing exclusively on the U.S.-located sections. In these pieces Melville introduces agriculture as one of the forces responsible for the abuse of U.S. laborers. The struggling farmers of "Poor Man's Pudding" are barely subsisting while their labor increases the wealth and comfort of figures like Squire Teamster. Meanwhile, the "Maids" of "The Tartarus of Maids" give Melville an opportunity to make his most pointed criticism against the unification of factory and farm. Unmarried women work in a paper factory, preparing packets that Melville's narrator ultimately uses in his seed-distribution business, a poignant example of nineteenth-century U.S. agri-expansion.[51] While Melville is primarily known as a sea-based author, his land-based narratives show his concern with the development of an expansive agriculture, which is just as fierce as any other of his cultural criticisms.

Henry David Thoreau suggests key reforms in agriculture and diet in both *Walden* (1854) and his later sketches published posthumously in *Wild Fruits* (2001). In his work U.S. producers have become part of an economic chain in which they must produce labor to purchase their food, even though in many cases easily accessible local foods are available to them. During Thoreau's time agriculture had joined economically with the Industrial Revolution, and food had become, further, a commodity. In "Local Beans, Apples, and Berries," I argue that Thoreau sought to restructure this national agri-expansion with a return to a localized agriculture and harvesting movement that incorporates regional, mostly vegetable, foods like the northeastern U.S. white beans, wild apples, and huckleberries, both in production and consumption. In *Walden* Thoreau writes of his experiment in growing beans, a specifically nonexpansionist crop; he anticipates the locavore and slow foods movements by over a century for many of the same reasons that have remained significant regarding global agriculture. This agricultural reform is continued in Thoreau's later writings on wild apples and huckleberries. In these later examples, collected in *Wild Fruits*, local (though not necessarily native) foods are democratically available, therefore far cheaper than exported items purchased from a store. They are also set apart from the exploitative economy that develops into a major part of U.S. agriculture. Thoreau argues against a move toward the privatization of the commons, represented by the berry fields of his region; he fears that removing democratic accessibility to certain foods would damage the United States. In these pieces Thoreau challenges U.S. agricultural practices by experimenting in a simplified mode of production and consumption.

Harriet Beecher Stowe expanded on Thoreau's local dietary and agricultural experiments. She wrote about agriculture, diet, and the nation from the antebellum period through Reconstruction, using her orange grove in Florida as an example of regional agriculture, advocating for the consumption of regional foods as way to reunite the nation in the years during and following the Civil War, as I show in "Fruits of Regionalism." Speaking directly to U.S. women, Stowe emphasized the power this population possessed to bring about domestic reform and thereby to transform U.S. agri-expansion. Stowe used the orange as a food crop and as a symbol of the changing region of the South both before and after the Civil War. First, she used oranges in key scenes in *Uncle Tom's Cabin* (1852) to link the fruit regionally with the South and with slavery. During the Civil War itself, Stowe advocated the consumption of U.S. foods as a way to encourage domestic unification in general, publishing a series of sketches focusing on the "lighter fare" of domestic consumption in *House and Home Papers* (1865). Even in this lighter commentary, Stowe brings the issues of nation, expansion, retention, and economics into the domestic arena. Her *Oldtown Folks* (1869) includes a chapter on the celebration of the Thanksgiving Day feast that continues her food-related goals. Finally, Stowe's regional writings during her time in Florida, collected in 1873 in *Palmetto Leaves*, provide examples for U.S. investors—including newly emancipated African Americans—to produce oranges for a regional U.S. market, as opposed to global imports. With the symbolic and physical production of oranges, united with her educational and religious mission in Florida, Stowe hoped to assist the emancipated South through agricultural regionalism. Her works include yet another food-related call for domestic production and consumption as a way to reunite the nation after the Civil War.

Following Stowe's domestic agricultural project, Mark Twain demonstrated the development of a nineteenth-century U.S. agri-imperialism, as an end-of-the-century version of agri-expansion. In "Sweet Empires of Labor," I show how Twain focused on one crop—sugar—and its effects on imperialism in order to discuss the expansion of U.S. agriculture and global power between the Civil War and the Spanish-American-War eras. In 1866 Twain actively promoted U.S. agri-expansion, writing a series of letters from Hawaii to encourage U.S. industries to invest in sugar plantations on a global scale. Toward the end of his writing career, he traveled around the world, witnessing British imperialism as it connected to global sugar-producing nations. During his tour of the British Empire, which would result in *Following the Equator* (1897), Twain researched the cruelties of the "coolie trade" between the Pacific Islands and the sugar plantations of Australia and enjoyed a recuperative stay among the sugar fields of Mauritius, reminiscent of his earlier travels among similar fields in Hawaii. Twain's travels in the British Empire became one area in which to demonstrate his ultimate sea change regarding imperialism in general and U.S. imperialism specifically. Twain might have experienced literary empathy regarding his earlier advocacy of coolie labor during these later travels. He was able, through his sugar-related expeditions, to relate the African Americans significant to his childhood to the Chinese and Pacific Islanders, through their shared status as diasporic laborers in the global sugar industry. The trajectory of Twain's writing shows his development as a national critic, from a supporter of U.S. expansion through its sugar business to an anti-imperialist critic of a nation whose tendencies—including sugar-based agri-expansion—became disastrous to other cultures following the Spanish-American War.

Further exploring U.S. global agricultural interests, Frank Norris provided an example of the global wheat trade at the dawn of the twentieth century. Norris showed, perhaps more clearly than anyone discussed in this book, the interconnectedness between U.S. economics and agriculture. Recognizing the dangerous supremacy of large U.S. agri-expansion, Norris argued against this movement, connecting it to a new age of empire ushered in by the end of the Spanish-American War. In "The Wheat Strikes Back," I maintain that Norris used wheat as a metaphor for a natural corrective against an exploitative U.S. agri-expansion at the beginning of the twentieth century. In Norris's epic the wheat itself rises up against key figures of capitalism, and those who have been oppressors are themselves ultimately destroyed. In his short story originally published in 1902, "A Deal in Wheat," Norris shows the trajectory of both wheat and farmers during a period of intensification in agriculture. In *The Octopus* (1901), Norris focuses on the physicality of the wheat extensively, making it into a character in its own right. Then, the wheat that avenges California farmers at the end of *The Octopus* becomes the vehicle for U.S. economic power in *The Pit* (1903). In every case the wheat—symbolic of the forces of nature—punishes key characters that most represent agri-expansion at the turn of the twentieth century. As an arguable early critic of globalization, Norris describes the wheat as a force ultimately more powerful than even the railroad or the Board of Trade, and this makes his epic a work that suggests an eco-critical reading against aggressive U.S. policies at the turn of the twentieth century.

Finally, I demonstrate the connection between nineteenth-century texts and twenty-first-century economics in agriculture. I describe what has become of the crops discussed—the dairy, wheat, fruit, beans, and sugar—at the global level. New muckraking texts continue to challenge large-scale, intensive agriculture. I provide three examples—nonfiction and fiction—of new reform movements challenging a twenty-first-century agri-expansion that is a direct result of its nineteenth-century predecessor. Anna Lowenhaupt Tsing discusses local harvesting practices in Borneo, Bill McKibben presents an organic movement in Bangladesh, and Ruth Ozeki fictionalizes the Monsanto genetic modification experiment using a rural farming town in Idaho as her background. Perhaps the stakes are even higher in these modern agricultural settings. Together, these authors show similarities to the nineteenth-century efforts described in *Beyond the Fruited Plain* as well as a hopeful praxis for small successes against the twenty-first-century globalization of agriculture as it remains a central issue in U.S. culture and history.

Indeed, culture and history could be described as a helix. Elements repeat, but a general progress is being traced at the same time. The twenty-first century is not a pinnacle standing above and apart from all that came before it. At the same time, neither is it repeating a pattern that has not changed in human history. In this manner agri-expansion has been a recurring theme in U.S. literature for hundreds of years. *Beyond the Fruited Plain* shows that the current level of interest in food and agriculture is hardly a new development in U.S. literature and culture. At the beginning of the era of intense U.S. territorial growth, cultural critics challenged the food production methods of the nation and suggested alternatives that would best aid the farmers themselves. The fruited plain is, indeed, a primary motif in the nation's history. The United States developed the plains, farmed them, and pushed them beyond the continental and onto the global stage. The writers I discuss offer alternatives to this aspect of U.S. expansionism by exploring the political dimensions of agriculture, examining the production and producers of food. Their texts navigate the move away from a self-sustaining to a more intensive agricultural system while focusing on issues of class, race, and gender in nationality. Meanwhile, they attempt to correct this agri-expansionism through the advocacy of dietary and agricultural reform at the domestic level. They advocate eating locally produced food, reforming industrial agriculture, and supporting U.S. labor, as part of the cultural history of environmentalism. Even after the victimization, abuses, and failures to reform seen throughout the works discussed in *Beyond the Fruited Plain*, there remains the theme of hopeful positive action through literature.

1

Expanding Agriculture

Do you want to know how I pass my time?—I rise at eight—thereabouts—& go to my barn—say good-morning to the horse, & give him his breakfast. (It goes to my heart to give him a cold one, but it can't be helped) Then, pay a visit to my cow—cut up a pumpkin or two for her, & stand by to see her eat it—for it's a pleasant sight to see a cow move her jaws—she does it so mildly & with such a sanctity.—My own breakfast over, I go to my work-room & light my fire—then spread my M.S.S on the table—take one business squint at it, & fall to with a will. At 2 1/2 P.M. I hear a preconcerted knock at my door, which (by request) continues till I rise & go to the door, which serves to wean me effectively from my writing, however interested I may be. My friends the horse & cow now demand their dinner—& I go & give it them.

HERMAN MELVILLE, *Correspondence*, 174

In this letter to friend Evert Duyckinck, Herman Melville describes his account of life on his farm, Arrowhead, where his manual and intellectual labors unite. In this homely description, work and farm chores are equated in importance. Melville privileges the domestic, even the local, when he describes pumpkins—a native food—as the lone garden product. The most frankly philosophical element of this passage is his description of a cow eating a pumpkin "mildly" and "with such a sanctity." Melville was well acquainted with the life of a farmer, in fact. The author known for his sea narratives spent far more of his life on a farm than on the sea. *Moby-Dick* (1851), *Pierre* (1852), and most of his short stories, among other writings, were published while Melville and his family lived at Arrowhead, outside Pittsfield, Massachusetts. During this time Melville's life as a writer to some extent followed the rhythms of a working farm. While Melville would struggle financially at Arrowhead, he also idealized the agricultural lifestyle, especially when combined with his writing, his "business squint." Therefore, Melville used his experience both as a farmer and an author to approach agricultural themes in the scope of national expansion and its effects on farming families.

Melville has largely been read as a critic of nineteenth-century U.S. imperialism and of the early stages of globalization on the basis of his descriptions of cosmopolitan sailors on board whaling ships and men-of-war. Meanwhile, Melville has also contributed a large body of work dealing with specifically domestic affairs, often set in the rural Berkshires of Massachusetts. In letters to friends, he describes the raising of cows, haying, harvesting apples, and other agrarian chores. Melville turns his critical lens as well to the struggles of farming families as they attempt to navigate the development of an intensifying form of agriculture during this period of U.S. history. In the same way that Melville's sea-based novels criticize U.S. globalization, his domestic writings also challenge the nation's project as it expands, intensifies, and industrializes agriculture. Food production is an important area of development during this time—one that is directly connected to economic and territorial expansion as well as to industrialization, urbanization, and capitalism. Farming families suffer both at the hands of quasi-feudal landlords as well as in the urban settings where they become wage laborers. Focusing on farmers suffering on land, as opposed to workers at sea, Melville challenges the nation's agri-expansion and shows the plight of rural farmers during this period of revolution in U.S. agriculture.[1]

Theories of agriculture in U.S. literature, such as the pastoral works of Raymond Williams and Leo Marx, are helpful in developing a richer understanding of Melville's works. Williams connects agriculture and capitalism with imperialism in Britain during that nation's Industrial Revolution in a way that applies to the United States in the nineteenth century.[2] Focusing specifically on U.S. literature, Marx further describes the pastoral as a useful method to discuss literary representations of U.S.

politics dating from the nation's earliest foundations. Marx notes that the romantic ideal of an agricultural landscape is seen in the writings of several nineteenth-century authors and uses Melville as a primary example.[3] Marx argues that Melville's *Typee* (1845) focuses more on an escape from the industrialized West of the mid-nineteenth century and less on an example of an "Emersonian Young American."[4] This theme becomes prominent in Melville's later works relating to rural U.S. farms, as he critically examines both the flight from urban life to an idealized landscape and the contrasting exodus from these rural farms to U.S. urban centers. Melville ambivalently challenges antebellum assumptions about expansion and urbanization as well as the idealized image of the rural landscape as related to agriculture.

U.S. history directly influences Melville's domestic agricultural critiques of the national project during agri-expansion. The early nineteenth century introduced the United States to the global stage economically after the chaos of a series of imperial wars and revolutions had weakened European countries between 1793 and 1815. As European nations found themselves financially and politically drained as a result of these wars, they turned more regularly to the United States to supply them with basic commodities, like food and other consumables. U.S. entrepreneurs quickly took advantage of available opportunities in what was a major development in U.S. globalization, initiating an era of aggressive economic expansion that preceded the territorial stage of expansion later named "manifest destiny."[5] John Jacob Astor, the first U.S. millionaire, amassed his wealth through trade during this period, establishing the American Fur Company in 1808, over a decade before the opening of the Erie Canal. The United States thus was already exploiting available north–south and east–west trade routes in a manner that intensified throughout the nineteenth century, helped by national policies promoting aggressive expansionism.[6] In the first half of the nineteenth century, the increase in trade spanned the northeastern region of the United States. Meanwhile, technological advances turned artisan laborers within the home into far more productive laborers in factories that developed quickly as part of the U.S. Industrial Revolution, and agriculture evolved in stride.[7] A greater population of nonagricultural workers fueled the mechanization of production, resulting in a corresponding revolution in agriculture. This revolution culminated in the years leading up to and during the Civil War, which brought about another large-scale change in U.S. agriculture.[8] In his domestic writings, Melville responds to the cultural and political drive for, not only greater expanses of territory, but also the exploitation of available resources and people as U.S. agriculture developed.

Melville furthermore responds to the agricultural reformers and communities that farmers increasingly turned to in their desperation. These societies were designed to provide traditional farmers with opportunities to share information and innovations with their neighbors in an effort to stay economically competitive against the larger, cheaper farms of the West. Melville's uncle and cousin were active in the Berkshire Agricultural Society, to the point of holding important positions in the institution. Founded in 1811 by Elkanah Watson, a Scottish immigrant with a flair for business and farming, the regional agricultural society was designed to foster a spirit of friendly competition through which farmers could share ideas that would elevate the entire community. He promoted the institution of regular county fairs, and these became universally popular. Decades after Watson founded his agricultural society, Melville would describe a youthful summer trip to Pittsfield, Massachusetts, that included a visit to the area's annual "Cattle Show and Fair."[9] Watson encouraged his society to "individually determine to contribute our mite to the best good of our common hive—and let the man stand immortalized in our annals, who can by his talents, or industry, cause 'two blades of grass or two ears of corn to grow where only one grew before.'"[10] Watson focused his energy on the raising of cattle and sheep, specifically looking to promote the manufacturing of wool as an economic goal for the area. An innovator, he developed the Merino sheep for U.S. production, considering them ideally suited to the rugged terrain of the Berkshires, with its somewhat depleted soil. Watson's suggestions were greeted eagerly in the community, and local farmers agreed that such specialization and innovation, together with crop intensification, were the best way to keep northeastern U.S. agriculture up-to-date with the Industrial Revolution and westward expansion. Watson noted the importance of joining forces with "all that portion of the Commonwealth lying west of Connecticut river,"[11] and his theories became so popular that he was invited to found a similar society in Otsego County, New York, in 1815. Both the Berkshire and Otsego agricultural societies influenced Melville, as the issues facing the nation regarding expansion and changing technologies in agriculture were occurring in Melville's home state throughout his early life. They continued to have a lasting effect on Melville as a writer as well.

Even before Melville experienced firsthand the harsh injustices involved in global imperialism and the economics of whaling, he had experienced the difficult realities facing U.S. rural farmers during a time of economic crisis. His uncle, Thomas Melvill Jr. (Herman's mother added the "e" to the family's last name), was an all-too-common figure in the early nineteenth century: a farmer who was not successful enough to make the agricultural life as appealing as its image. Melvill was connected to Watson's society and thus to the agricultural reform movements taking place in the United States during this time. He won a cattle show plowing contest in 1818 and was named president of the Berkshire Agricultural Society in 1835. In an 1815 report to the Berkshire Agricultural Society, Melvill emphasizes the importance of innovation in agriculture: "Discoveries made in the cultivation of the earth, are not merely for the time and country in which they are developed, but they may be considered as extending to future ages, and ultimately tending to benefit the whole human race."[12] In this way the elder Melvill encourages contemporary methods being applied to husbandry; he notes that their addition will aid posterity—"the whole human race." Melvill believes that agricultural innovation is universally beneficial. He notably does not call for a regional or national proprietorship. Yet, while Melvill calls for a globally available agriculture development, he quickly turns to nationalistic language—echoing President Washington's December 1796 speech to Congress. Melvill connects U.S. economics and politics to its farms, recommending agricultural improvements "not only as being of the first importance to mankind, but as the firmest basis of our national independence and posterity."[13] Politics and economics are related to the farmer. By 1815 the farmer was lauded by agricultural reformers as a primary developer of national wealth and the political security that came with it. Farmers are the focus not only of Melvill's speech but also an economic reading of agricultural innovations. These innovations, community-building activities, and societies become some of the areas in which farmers develop into stronger national figures.

The young Herman Melville romanticized the poetic figure of his uncle in his writing. While haying together, Melville observes his uncle "pause in the sun, and taking out his smooth-worn box of satin-wood, gracefully help himself to a pinch of snuff."[14] Before his time as a Berkshire farmer, Melvill had traveled in Europe, and he had lived among European nobility. This contrasted fiercely with his poverty as he tried to make a living from the land. Melville notes this as he describes his uncle "making some little remark, quite naturally, and yet with a look, which—as I now recall it—presents him in the shadowy aspect of a courtier of Louis XVI, reduced as a refugee, to humble employment, in a region far from the gilded Versailles."[15] Melville makes a picturesque image of his uncle, a man who had toured the splendors of Europe before falling upon reduced circumstances and into the relative obscurity of life as a farmer. Melville brings these elements of an ironic depressed state to what would otherwise be a classic image of a farmer resting. In this case the farmer is touched with regret for his relative poverty and obscurity, an image that does not fit with the U.S. agrarian ideal.

Melvill epitomizes the dangers of following the advice of agricultural reformers during the Industrial Revolution. In 1834, as Melvill struggled to make a living on his farm, he wrote to family friend and Herman Melville's future father-in-law, Lemuel Shaw. In this letter Melvill complains of his and his wife's poor health, which makes them unable to be as diligent as they would like to be with their farm or their connected dairy. He writes, "It would be most conducive to the interest & comfort of the family, to dispose of all the Cattle, except 2, or 3 Cows, and invest the proceeds in Sheep . . . inasmuch as the care of this kind of Stock, requires much less hard labor, both out of, and in doors, than is necessary for Horned Cattle."[16] In this passage Melvill describes a familiar agricultural theme, especially for a farmer who lacks the talent and industry to become a great producer. In his decision to turn to the husbandry of sheep rather than cattle, Melvill follows the recommendations of Watson in his speech to the Berkshire Agricultural Society, advice he would promote in his own speech in 1815. However, this advice did not save his farm, and Melvill ultimately moves with his family to Galena, Illinois, falling into the seeming inevitability of farming the expanding lands of the U.S. West. Ironically, a series of natural and unexpected tragedies affected this endeavor too: bad weather caused him to lose a crop of turnips, and his cattle suffered from a series of illnesses. Such events forced Melvill to seek a bank loan during the Panic of 1837, a time when banks across the Northeast were making it more difficult to obtain credit. Eventually, he found himself in debtors' prison after a career of failing at agriculture.[17] Melvill emerges as an example of the failing agrarian figure in the nineteenth-century United States. The reforms promised by Watson through his agricultural society were ultimately not enough for farmers like Thomas Melvill Jr.

Herman Melville would return to the idea of agricultural reform again after the period of sea travel that significantly influenced his writing. He revisited the Melvill family farm, managed at this time by his cousin Robert, in 1848. By this visit Melville was a married man, on holiday from his domestic duties. Melville's cousin Priscilla notes "his manifesting 'so much constancy toward the object of his *first love*, our *Berkshire* farm—as to *tear* himself from the idol of his heart' (that is to say, Lizzy) 'to indulge again in the unfetter'd freedom of Batchelor ways.'"[18] In 1850 Melville traveled around the Pittsfield region with Robert to gather information to include in a report for the Berkshire Agricultural Society. Robert was the Viewing Committee chairman of the society, and one of his duties was to survey the crops of the region.[19] This excursion led to a youthful mock report written by Melville and published under Robert's name. Herschel Parker describes Melville as having "amused the whole family by writing out a spoof agricultural report for Robert to sign. . . . What Herman dashed off was a gleeful parody of the language of Progress, much to his own pleasure and that of the family."[20] Melville's mock report was printed in his local paper, the Pittsfield *Culturist and Gazette*, in 1850. It is a satire of the kinds of official reports being published at this time, by writers like Watson and even Thomas Melvill Jr. Melville ironically applauds local farmers as they apply the agricultural techniques of the day. He writes that "apple, pear, peach and plum" trees grow along with "extensive embellishments" of forest trees.[21] The orchards are not as striking to this observer as the native forests that encircle them in this passage. Indeed, though his inflated rhetoric is mocking in tone, he states a fact when he comments on "the contrast between the present appearance of many parts of the County, and that which they exhibited but a few years ago" and the "admiration" that must be felt by "every beholder, who has a mind capable of estimating the value of useful improvement"; these prove "most conclusively, that the efforts of the Society have not been in vain" (*PT*, 449). Melville does not seem to challenge the opinions of such societies, as much as to gently tease them as the dominant belief system of the time in the region. He makes fun of the quasi-imperialistic language of such reports as well, at a time when he had recently experienced and written about the dangers of Western imperialism in the Pacific. Melville applies the tone of the nineteenth-century agricultural reformers in order to draw attention to their flaws as he begins his own project based on domestic agriculture and literature.

Melville's mocking tone changes later in his report, when he earnestly calls for a reduction in the seed crop size of corn. He discusses the development of corn production: "Frequently has their [the committee's] attention been attracted by the many new and commodious dwellings—by the new and well-filled barns,—by plantations of thriving trees,—and by the numerous, extensive and well cultivated fields of Corn" (*PT*, 449). At first he presents an agrarian image of the U.S. farm. However, by the end of his report, he challenges the methods being used in these agricultural societies: "The examination of the corn crop has convinced the committee that a gigantic stalk is not pre-requisite for a large ear, but that on the contrary, a greater number of ears of a given size can be produced per acre, with equal, if not greater facility, upon stalks of much less dimensions, thereby materially diminishing the hazard of the crop and the exhaustion of the soil" (*PT*, 451). In this passage irony is presumably mixed with truth in his criticism of an intensive form of agriculture and its effects not only on farming families but also on the land. The idea of not choosing the biggest ears of corn for seed, but rather turning to heartier, smaller forms, would sound comical to an audience of the 1850s that had immersed itself in agricultural reform journals of the kind written by Watson and Melvill. The focus of such journals was on maintaining farms in the Northeast that could compete with the lands of the West. Melville here makes a joke that his readers would understand as one; however, he also makes a point that the manner of farming corn during this time may not be truly sustainable. Indeed, it might lead to an "exhaustion of the soil" that would eventually hurt farmers, as they would not be able to produce the quantity of corn they needed. Melville challenges arguments made by earlier reformers, and in his mock report, he begins to show his engagement with the farmers of the Berkshire community, even before he officially lived there.[22]

Melville's history in the Berkshires and his concern with rural country life as a writer was part of a growing trend in U.S. literature during the antebellum period. Indeed, the Berkshires had become a fashionable area for writers to own country farms. Nathaniel Hawthorne lived in a moss-encrusted red cottage nearby with his family; meanwhile, Oliver Wendell Holmes and Catherine Sedgwick also owned country homes in the area. Holmes was well-acquainted with the Melvill/e family and had written poetry about Thomas Melvill Sr.[23] Moreover, Henry David Thoreau had recently published *A Week on the Concord and Merrimack Rivers*, set in the Berkshires. In this work Thoreau romanticizes Saddle-back, or Greylock, Mountain, the same mountain to which Melville would dedicate *Pierre*. Though Melville's friends criticized the transcendentalist tone of *A Week*, they understood the benefits of being allowed to describe rural life in literature. Melville was not writing about the Berkshires because of a lack of more suitable material;

the agricultural elements of his works written during this stage of his career were intentional, part of his own domestic project.

Melville ultimately lived at Arrowhead from 1850 through 1862, when he sold his farm and, after a yearlong stint in town at Pittsfield, returned to New York City. In a well-known letter to Duyckinck, Melville writes of having "a sort of sea-feeling here in the country."[24] Melville indeed invites comparisons between his sea-based and domestic writings. He embraces elements of the agricultural life and is able to speak about it with as much experience and as critical a lens as he does the sea life. In a note to Hawthorne, he adds, "I am now busy with various things— not incessantly though; but enough to require my frequent tinkerings; and this is the height of the haying season, and my nag is dragging me home his winter's dinners all the time" (*C*, 199). Agricultural themes run throughout Melville's land-based writings and are seen as early as his comparisons of Western and Polynesian civilization in works like *Typee* and *Omoo* (1847). Laurie Robertson-Lorant calls Melville "ideologically egalitarian but patrician to the core," adding that his cultural work reflects issues of slavery, expansion, globalization, and industrialization.[25] These issues are present in Melville's farm-connected writings as much as in any other of his works. Melville criticizes a U.S. economy that abuses the poor within a system of developing capitalism, and he implicates U.S. consumers themselves as part of that expanding U.S. economy. The Polynesians and Yankees in *Typee* and *Omoo*, the farming families of *Pierre*, and the Coulters and the factory maids of his poverty diptych stories are part of the larger structure of the developing nineteenth-century U.S. market-based economy, specifically as it moves toward agri-expansion. While not entirely supporting the quasi-feudal system of the tenant farmers of the early nation's history, Melville deliberately criticizes the development of agri-expansion and its effects on the small-scale farmers of the northeastern United States.[26]

BREADFRUIT AND CATTLE IN THE PACIFIC

Melville develops some of his early complaints against the industrialization of production in his travel narratives *Typee* and *Omoo*, in which he discusses agricultural issues in the larger context of Western imperialism. He connects patterns of production and consumption through capitalism through fields as disparate as agriculture, industry, and trade. He uses these early narratives to challenge a Western system of global imperialism already threatening the relatively idyllic agrarian lifestyle of cultures like the Typee. While the Typee were invariably less wealthy than rich Westerners, specifically the wealthy of the United States, they were also less poor than the nation's underprivileged. Melville was struck by the realization that in the West, specifically Europe and the United States, technological advances had made numerous aspects of life easier than they were in several of the island nations of the Pacific. However, the fact remained that more Westerners seemed to suffer from hunger and other forms of want than did the Typee, who were provided with food as a community more equably. Later, after experiencing the romanticized breadfruit harvests and fishing expeditions of the Typee, Melville spent time on a farm on the island of Imeeo, modern-day Mo'orea. Here, he helped to grow yams and sweet potatoes, in addition to the breadfruit already described.[27] Melville's descriptions of these experiences are among his most interesting arguments against Western imperialism in the Pacific, specifically as they relate to U.S. concepts of agriculture and expansion. His experiences of South Pacific agriculture—and of labor there in general—are helpful to demonstrate an early challenge to the development of agri-expansion within the United States.

Melville criticizes Western expansion in Polynesia in his descriptions of various forms of agriculture. In *Typee* as well as throughout *Omoo*, Melville describes a new form of imperialism, one that is based on economics rather than earlier forms of colonialism. The South Pacific region was seen as strategic to trading routes throughout Asia. During the first half of the nineteenth century, European countries used economics as their mode of control in the South Pacific, rather than relying on outright war among rival European colonial powers. Developing U.S. imperialism has more in common with its European counterparts than is often thought. One way that the imperializing nations of Europe were able to sufficiently control the people of Polynesia, especially at a time when they did not have an economic system comparable to that of Europe and the United States, was through control of their food systems. Elements of this struggle for agricultural control can be seen throughout *Typee* and *Omoo*.

In *Typee* Melville contrasts Polynesian and Western culture. In many cases Western "civilization" is found wanting when compared to the communal "savage" existence he finds among the Typee. Melville examines the Typee food production system, their harvest, and their distribution. While the Typee are not farmers in the sense that the term is understood in the United States, they follow an agrarian lifestyle in which they live on the fruits of communal harvests. Indeed, they survive primarily on the harvest of one key foodstuff, the breadfruit. Melville writes, "When the fruit of the hundred groves of the valley has reached its maturity, and hangs in golden spheres from every branch, the islanders assemble in harvest groups, and garner in the abundance which surrounds them. The trees are stripped of their nodding burdens."[28] The harvested breadfruit is processed and stored in much the same way as U.S. cereal crops, as a reliable long-term food source. Melville realizes, "Were it not that the bread-fruit is thus capable of being preserved for a length of time, the natives might be reduced to a state of starvation" (*T*, 117). This critical culinary staple is prepared into dishes like "kokoo," "Tutao," "Amar," and "Poee-Poee," which Melville describes for his readers (*T*, 116–17). In Melville's portrayal the Typee are able to harvest, store, and prepare breadfruit with less toil than that involved in expansionist U.S. farming. They support their entire community with this harvest as well. All are able to eat, and none—in Melville's experience—suffer disproportionally for the want of food. His idealized description of the Typee harvest time is contrasted tellingly with the more difficult harvests and farming experiences of some U.S. communities of the nineteenth century debated in the speeches and writings of figures like Elkanah Watson.

Furthermore, Typee labor is also contrasted with nonagrarian U.S. laborers, those who do not have the security of being in control of the production of their own food and often suffer for the lack of it. Melville looks next at the Typee harvest of fish. As opposed to working in factories, the entire community engages in regular fishing expeditions. Melville writes, "Four times during my stay in the valley the young men assembled near the full of the moon, and went together on these excursions. . . . During their absence the whole population of the place were in a ferment, and nothing was talked of but 'pehee, pehee' (fish, fish)" (*T*, 206). At regular intervals the society turns its focus to the act of fishing. Melville is struck by the sense of solidarity evinced even in the seemingly menial task of fishing: it is not a solitary event for the Typee, as it would be to a larger degree in the United States, but a truly communal affair. The distribution of the harvest was similarly a community engagement: "The fish were under a strict Taboo, until the distribution was completed, which seemed to be effected in the most impartial manner. By the operation of this system every man, woman, and child in the vale were at one and the same time partaking of this favorite article of food" (*T*, 207). Melville observes what he takes to be a democratic distribution of a staple harvestable foodstuff and the "favorite article of food" of the entire group. He takes care to mention that "every man, woman, and child" are fairly served. Whereas the U.S. workers focus on individualism and a drive for wealth, Melville shows the Typee as jointly engaged. Melville describes the Typee as a community in which no individual is left wanting while others consume; furthermore, no one eats a disproportionate share in comparison to the rest. Melville appreciates certain aspects of this culture, like its attitude toward the necessity of food and the manner of obtaining and distributing it. He argues that in such a society, there is in some ways less of a drive for other luxuries such as those that Westerners in general and U.S. Americans in particular depend upon.

Melville continues to challenge Western imperialism in his description of the agricultural destruction of the Typee. He ironically contrasts Western civilization and Polynesian savagery in passages that show foodstuffs like breadfruit: "The spontaneous fruits of the earth . . . remorselessly seized upon and appropriated by the stranger, are devoured before the eyes of the starving inhabitants, or sent on board the numerous vessels which now touch at their shores" (*T*, 196). He contrasts Polynesian harvesting with the agri-expansion of the United States and other Western nations. The Typee harvest "spontaneous fruits" that are deemed relatively easy to procure. However, Western agricultural and imperial interests are militaristic in their seizure of the harvest, "devouring" the literal fruits of their victory. Polynesians are then told by the Western strangers "to work and earn their support by the sweat of their brows!" (*T*, 196). The seemingly idyllic, agrarian life of the Typee is systematically being transformed into a more labor-intensive one, more like that of the colonies of Western imperialism. Meanwhile, as opposed to having enough to eat based on relatively mild labor, the Typee following Western expansion are left to labor extensively for wages or starve. This change, one that Melville will return to in his land-based writings, is not one he considers to be progress.

Melville's discussion of the agricultural patterns in *Typee* is seriocomically contrasted with the Westernized farming on Imeeo as described in *Omoo*. While island hopping, Melville's narrator and his traveling companion, Dr. Long Ghost, meet a pair of twins who convince them to visit a working "Yankee" farm on Imeeo. On that island two former sailors have taken up farming: "The cleared tract which they occupied, comprised some thirty acres, level as a prairie, part of which was under cultivation."[29] Though physically and culturally from alternate parts of the Western world—Britain and the United States—these men have a similar attitude toward farming in Polynesia: "In most matters, Zeke had his own way. Shorty, too, had imbibed from him a spirit of invincible industry; and Heaven only knows what ideas of making a fortune on their plantation" (*O*, 204–5). The U.S. American has convinced the Cockney to approach agriculture with a U.S. spirit of industriousness, the same zealousness that during this period has been changing the lands of the territorial U.S. West into regularized farms. The pair works according to a Westernized idea of industry in order to make a prairie-like farm in the islands of the South Pacific. In the same spirit, the pair is farming not for subsistence, but rather as a speculative endeavor; they want to make a "fortune," rather than a "living," through farming. Of course,

Melville's narrator and Long Ghost have lived among the Pacific Islands long enough to be wary of this kind of Western industry: "We were much concerned at this; for the prospect of their setting us in their own persons an example of downright hard labor, was anything but agreeable. But it was now too late to repent what we had done" (*O*, 205). The island hoppers are scared of this degree of industry on behalf of a speculative U.S. agricultural model. By this point they prefer a communal harvest. Meanwhile, Melville uses the industrious pair of farmers to exemplify his concern with expansion and its connection to agriculture.

The industry of Zeke and Shorty is demonstrated most fully in the scene when they must prepare the soil for tillage. They work to change the growing conditions of the island to something presumably more fitting for farmlands of the northeastern United States. In a labor-intensive manner, they dig up roots and hoe the soil. First, Melville describes the proofs of their previous labor: "The surface, here and there, presented closely amputated branches of what had once been a dense thicket" (*O*, 206). Zeke then returns to his physical labors: "After loosening the hard soil, by dint of much thumping and pounding, the Yankee jerked one of the roots, this way and that, twisting it round and round, and then tugging at it horizontally" (*O*, 206). Indeed, this would be work done by horse or oxen in the United States. But in Imeeo the land is too lushly forested for such beasts of burden to adapt, so the men must do the work themselves. Even the tools used must be first adapted to the unfamiliar terrain; tools that Melville's narrator expects to find are in fact not useful here. In this way the farmers are fighting against the natural terrain and topography of the island in order to make it more like the farms of the United States. They are trying to make the land itself assimilate into an expanding economic and territorial plain. The "dense thicket" of the forest will eventually give way to the handheld plow, completing the agricultural assimilation process. Melville's portrayal is humorous in the way that it shows the difficult labors of the Yankee and the modes to which the travelers go to avoid them, but underneath this humor Melville aptly depicts the way the United States uses agriculture to further its expansionist project into the Pacific.[30]

Melville follows this discussion of Imeeo farming with another anecdote describing the fate of cattle and other livestock in Polynesia. As livestock husbandry is one of the primary kinds of U.S. agriculture, this description also provides a useful look at another element of U.S. agri-expansion in the Pacific. Melville establishes the history of cattle on certain Pacific Island nations: "Some fifty years ago, Vancouver left several bullocks, sheep, and goats, at various places in the Society group. He instructed the natives to look after the animals carefully; and by no means to slaughter any, until a considerable stock had accumulated" (O, 209). This representative of European imperialism offers the cattle and other animals as a gift to the native populations of Polynesia. However, in many cases, this gift brought unexpected and often negative consequences, depending on the specific situation of the nation involved. Melville writes that the Imeeo cattle "coming of a prolific ancestry, are a hearty set, racing over the island of Imeeo in considerable numbers; though in Tahiti, but few of them are seen. At the former place, the original pair must have scampered off to the interior, since it is now so thickly populated by their wild progeny" (O, 209). On Imeeo the cattle have become harvestable. They have become much like other forms of game, and they complement the agricultural lifestyle of Zeke and Shorty, who are given permission to hunt as many as they like: "The herds are the private property of Queen Pomaree; from whom the planters had obtained permission to shoot for their own use, as many as they pleased" (O, 209). In this case the Western farmers are able to supplement their agricultural fortune-seeking with free access to as much meat and corresponding hides as they can use for consumption or, presumably, trade.

On the other hand, in a nation like Hawaii, Vancouver's cattle gift had dramatic consequences. The Spanish in Hawaii were given consent by King Kamehameha III to hunt as many cattle as they would like. Melville writes, "It was not until the arrival of a party of Spanish hunters, men regularly trained to their calling upon the plains of California, that the work of slaughter was fairly begun" (O, 211). The Europeans and Hawaiians had discovered a desire for capital as opposed to a traditional harvesting system. They stopped hunting the cattle for their meat and were interested rather in their hides. In this way the Hawaiians became manipulated further into Western imperialism, first of Europe and eventually the United States. Kamehameha III was "receiving one of every two silver dollars paid down for their hides; so, with no thought for the future, the work of extermination went madly on" (*O*, 211). Soon, however, the Spaniards proved too efficient at hunting. After nearly destroying the islands' stock of cattle, Kamehameha III made a desperate "taboo" of the remaining numbers, hoping to reestablish them. Melville leaves his narrative there; the ten-year embargo "not yet expired" (*O*, 211). In *Omoo* Melville argues that Vancouver's action is actually a form of control, a way for the native populations of Polynesia to grow more Western in their desire for exploitative wealth as opposed to a harvest-based lifestyle, exemplified by the Typee's breadfruit harvest.

Certain apocryphal accounts help to substantiate Melville's narratives in *Typee* and *Omoo*. In much the same way that the real person behind the character of Toby supported Melville's *Typee*, the twins who lead Melville's narrator and Dr. Long Ghost to the farm in Imeeo were also based on real people. One of these brothers, William Libbey, wrote a journal of his own about his time working on the Imeeo farm, one that corroborates Melville's tale. This secondary text provides additional information about the situation for Yankees in Polynesia and their agricultural ventures there. Whereas Melville describes a harsh form of farming against an inhospitable tropical landscape, Libbey writes that the farmers had succeeded in planting potatoes by this point. He adds that they had also cleared more than two acres of guava, "burrow" trees, and other native plants to do so.[31] The agricultural work being performed at this point in the narrative, and in the history of the United States in Polynesia, is of a particular kind. In this instance the native guavas, harvestable fruit that could sustain the people with relatively mild labor, are replaced with potatoes and the augmented cattle. These facts support Melville's discussion of the West in Polynesia during expansion, and his agricultural critiques become useful further when he returns to farmers and farming as a topic for his land-based texts set in the United States. In these later works, Melville again connects agriculture and U.S. politics via the harm they cause to the poor. Melville once more compares forms of labor—specifically as regarding food production and distribution—strikingly in *Pierre*, as he describes the fate of rural farmers in the Berkshires following the anti-rent movement of nearby New York State.

DAIRIES AND TENEMENTS IN *PIERRE*

Pierre; or, The Ambiguities is the first novel that Melville wrote specifically about domestic issues. Melville criticism has focused on his powerful discussions of race, class, and nationalism in his other works, but far less so in *Pierre*. However, the historical connections are equally significant in this novel, though focused more on domestic issues than on the globalism described in his sea-based narratives. *Pierre* has been read as a psychological semiautobiography.[32] The main character declines into tragedy throughout the novel in a way that focuses on his internalizations of guilt on various levels. At the same time, many of the historical and cultural issues present in other Melville works, like *Moby-Dick*, also appear in *Pierre*. In this case Melville engages with agricultural production and production in general during a time of national expansion. He plants agricultural themes throughout his novel, as in the case of Pierre's family name, Glendinning, a name that represents the clash between rural and urban, agrarian and mechanized lives, as more glens ring with the din of industry. Even Melville's language in the novel reads as an exercise in expansionism, like the national policy he criticizes. Long a difficult work for audiences to appreciate or even to understand, *Pierre* remains largely unknown to the general reader. Called "probably the funniest tragedy ever written, and certainly the greatest potboiler of all time" by Robertson-Lorant, *Pierre* is a novel that discusses the lives of rural farming families, all of whom are forced to confront urbanization and the loss of their traditional ways of life.[33] In the novel at least one member of every family must transition from farmer to wage laborer in the city. In almost every case, and for a variety of reasons, this change results in tragedy for the families involved. Two characters Melville describes in detail are Isabel Banford and Charles Millthorpe. Isabel is Pierre's long-lost half sister and potential love interest, while Charles is a former acquaintance now living in the city. These characters contrast significantly against characters associated with the status quo: Pierre's fiancée, Lucy Tartan, and his aristocratic cousin, Glendinning Stanley. While *Pierre* is a psychological thriller that deals with incest, heredity, charity, and the process of writing literature, it is also a novel that confronts key national issues, like the rise of agri-expansion. In this way Melville allows the reader to understand more about the change from an agrarian-based economy to a wage-based one during a period known for agricultural conflict in the rural Northeast.

Melville wrote *Pierre* while working on his farm in the Berkshires, doing farm chores such as harvesting apples and haying, in addition to raising his family.[34] When Melville describes *Pierre* to Sophia Hawthorne, he turns to agrarian images, calling his novel about domesticity and production a "rural bowl of milk" as opposed to the "bowl of salt water" that had been *Moby-Dick* (*C*, 219). Melville is concerned with land, nobility, democracy, and agriculture in this novel, appreciating the Berkshires enough to set the early part of *Pierre* in that region, named Saddle Meadows. Moreover, the idea of lineage was a potent one for Melville, whose family had lost its ancestral farm before he began writing his rural novel. Significantly, the narrator describes Pierre's lineage extensively in the early sections. Himself a gentleman farmer and a member of declining aristocracy, Melville is perhaps uniquely able to link the concerns of working farmers and landed gentry in the Berkshires during this period. He draws the character of Lucy to show Pierre's potential future, in which he marries and is allowed to maintain his tenant-based lifestyle affiliated with the imperial Mrs. Glendinning. On the other hand, Isabel is a harbinger of the changes brought about by the rebellious tenant farmers. In this novel that pits rural against urban settings, rural-turned-urban figures like Isabel symbolize crucial aspects of farming families during this time. Never destined for great wealth, Isabel falls even lower in status over the course of the novel, though her claims for nobility may be as high as Pierre's own. This theme of misplaced nobility in agricultural settings is continued later in the figure of Mr. Millthorpe. Contrasted with Glendinning Stanley, a cousin who personifies Pierre's lineage, Millthorpe and his family represent the class of farmers who deserve more than they receive. The main character feels guilty throughout the novel because of his direct connection to the patronage system and his loyalty toward the anti-rent movement during the first half of the nineteenth century. In such a reading, the descriptions of certain characters are historically connected to a contentious time in the history of U.S. agri-expansion.

Pierre was written against the backdrop of the anti-rent movement during the first half of the nineteenth century. This movement was a response to the quasi-feudal system in place in rural New York State through the nineteenth century. Stretched tenant farmers of rural New York refused to pay rent on land they could no longer afford; they acted in response to the economic situation resulting from U.S. expansion, especially following the Panic of 1837. The development of intensive agriculture and the market revolution greatly affected rural farmers in the Northeast. In many cases the system of tenant farming was considered a safe alternative to the development of a market-based agricultural economy. Landlords encouraged this belief among their tenant farmers for self-serving reasons. The tenants would observe a rent-day ritual, show feudal respect to the landlords in social settings, and perform manual labor when requested. In exchange for this, landlords protected the lands of the community.[35] After 1837 landlords had their own financial security in doubt. Many had lost money speculating on railroads and land opportunities in the West that had failed to produce profits. In response, they grew harsh against their tenants, who in turn felt they had little choice but to protest. The farmers who made up the majority of the anti-rent movement particularly protested the concept of their annual "rent," which was really a "tribute" to their landlords in the form of time, money, or crops that they may not be able to spare. The anti-renters took on a revolutionary attitude, rioting and even dressing in Native American–influenced clothing during their protests—giving their cause some of the spirit of the Boston Tea Party.

These anti-rent "wars" peaked between 1839 and 1846 and resulted ultimately in the abolishment of the feudal farming system in the New York State Constitution.

Moreover, the anti-rent movement had a broad influence on neighboring communities. While it was centralized in upper New York State, it also affected the surrounding counties, including the nearby Berkshires in Massachusetts. In fact, these regions shared much agricultural history. The same Elkanah Watson who founded the Berkshire Agricultural Society in 1811 helped to found the Otsego County Agricultural Society in New York State in 1817. The New York society, under Watson's guidance, promoted agricultural specialization much as its sister organization in the Berkshires did, focusing on dairy, wool, and hops as suitable crops for the region. It also encouraged the use of additional fertilizers to make the depleted soils more productive, as well as annual agricultural fairs to foster a competitive community spirit.[36] In this way the agricultural societies of the Berkshires and Otsego County were nearly simultaneous in their specialization and intensification of agriculture and its effects on farmers—an agricultural equivalent to the expansion of the nation and its economy. However, the agricultural societies' examples of competitively developing advanced methods of agriculture did not make the actual living situations better for the farmers in the rural Northeast. While the previous arrangement seemed—and was—antidemocratic, the commercialization and intensification of agriculture did little to help matters for rural farmers of the anti-rent movement themselves.

The anti-rent movement was a significant enough disturbance that the New York state government sent military reinforcements to assist landowners in 1839. Then, in 1845 the government supplied three hundred troops to rural New York to help collect delinquent rents.[37] This military response is represented in the early pages of *Pierre*: "three hundred men-at-arms . . . have been sent out to distrain upon three thousand farmer-tenants of one landlord, at a blow. A fact most suggestive two ways; both whereof shall be nameless here."[38] Furthermore, Samuel Otter observes that Melville repeats so "long as grass grows or water runs" twice in reference to President Andrew Jackson's infamous 1829

message to the Creek Nation.[39] Melville turns his most psychological novel into a political commentary about rural U.S. farmers during
Jacksonian expansion, connecting rural farmers and the Creek Nation
in terms of government hypocrisy. The agricultural system at this time
becomes incorporated into the larger national system. Melville himself
was descended on his mother's side from the Van Rensselaer family,
one of the culprits of the anti-rent conflict. Thus, his potential familial
guilt appears throughout *Pierre* in an economic fashion through his
associations and references to the movement, as well as through his
sympathetic portraits of the rural farmers contrasted with the haughty
and unforgiving Mrs. Glendinning. Indeed, Mrs. Glendinning is represented as a villain not only through her incestuous jealousy over her son's
choice of marrying independent of her decision, but also through her
cruelty to her tenant farmers and strict adherence to a formal class-based
social code. Melville, meanwhile, wants his readers to sympathize with
struggling farmers like Isabel, Mr. Millthorpe, and even Delly Ulver.
These figures are described as victims based on their placement within
this quasi-feudal system and their struggle to escape that system by
moving to the city. In theory, even Pierre's great action in the novel—
supporting a sister even though this means losing his own economic
status and comforts of nobility—becomes a direct response to Melville's
anxiety of influence. Pierre wants to appear noble in the manner of his
honored ancestors, while at the same time making up for some of their
questionable actions.

Isabel Banford, Pierre's newly discovered sister, is related to the agricultural history of the Berkshires, including and beyond the anti-rent
movement. Though she comes from Europe, Isabel largely associates
herself with farms and farm life once in the United States: "But this
other house . . . There were cultivated fields about it, and in the distance
farm-houses and out-houses, and cattle, and fowls, and many objects
of that familiar sort. This house I am persuaded was in this country;
on this side of the sea" (*P*, 118). This rural farm represents the beginning of Isabel's awareness, in fact, as her time in Europe is spent in
near-animalistic conditions, whether in the European wilderness or in

an asylum. For Isabel, coming to the United States equals an agrarian familiarity. Moreover, Isabel finds her place and purpose in this nation among farming families. In addition to her quest to find her family, Isabel is taught the common female tasks associated with farming: "Now that was my residence, the farm-house. They taught me to sew, and work with wool, and spin the wool; I was nearly always busy now" (*P*, 122). Continuing her list of farm chores, she describes "milking the cows, and making butter, and spinning wool, and weaving carpets of thin strips of cloth" (*P*, 125). Isabel becomes a part of the U.S. farming class, helping to produce the dairy and wool that would be commonly associated with a northeastern farm in the first half of the nineteenth century. Watson's agricultural recommendations to both the Berkshires and Otsego County agricultural societies included a focus on raising dairy cattle and Merino sheep for their wool. Watson promised that such animals would do well in the hilly terrain of the Berkshires, and this advice is acted upon through the farming figures of Isabel and the Ulvers. In this way Isabel acts out the influence of reformers on northeastern farmers.

In Isabel's case this agricultural experience and skill eventually allows her to be introduced to her brother. She works at "the rented farmhouse of old Walter Ulver, father to the self-same Delly, forever ruined through the cruel arts of Ned" (*P*, 111). The Ulvers are tenant farmers under the patronage of Mrs. Glendinning, who uses her control—even over the parsonage—to force Delly Ulver to leave the village after the young woman becomes pregnant out of wedlock. Isabel is connected directly to the plight of the rural farmers by her placement, both in the focus on rural agriculture as well as in their lack of control over their own lives, in this case under the feudalistic Mrs. Glendinning. Moreover, the setting of the early conversations between Pierre and Isabel take place at the Ulver farm. The Ulver cottage has been compared to the red "moss-incrusted" farmhouse Hawthorne lived in when he was Melville's neighbor. In addition, Melville focuses on the image of the "lowly dairy-shed; its sides close netted with traced Madiera vines; and had you been close enough, peeping through that imposing tracery, and through the light slats barring the little embrasure of a window, you might have seen the gentle and contented captives—the pans of milk, and the snow-white Dutch cheeses in a row, and the molds of golden butter, and the jars of lily cream" of the Ulver dairy (*P*, 110). At a key point in the novel, when Pierre comes to take Isabel and Delly, as his wife and maid, to the city, Isabel stands "without the little dairy-wing, occupied in vertically arranging numerous glittering shield-like milk-pans on a long shelf, where they might purifyingly meet the sun" (*P*, 188). This image takes on a nostalgic tone as the future of the trio in the city is represented far less appealingly.

This final image of a woman standing outside of a rural country dairy is contrasted with the early descriptions of the city. Isabel tells Pierre, "I like not the town. Think'st thou, Pierre, the time will ever come when all the earth shall be paved?" (*P*, 231).[40] She appears to worry that her farm-based knowledge will lose its usefulness in an urban setting. Pierre mollifies her childlike question by saying that the city can never consume all of the country. However, the image the reader is left with is one in which urban spaces threaten the country. In this way, then, Isabel, and to a lesser extent Delly, represent another element of the cause of tenant farmers during Jacksonian expansion. Part of Pierre's particular journey through the course of the novel is determined through his connection to a specific agricultural history. In this reading, whether or not Isabel is really Pierre's family, she becomes his responsibility during his reckless attempt to right the quasi-feudal landowner system by moving to the city. The agrarian life of his childhood is no longer an option: that system is truly broken. Instead, he turns toward the city, as countless rural farmers have done before him, farmers like Charles Millthorpe. Unfortunately, the young Millthorpe and the other transplanted farmers often find that the urban system is at least as damaged as the agrarian one.

Charles Millthorpe gives another example of the plight of the rural farmer during early agri-expansion. He is as strictly contrasted with Pierre's cousin, Glendinning Stanley, as Isabel is with Lucy. If Glen is associated with the aristocracy, the young Millthorpe represents the urbanization and change befalling the farming families of this time. Melville describes him:

> Millthorpe was the son of a very respectable farmer—now dead—of more than common intelligence, and whose bowed shoulders and homely garb had still been surmounted by a head fit for a Greek philosopher, and features so fine and regular that they would have well graced an opulent gentleman. The political and social levelings and confoundings of all manner of human elements in America, produce many striking individual anomalies unknown in other lands. Pierre well remembered old farmer Millthorpe:—the handsome, melancholy, calm-tempered, mute, old man; in whose countenance— refinedly ennobled by nature, and yet coarsely tanned and attenuated by many a prolonged day's work in the harvest—rusticity and classicalness were strangely united. The delicate profile of his face, bespoke the loftiest aristocracy; his knobbed and bony hands resembled a beggar's. (*P*, 275)

The elder Millthorpe represents one element of U.S. agrarianism. He is a poor but noble farmer, possibly a fictionalized representation of Thomas Melvill Jr. However, he is eventually ruined through Mrs. Glendinning's harsh feudal system, in a further connection to the region's anti-rent history. Unable and unwilling to assist the Millthorpe family while they must farm land that is unsustainable for their needs, Mrs. Glendinning ultimately is the cause of Mr. Millthorpe's decline and eventual death and the desperate course of action of his son and family.

After his father's decline into poverty and death, Charles Millthorpe brings the rest of his family to the city, hoping to better provide for them as a wage laborer than as a failing farmer. Charles represents, like Delly or Isabel, the few alternatives available to rural farmers once they move to the city. Melville writes that the young Millthorpe "sold the horse, the cow, the pig, the plow, the hoe, and almost every movable thing on the premises; and, converting all into cash, departed with his mother and sisters for the city; chiefly basing his expectations of success on some vague representations of an apothecary relative there resident" (*P*, 279). Moreover, Charles seems to be having some success in the city. His story is not a tragedy; rather, "some mysterious latent good-will of Fate toward him, had not only thus far kept Charles from the Poor-House, but had really advanced his fortunes in a degree" (*P*, 279). For example, Charles helps Pierre find housing at the Church of the Apostles tenement, where he resides. Melville's description of Charles's advanced fortunes is ambiguous, however. While Melville maintains that Charles works for a "very large, and hourly increasing business," such descriptors ring hollow when they are combined with the images of "empty pigeon-holes" and an "unopened bottle of ink" in his "small dusty law-office," which illustrate a relative lack of productivity (*P*, 280). Furthermore, Charles is both working and living at the Apostles, a situation that implies that he has not reached full economic success in the city. Following Melville's theme of the egalitarianism of the anti-rent movement, though, Charles embraces the attitudes available in the city as opposed to at Saddle Meadows. "Pierre was at first somewhat startled by his exceedingly frank and familiar manner; all old manorial deference for Pierre was clean gone and departed" (*P*, 280). Melville returns his reader to the earlier feudal farming system rebelled against by the anti-renters, in which tenant farmers were expected to act in deference to their patrons, in this case the Glendinnings. Charles Millthorpe shows the ambiguous choices available to poor farmers and wage laborers alike during this period. While the country was by no means a perfect land, ruled by often-harsh landlords, the city is similarly flawed, ruled by the owners of corporations and factories and, moreover, depriving workers of exercise, nature, and society available in the country. Ultimately, Melville makes Charles and Nelly his surviving characters. These farmers-turned-city-laborers outlive Pierre, Isabel, Lucy, Glen, and Lucy's brother after the tragedy at the end of the novel, in perhaps Melville's most democratic statement of the story.

In the novel Pierre progresses from an idyllic baronial life to one of abject poverty in the city. Melville focuses on this ironic povertiresque in the work: "If the grown man of taste, possess not only some eye to detect the picturesque in the natural landscape, so also, has he as keen a perception of what may not unfitly be here styled, the *povertiresque* in the social landscape" (*P*, 276, Melville's italics). He compares "the dismantled thatch in a painted cottage of Gainsborough" to "the time-tangled and want-thinned locks of a beggar" (*P*, 276). In a passage echoed in "Poor Man's Pudding and Rich Man's Crumbs," Melville puts in harsh and cruel relief the "Optimist" philosophy that would "deny that any misery is in the world, except for the purpose of throwing the fine *povertiresque* element into its general picture" (*P*, 277, Melville's italics). Farmers like Mr. Millthorpe become removed from their poverty and into the landscape as aesthetic objects in this philosophy. Mrs. Glendinning shows herself to be the villain of the piece not only by disowning Pierre, but also through her acts against Delly and Mr. Millthorpe. Indeed, she never thinks critically of her own actions, instead using the "Optimist" philosophy when describing Millthorpe as "noble" in spite of his poverty, as opposed to offering him material assistance. Mrs. Glendinning once more represents the failed system that forces farmers away from the means of producing their own food and to the cities where they live at a remove from their basic necessities—even further under the control of a wealthier class. In this manner a farmer like Mr. Millthorpe is connected to the Typee in Melville's earlier text and to others who are removed from their agrarian lifestyle and suffer for it. However, even the city does not provide a lasting refuge for Pierre, Isabel, or Lucy. It is only through the characters of Charles and Nelly that Melville gives hope for anti-rent farmers in *Pierre*.

Melville encourages a domestic reading of *Pierre*. His intended audience was originally a female readership like his own family and Sophia Hawthorne. Indeed, both Nathaniel Hawthorne and Melville wrote domestic novels following an 1851 visit to a Shaker settlement in nearby Hancock; as Melville was writing *Pierre*, Hawthorne worked on *The Blithedale Romance*. Thus, the domestic and agrarian elements of both works are doubtless intentional. As in the domestic novels that influenced Melville, Wyn Kelley adds, there seems to be a "cover story" in *Pierre*, much as there would be in contemporary women's novels, and underneath this "it works out sensitive personal issues or presses an urgent social agenda under a socially acceptable guise."[41] While *Pierre* did not succeed at publication in finding an "acceptable guise," Melville does succeed at making a critical commentary on society in his novel. These two examples of farmers-turned-city-dwellers following the anti-rent movement highlight some of the larger issues of Melville's other works. In a discussion that will continue into his short stories, Melville focuses on the rural farming class to challenge those who read the poverty around them in aesthetic as opposed to sociological terms. Melville's depths of ambiguity appear once again in his tragic discussion of farmers forced into the cities and the rural forms of oppression that drive them there. The anti-imperialism that Melville is known for appears in *Pierre* and again as a class-based discussion of rural farming communities in "Poor Man's Pudding and Rich Man's Crumbs" (1854) and factory workers in "The Paradise of Bachelors and the Tartarus of Maids" (1855). In these works Melville shows the effects of agri-expansion on small farmers who are often forced into industrial forms of employment once farming is no longer tenable.

TREES AND SEEDS: FARMERS AND FACTORY MAIDS

Elements from *Pierre* continue into Melville's short stories. His concerns with agricultural conditions and their effects on U.S. farmers are again found in the U.S.-based portions of the diptychs "Poor Man's Pudding and Rich Man's Crumbs" and "The Paradise of Bachelors and the Tartarus of Maids." One of the "promises" of the United States during the nineteenth century was as an idealized democratic state, one that provided the potential for wealth for the U.S. worker in developing industries transitioning away from an agrarian economy. In reality, however, the dream of acquiring wealth within the expanding U.S. borders of both territory and trade often did not come true for U.S. laborers. While people in the United States hoped to work for something beyond material necessities like food, they were themselves often materially used up within the nation. Melville responds to the hypocrisy that permeated the United States during this time in a series of diptychs in which the ideas of charity and economics become central themes. Though the United States claimed to be an "empire for liberty," the fact was that the rich ate their fill and left their inedible leftovers to the poor, who were in turn fed into the system of capital via their labor—agricultural and otherwise. In both of the U.S.-based halves of these diptychs, the poor are shown to suffer—even to the point of death—as they must continue to labor. For example, in "Poor Man's Pudding," the first half of the diptych "Poor Man's Pudding and Rich Man's Crumbs," Melville shows the contradiction between the dying Coulters and the landowning Squire Teamster.[42] The squire, who has a comfortable home farm, is using up the labor of the Coulters, as Mr. Coulter must harvest trees for the squire's domestic use. In other words, even as the Coulters waste away, they must keep working. Melville shows that the economic system that has been brought about as an effect of developing agri-expansion does not work. Nature is not going to take care of people when their poverty is not natural, but rather is caused by the conditions of available employment as the nation moves from an agricultural to a factory-based system.

In "Poor Man's Pudding," Melville speaks particularly of the United States and how it treats rural farmers. Set in the year 1814, this story takes place before the aggressive U.S. push into territory and agriculture.[43] However, this choice of dates more closely links the United States with European imperialist nations, showing that Melville appreciated the fact that the United States had become comparable to these empires. Following the War of 1812, technological advances made it possible to acquire food more cheaply from the interior of the expanding nation. Villages moved away from self-sufficiency to an agricultural system through which surplus products were traded for cash and other goods as recommended by the agricultural societies of the time.[44] The nation was transforming from agrarianism to a market-based economy, and many of those agricultural jobs were transformed to factory work, through which laborers produced a different kind of surplus than those encouraged by Watson's Berkshires and Otsego County agricultural societies.[45] Melville uses elements of his intricately detailed knowledge of industry, previously seen in his sea-based novels, into his land-based stories. In so doing, he is able to challenge the narrative of economic progress and the exploitation of the worker that accompanied this particular phase of nineteenth-century U.S. expansion as the nation moved from an agrarian to urban economy. In addition, the story is a satire of society's conception of charity to the poor. Using his theory of the povertiresque, defined in *Pierre*, Melville demonstrates the failures of that system.

Melville's diptych uses a nameless narrator and his friend, a poet named Blandmour, to challenge the status quo of social charity in this era of early agri-expansion. Blandmour demonstrates his overt blindness to true economic injustices in his description of the natural remedies for the poor as opposed to social ones—thus relieving the wealthy of any responsibility for existing conditions. Blandmour artistically renames basic needs in the hopes of euphemizing the horrors of poverty and a poor family's lifestyle. Water becomes a "Poor Man's Manure," "Poor Man's Eye-water," and "Poor Man's Egg." Indeed, water is the most often-repeated image throughout the sketch. The "economically contrived" uses of water that Blandmour finds are actually insufficient substitutes for the real foods and basic needs the resource is being forced to replace (*PT*, 290). Water feeds and fuels, but it also chills and eventually kills the Coulter family; the positive aspects of water delineated by Blandmour do not redeem it for them. The narrator notices that "the wind drives yonder drifts of 'Poor Man's Manure' off poor Coulter's two-acre patch here, and piles it up yonder on rich Squire Teamster's twenty-acre field" (*PT*, 289). The "Poor Man's Manure" is failing the Coulters—and is watering the rich man's field instead. Even in the freely provided natural resources, the Coulters are not provided for. Because of this, they have less to eat, as their fields are not able to produce enough food. The Coulters are being systematically driven from a more sustainable agricultural way of life toward a wage-based system that is not tenable.

However, the narrator is no more helpful in terms of actual assistance toward the family he visits, the Coulters.[46] As a gentleman and so a part of the same class as the estate-owning Squire Teamster and poet Blandmour, the narrator finds himself appreciating the povertiresque figures as Blandmour presents them.[47] As part of this touristic appreciation of the U.S. working poor in agriculture, the narrator decides to visit the Coulters, a farming family who must also hire out their labor to their landowner, Squire Teamster. During his visit the narrator begins to mimic Blandmour's way of turning the very symbols of poverty into romantic images, trying the Coulter's "Poor Man's Pudding," calling the green shavings of trees "Poor Man's Matches," and dubbing Mr. Coulter's long walk back to work a "Poor Man's saunter" (*PT*, 292, 294). Though the narrator is honestly disturbed by the poverty represented by the inedible meal offered to him, his description of the Coulter family in the end mirrors Blandmour's povertiresque attitude. They are seen as honest, hardworking, impoverished, and trapped in an aspect of agri-expansion. Melville shows that the narrator is an actor within the class system that uses the Coulter family's labor to help the national project further described in povertiresque terms. Moreover, the meal the narrator tries to eat during his visit is made up of "salt pork, rye-bread, and pudding" (*PT*, 293). The narrator declares it "impossible" to eat the pork and pudding with their "mouldy, briny taste" and "yellowish crust" and finds himself "half choked" after trying to eat a few bites (*PT*, 294–95). As he finds most of their food inedible, he instead eats their rye bread, their only healthy food. As opposed to going hungry, or suffering what the poor must suffer when eating unhealthy food, the narrator eats the Coulters' best food, depriving them of what could actually keep them healthy. In this manner he makes them even worse off and hungrier than they were before. Furthermore, he does not offer them compensation for the meal, citing his concern for their pride as his excuse for not doing so. In this way he mimics Mrs. Glendinning's povertiresque attitude toward Mr. Millthorpe in *Pierre*. The Coulters have no opportunity to replace the foods that the narrator has eaten, and they have less food and fewer financial resources than before the narrator visited them. Therefore, his touristic incursion on their hospitality has cost them disproportionally. Like the squire, the narrator's actions keep the farming class struggling within a developing economic and agricultural framework, in a manner that invokes elements of the anti-rent movement. Instead of being able to farm their own land, they become laborers working for the squire. The development of a new kind of agriculture fundamentally harms them.

The Coulters as farmers are embodied as failed producers of agricultural commodities. Though Mrs. Coulter tries to feed her family with the production of her body, first with her breast milk and eventually by weeping into her cooking, her children still die. Mr. Coulter alone seems to have a strong enough appetite to eat her food, which would otherwise be considered unfit for human consumption, and his appetite comes from laboring for long hours on a daily basis. He eats as much of the briny pudding as his short break will allow: "one—two—three mouthfuls must do me" (*PT*, 294). Whether because of the time allotted for his break or the truly inedible quality of the pudding, he can eat only three bites. Mr. Coulter is the opposite of his wife, representing another aspect of poverty as it plagues the bodies of U.S. workers. Physically strong, he is desperate to remain that way. He tells the narrator that he asks only to avoid "the rheumatiz and other sickness," as any such illness would be the literal death of himself and his family (*PT*, 293). His body is the only commodity he has to offer, but even so he fails to support his family through its labor. The connection between his body and labor remains, however. When he is unable to farm, he hires himself out to fell trees at wages, and he is literally becoming treelike. As he first enters the shanty, he is described as a tree emitting sap: "He turned toward his wife, inquiringly, and stood stock-still, while the moisture oozed from his patched boots to the floor" (*PT*, 293).[48] The production of his labor is what the squire uses to fuel his home, consuming any heat from Mr. Coulter's watery existence. Though he might not consider himself as blind to the plight of others as Blandmour or the squire, the narrator falls under the same category as being one who is clearly warm, fed, and sheltered when others are not. This issue of culpability is presented more completely through the concluding image of the story: the narrator sits by a warm fire with Blandmour and his family, an image contrasted at once to the Coulters' cabin. The fire at Blandmour's home is warm and dry, while the Coulters' fire is insufficient and created by the lesser leavings of the tree. Finally, the wood at Blandmour's is cut by one of countless Coulter-like laborers, would-be farmers forced into laboring for wages in factory work and other menial jobs. The result of this combined bodily labor—the physical bodies that create the labor—fuels the fires of squire-like families throughout the nation.

The narrator visits the Coulters in order to experience a romanticized version of Melville's povertiresque, to feel good about himself and his place in the U.S. system of labor, which mirrors the plight of workers anywhere, northeastern paper mills, for example. Becoming aware of the inequality in this developing system of expansion, he does absolutely nothing to ameliorate it. To his credit, though, he is profoundly moved by his experience; he admits that he "won't mention the word" that occurs to him after what he has seen (*PT*, 296). The narrator must become speechless by the end of his experience with the Coulters given what that experience has taught him about the United States at this stage of agri-expansion.[49] He sees finally and fully the poverty of the U.S. working class—the very citizens promised better lives through industrialization and the progress moving the nation from a mostly agrarian economy to a capitalist system. The promise implied in the nineteenth-century United States does not deal with the bodies of farmers, no longer able to sustain themselves directly from the land and forced to become hired laborers.

Melville continues his theme in which the bodies of the workers fuel U.S. expansion, specifically agri-expansion, in "The Tartarus of Maids" portion of the diptych "The Paradise of Bachelors and the Tartarus of Maids." In this story the workers at a northeastern paper factory are all maids, unmarried women, who have moved from an agricultural to a factory-based form of living. Melville shows the industrial poverty in an environment where women are being bled dry by vampiric anthropomorphized machines of industry. In his travels Melville had been confronted by the often-degrading move from agriculture to mechanized factories, a move by which nonhuman machines and their owners efficiently grew stronger off the lives and bodies of the workers tending them. Melville visited local paper mills in 1851 and modeled "The

Tartarus of Maids" to some extent on that experience.[50] He discusses the rise of the factory and its implied connection to the development of large-scale farming in this story.

The product resulting from the bodily labor of the maids in this instance is paper—a material necessity for Melville's narrator in his seed-distribution business. The once again nameless narrator is a "seedsman" who looks to expand his business, connecting him to the expansion of U.S. agriculture.[51] Outside of the obvious sexual implications of the story and his role in it, this narrator is literally connected to the drastic changes occurring in agriculture within the United States during the nineteenth century. The narrator is a personification of U.S. expansion; he boasts of having customers for his agricultural product in "all the Eastern and Northern States" as well in "Missouri and the Carolinas" (PT, 324). The fact that he trades to the Carolinas and Missouri shows his direct involvement in the slave states and along the contested frontier; he is implicated in profiting from two of the most recognizable horrors in U.S. history—the internal imperialism of the slaves in the South and the wars against Native Americans in the West. This is the land-based parallel to Melville's well-known whaling empire of the sea. The narrator distributes seminal foodstuffs for capital gain across what is at this time the breadth of the U.S. territory, promoting specific kinds of seeds following recommendations like those made by Watson to his agricultural societies. The fruits of U.S. expansion are represented here as the actual seeds that will produce them. Furthermore, the narrator's clothes mark his attitudes regarding national policy. On his journey to the paper mill, looking for the best and most economical paper available, he dresses for the cold "well fitted with buffalo and wolf robes" (PT, 325). His business's growth has not led him to the Great Plains of the future United States or to the wilds of the Yukon Territory. All of these animal garments are, rather, ostentatious displays of his wealth that also make him into a wolfish figure, one that preys on the weak. He spends the duration of his visit at the paper factory pitying the fates of the tragic figures of the women workers. However, this pity and grotesque awe do not stop him from conducting his business there.

Melville emphasizes the narrator's culpability through his part in the fate of the women working in the paper mill.[52]

As "unproductive" members of society, these maids do not harvest seeds in their bodies to grow into productive workers through subsequent generations. Instead, they make paper for the envelopes that will contain generative seeds. The labor of these maids produces materials used to further a food-related industry that is expanding across the antebellum nation, one that will develop even more following the Civil War. The women are being apparently bled to death while working at this factory. This is seen in the image of a river running through the mill. Mineral deposits have caused it to be called "Blood River" by the local residents (*PT*, 324). It appears as though the river drains blood from the factory and so from the workers in the factory. Emphasizing the lack of female fertility through the symbolically red river, Melville shows that these women must become productive in their factory work instead. The vitality of the women working in the mill is incorporated into their material product: the paper. They become pale and blank-faced as animalistic machines consume them while producing healthy-looking paper. The "pale, blue" young women, without any protection from the elements, are markedly contrasted to their foreman, who is "dark-complexioned" with health and "well-wrapped" (*PT*, 327). Later the narrator notices that the faces of the women are "blank" and void of life—he uses the word "blank" six times in one sentence. Meanwhile, the note paper they make is "rose-hued" as if full of life (*PT*, 328). One woman is young and fresh faced as she places the blank pages into the machine. The other woman, as she gathers the finished product, is described as "ruled and wrinkled" (*PT*, 328). The women's lives are once again compared to the paper—only this time, it is imprinting on them in addition to itself. It is not stealing their blood, so much as aging them, stealing their vitality. The narrator is particularly struck as the women change places and the young woman thus becomes the "ruled" one and seems to physically change in front of him. The narrator notes, "I looked from the rosy paper to the pallid cheek, but said nothing" (*PT*, 328). As in the case of the Coulters, the spectacle of these factory workers—all women—within the development of agri-expansion and factorization has left Melville's narrator speechless.

As Melville's narrator wordlessly observes the lack of vitality among the factory women, he notes the corresponding animation of the factory machinery. The "iron animal" possesses near-human qualities, and the machine room has a "strange, blood-like, abdominal heat" (*PT*, 328, 331). The machine seems to be incorporating the lives of the women into itself and growing even more lively. To show this, Melville calls one woman "tame" when compared to the machine she tends (*PT*, 328). There are many iron animals within the paper factory humming satisfactorily as their human workers feed them. Melville shows this as part of the developing industrial agricultural economy: "Machinery—that vaunted slave of humanity—here stood menially served by human beings, who served mutely and cringingly as the slave serves the Sultan" (*PT*, 328). Not only are the machines likened to living things, they are raised above the workers who serve them. Furthermore, the only sound in the factory is the humming iron animal and the conversation between Cupid (the errand boy), the foreman, and the narrator. The machine produces a "low, steady, overruling hum" while the women are utterly silent; the narrator notes that the "human voice was banished from the spot" (*PT*, 328). Perhaps because of this silence, the narrator experiences "something of awe" watching the machine busily at "its play" (*PT*, 333). Melville has taken the image of the sublime and made something grotesque out of it. The narrator feels awe toward the machine, not toward the natural world around him, but he does so for the same reasons that give nature its transcendence: it is eternal—the workers will sicken and die, but the machine will not falter. Melville's narrator feels a sublime realization about the seeming inevitably of the machines in the world of U.S. expansion, a world moving away from an agrarian and toward an industrial economy.

The women are not only slaves to this sublime and playful iron animal, they are also giving birth to the paper that comes out of it, and they ultimately become their own executioners while still in its service. The long passage focusing on the nine-minute production of paper has been compared to a woman's gestation period.[53] The women have produced paper offspring with the help of the same machine that drains their vitality as they create a grotesque new "life." The union of human and machine in this instance has created paper. As a sad-looking former nurse oversees this process, the narrator observes that she does not seem as interested in this industrial productivity as she should be. He then discovers that she works at the factory only because there is little work for a nurse in that area anymore. Like Mrs. Coulter in "Poor Man's Pudding," the women in "The Tartarus of Maids" are not successful at producing human offspring, so they produce foolscap paper for clients involved in the distribution of U.S. agri-expansion instead. By this point there are no longer enough young people left for the nurse to assist; she must tend the factory machines, as they are the community's only vital bodies. After the mechanized birth comes death, and this is also described in the story as women workers with "consumptive pallors" cut sheets of paper with ominous-looking scythes, in the process of becoming "their own executioners" (*PT*, 330). The narrator meditates on the gallows-like scene as the women cut the paper using their fatal blades; he realizes that this job will take their lives. By this point in the story, the paleness of their cheeks has been referred to repeatedly; however, this is the first moment Melville actually uses the term "consumptive." These women have a disease that will eat them from within. They are dying by slow steady degrees at the hand of an iron animal, a symbol of the connection between the Industrial Revolution and a new economy based on expansion. This economy corresponds to agriculture, and agri-expansion is a parallel development with factorization at this transitional period in U.S. economic history.

In "The Tartarus of Maids," Melville draws a parallel to the Lowell factory system of the early nineteenth century, one of the foundations of the economic growth of the United States during that period. The women producing this paper to be used for the fruits of empire are themselves used up, but their pain leaves its impression on the narrator: "Slowly, mournfully, beseechingly, yet unresistantly, they gleamed along, their agony dimly outlined on the imperfect paper, like the print of the tormented face on the handkerchief of Saint Veronica" (*PT*, 334). The tortured maids become saint-like, even Christ-like, in their misery as tools of agri-expansion. Melville writes "The Tartarus of Maids" entirely about issues of labor, including his own labor via his writing. As he does so, he brings issues of class and the inherent value of labor into the story.[54] Melville shows the often stark differences between the ideals of democratic societies—in both the agrarian and factory systems—and the reality for the working families trapped within systems as harsh as any within the nation's global influence, returning his readers to the image of the Typee that began his larger critique.

Part of Melville's focus in highlighting the culpability of capitalists like the narrators of "Poor Man's Pudding" and "The Tartarus of Maids" is in showing how prevalent their guilt is in the suffering of U.S. workers during the development of agri-expansion. In "The Tartarus of Maids," the narrator realizes that he buys the paper that these women have given their health and their lives to make. Melville demonstrates the conditions by which the development of factories can harm workers who used to be farmers, both in their body and mind.[55] Melville places himself directly in this conversation. He realizes that as a writer he is also to some degree culpable. He uses paper, he burns fuel, and he takes advantage of the products made by workers like the Coulters and the maids. Like any U.S. consumer of agricultural products, he contributes to a system that uses up the bodies of U.S. laborers.[56] The narrators in both "The Tartarus of Maids" and "Poor Man's Pudding" are men who consider themselves to be compassionate, and yet throughout the course of the stories, they are exposed as participants in an unjust system of U.S. economics at a time of agricultural revolution.

Melville shows that the workers in "Poor Man's Pudding" and "The Tartarus of Maids" are harmed in a similar fashion, related to their connection to developments in agriculture in the nineteenth century. As the Coulters are farmers turned into starving day laborers, the women of "The Tartarus of Maids" are consumptively bled to death to produce material that contributes to national agri-expansion. The narrator wonders at how it is "so strange that red waters should turn out pale chee—paper," stopping himself before he can fully commit to the grotesque by saying "cheeks" (*PT*, 329). Meanwhile, the humming machinery with its damp, abdominal heat can also be seen as a stomach that digests the women who spend almost all of their time within it. If the narrator is Actaeon, to some degree feeling the pain of his frostbitten cheeks (pain the workers are well past feeling), these women are like Jonah, living within the stomach of the great leviathan almost as literally as Tashtego's descent into the whale in *Moby-Dick*.[57] They are consumed through grotesque methods (both cyborg-like and sexualized) to help the nation in its business of producing food to increase its numbers and by extension itself. The Coulters work for a version of the feudal landowner and farmer in Squire Teamster, and the factory women are producing paper for seed envelopes that will help distribute food across the nation. The United States has turned food production into yet one more form of economic expansion, and the nation gains at the expense of its laborers. Much of the literature Melville writes during his time living at Arrowhead, while he works as a farmer and a writer, deals with the human cost associated with the development of agri-expansion.

CONCLUSION: THE ROSE FARMER

Writing from Arrowhead in 1851, Melville describes the modest, though fulfilling, rewards of the rural life in a philosophical letter to Hawthorne: "If I have done the hardest possible day's work, and then come to sit down in a corner and eat my supper comfortably—why, then I don't think I deserve any reward for my hard day's work—for am I not now at peace? Is not my supper good? My peace and my supper are my reward" (*C*, 211–12). In this way it would seem that throughout Melville's writing career, he had to some extent his own reward in life, and a much larger one in posterity. Melville's critiques of nation and imperialism have made him one of the most studied U.S. authors of the nineteenth century, and his writings are read throughout U.S. literature survey courses. The larger backdrop of Melville's writing is a world economy in which the United States is already expanding and incorporating more than it needs, whether breadfruit, whale oil, dairy, or other agricultural crops. In *Moby-Dick* Melville writes about one of the nation's earliest global industries, already putting a violent and in some cases cannibal price on the cost of whale oil for the U.S. consumer. For the workers on whaling ships—like workers in factories or on farms in the United States during this period—the figures of the whales they kill are reflected in their own harsh lives. Melville focuses the reader's attention on the physical exploitation of workers, connecting three key themes in the development of the country during the nineteenth century: bodies, labor, and exploitation.[58] Melville bids his readers, "For God's sake, be economical with your lamps and candles! not a gallon you burn, but at least one drop of man's blood was spilled for it."[59] In *Moby-Dick* Melville focuses on laborers and their abuses in a way that becomes even more significant in his later writings.

In one of Melville's late writings—a poem—he returns to the image of agriculture. In "The Rose Farmer," Melville's narrator is bequeathed "a farm in fee / Forever consecrate to roses."[60] The narrator must research the best way to produce a profit from that rose farm: to harvest the roses themselves or their attar. Melville's narrator returns to the antebellum issue of agri-expansion but ultimately decides, "For wise employment, / Repute and profit, health, enjoyment, / I am for roses—*sink* the Attar!"[61] The narrator decides ultimately to enjoy the crop itself, as opposed to the more materialist commodity. At the end of Melville's writing career, he remained concerned with market-based production as opposed to an idyllic model. In addition, symbolizing his career as a writer, this is a direct comment on U.S. agricultural policy during the early stages of expansion. Melville's examples of production as they effectively destroy—even consume—the U.S. farmer and factory worker challenge the early stages of U.S. globalization.

2

Local Beans, Apples, and Berries

When La Mountain and Haddock dropped down into the Canada wilderness the other day, they came near starving or dying of cold, wet, and fatigue, not knowing where to look for food nor how to shelter themselves. Thus far we have wandered from a simple and independent life . . . Talk about tariffs and protection of home industry, so as to be prepared for hard times and wars! Here we are deriving our bread stuffs from the west, our butter stuffs from Vermont, and our tea and coffee and sugar stuffs (and much more that we stuff ourselves with) from the other side of the globe.
HENRY DAVID THOREAU, *Wild Fruits*, 243

Henry David Thoreau questions the drastic changes in U.S. agriculture and consumption in this passage from a posthumously published work on the wild fruits of the Concord region of Massachusetts. He does so in a way that relates food production and consumption to the nation's drive for greater territory during the nineteenth century. The adventurers of Thoreau's example are unable to sustain themselves in the woodlands of Canada because they lack the appropriate knowledge to harvest the foods of that area; the luckless travelers "might have had several frogs a piece if they had known how to find them."[1] Thoreau connects their ignorance to the larger issues of "tariffs" and "home industry," extrapolating from this example to a larger commentary about the United States as a whole during this time of agri-expansion. Thoreau notes that "we" have complicated "our" lives detrimentally from the most useful and "simple" kinds of knowledge, and instead of local foods, then, U.S. consumers turn to "bread stuffs" and "sugar stuffs," as well as the other

67

foods we "stuff ourselves with" from the newly acquired territories in the West and from "the other side of the globe." Thoreau challenges the agricultural and dietary practices of the United States during the nineteenth century, as the nation already had become engaged in the global food trade. The food that the United States consumed was coming from farther away than ever before, from lands messily acquired over a short period. Throughout his writings Thoreau warns against the dangers of what he sees as an excessive form of agriculture already established by the antebellum period.

Thoreau writes of reforming agri-expansion and its influence on the U.S. diet, comparing agriculture to nineteenth-century expansion directly. In both *Walden* (1854) and the later sketches now compiled in *Wild Fruits* (2001), Thoreau experiments in local farming and dietary practices. Within these experiments in what might now be called sustainable agriculture, Thoreau treats two forms of localized farming, the individually maintained bean field and the huckleberry-gathering community. To these he adds a dietary element that consists of mostly vegetable foods. To help direct him toward this simplified consumption and local agriculture, Thoreau looks to the natural world, as opposed to agricultural societies and their recommendations. In fact, the woodchuck—long appreciated as a comic symbol of Thoreau's baser appetites—comes to act as a model of sustainable food-gathering, in serving as both Thoreau's vegetarian guide and his failed hunting experiment. In looking to the production and consumption of local foods as his idea of a cure for the national disease of an exploitative agri-expansion, Thoreau turns to neighboring flora and fauna to demonstrate that his own practices are useful models for other U.S. consumers. Thoreau's experiment in simplified consumption, then, is a reevaluation of the national diet and agriculture during this time of national expansion, and his personal example becomes a counter to the tragedy of the epigraph's doomed adventurers.

There remains significant work to be done on Thoreau's writing in terms of his agricultural and dietary praxis. Pierre Bourdieu maintains that those richer in cultural than economic capital tend toward asceticism and originality in their culinary tastes. Thoreau's life and writings were arguably prone to asceticism. Also, his need for originality of thought and a disdain for the judgments of his neighbors make Thoreau a figure socialized toward independent reform projects. Thoreau privileged simplicity, individuality, and creativity in his lifestyle, and the agricultural experiments described in *Walden* and *Wild Fruits* follow this preference. He opposed the technological, economic, and industrial developments in agriculture promoted by early agricultural figures like Henry Colman, even though most U.S. farmers at the time embraced them. Furthermore, Thoreau challenged the "fat cats" of the middle class of the nineteenth century, whose newly developed consumption habits too closely mirrored U.S. expansionism.[2] Bourdieu's analysis of twentieth-century France, then, is useful to a discussion of Thoreau's nineteenth-century northeastern United States. Thoreau also highlights agriculture, not traditionally a popular topic, as a subject worthy of critical discussion.[3] He, however, would make fieldwork a rich source for his literature, becoming a role model for future authors and reformers. Thoreau writes of his farming experiment, including episodes that describe a seriocomic battle with a local woodchuck. Moreover, to counter the overall national expansionism, specifically as connected to agriculture, Thoreau turns to the level of the individual, engaging in this cultural theorizing in domestic agriculture. *Walden* shows Thoreau's personal vision of agriculture and its reform, while *Wild Fruits* displays his ideas for society more broadly. Throughout, he argues that it is better to grow foods that can be recognized and used by the community, with smaller and sustainable local harvests, in order to prevent the ignorance of the ill-fated Canadian adventurers.

Thoreau writes in response to the changes in U.S. farming during the first half of the nineteenth century. Agriculture is directly connected to the politics of the nation. Newly acquired agricultural lands in the West made available a greater variety of foodstuffs to a greater number of citizens. The Indian Removal Act of 1830, subsequent Indian wars, and the conclusion of the U.S.-Mexican War in 1848 showed that the United States was willing to bloody itself in its drive to acquire greater expanses of land during the first half of the nineteenth century. These lands were often developed into farms and ranches, and the foods produced in these new U.S. territories were then transported back to the industrialized East. Developing technologies made the transportation of food from these ever-widening territories possible, through the use of steamboats, clipper ships, and railroads. The Erie Canal opened in 1825, steam trains began running in 1830, and the United States had come to dominate ocean-trading routes by the 1830s.[4] Moreover, the Panic of 1837 created an economic depression that hurt small towns, as they lost their trade to urban centers. Meanwhile, legal acts like the Fugitive Slave Act of 1850 brought the question of national boundaries into focus. In summary, these historical factors created an environment that encouraged the expansion of agriculture to larger, cheaper tracts of land in the West. This development was ruinous to the small northeastern farmer, and by the 1850s the region was forced to revolutionize its agriculture, specializing crops and intensifying production, specifically. Northeastern farmers were feeling pressure to compete with the nation's trend toward agri-expansion, and they actively sought new breeds of crops that could be grown to trade at the national and global levels in order to do so. New borders were being drawn culinarily in order to adapt to the change in the nation's physical boundaries. Thoreau defines his ideal U.S. consumer as one who would challenge these agricultural developments by focusing on locally grown, mostly vegetable foods.

Thoreau was critical of the recommendations of antebellum agricultural reformers like Henry Colman, who suggested not that northeastern farmers focus on the local, but rather that they take intensive steps to maximize production in order to compete with the large-scale farms of the West. In his *Fourth Report on the Agriculture of Massachusetts*, published between 1838 and 1841, Colman notes that Middlesex County, the region including Concord, had traditionally based its agriculture on its proximity to Boston, relying on the fact that families often possessed homes in the country as well as in the city. Because of this arrangement, he observes, the area grew a limited quantity of a variety of fruits, vegetables, dairy products, and meat that could be marketed locally. Colman names the region a "garden culture" rather than a "field culture," noting the lack of market stability in its agriculture. He worries that the lack of exportable crops and the fact that this "garden culture" selection barely satisfies the local population place the Concord farmer in a precarious position. He argues for a greater intensity of crop selection, application, and production, adding that Concord farmers should select a smaller number of foodstuffs to grow more intensely.[5] One example of the successful application of Colman's theory is presented in the figure of Ephraim Bull. Bull, a Concord farmer, discovered and became successful producing the Concord grape, named after its hometown, a grape that has been used in juices and jams across the nation and the globe ever since.[6]

As with the example of the Concord grape, Colman pursued ways to increase farm production in regions like Concord for a larger consumer base. He urged farmers of the county to focus their attention on the production of corn and hay specifically, writing that corn "should be considered as the great crop of New England, and its cultivation ought to be increased tenfold."[7] By the 1840s English hay had become such a successful feed crop that farmers were clearing more lands to dedicate to hay exclusively.[8] Further, Colman compliments the "improvements" of the land of Lexington, Groton, Framingham, Concord, "and many other towns" in their "redemption of peat bogs and their conversion from sunken quagmires into most productive arable and grass lands."[9] In the U.S. West, the only land considered acceptable for harvesting or farming was the prairie, the land most suitable for grasses. This attitude became predominant in the Northeast as well, following advice from figures like Colman. Finally, Colman encourages Middlesex County to take advantage of agricultural societies, emphasizing the importance of annual meetings and fairs in order to encourage innovation and advances in production through the spirit of friendly competition. Applying such methods and focusing on specific crops would, he hopes, reestablish the county as a strong farming region.

Though Colman wrote his report in response to the real concerns of local farmers in a depressed economy, Thoreau emphatically disagrees with his suggestions. Thoreau does seek out agricultural advice for his various experiments with local, small-scale farming, but he looks to different sources for that information. His journal records his conversations with several Concord farmers, many of whom were close friends. George Minott was one of Thoreau's neighbors in Concord. A small-scale farmer, Minott had a local knowledge highly esteemed by Thoreau and Ralph Waldo Emerson. Thoreau discusses Minott in his journal more than anyone other than his friend, poet William Ellery Channing, the nephew of the Unitarian minister of the same name and brother-in-law of Margaret Fuller. In an early letter written from Staten Island on July 8, 1843, Thoreau writes of missing his friend Minott, noting that his memories "revert to those dear hills and that *river* which so fills up the world to its brim, worthy to be named with Mincius and Alpheus still drinking its meadows while I am far away. How can it run heedless to the sea, as if I were there to countenance it—George Minott too looms up considerably—and many another old familiar face."[10] In this passage Minott is the only person to be singled out. He is listed among the faces Thoreau finds himself missing, other friends, as well as the natural landscape around Concord. In addition to being able to read Thoreau's homesickness for Concord and his family into this note, this passage shows Minott as being an important person to Thoreau. Thoreau draws a parallel between the natural world and Minott; therefore, Minott's advice—stemming from a connection to the natural world—is privileged. Thoreau again comments on Minott's local knowledge and respect of the natural landscape, something lacking in Colman's report: "Minott adorns whatever part of nature he touches.... If a common man speaks of Walden Pond to me, I see only a shallow, dull-colored body of water without reflections or peculiar color, but if Minott speaks of it, I see the green water & reflected hills at once, for he *has been* there."[11] As in his early letter, Thoreau again places Minott with a natural aspect of the Concord region as a way to show his appreciation of the farmer's regional knowledge. Moreover, their lives remained closely linked through their deaths as well. Walter Harding notes that Thoreau died no more than six months after Minott, though he was a generation younger than his friend. Minott's passing took a particular toll on an already weakened Thoreau, one from which he never entirely recovered.[12]

Minott's experience is privileged in Thoreau's letters and journals in a way that the works of agricultural reformers like Colman never are. A country farmer rather than a sophisticate, he is described as having a useful knowledge base about all things natural in the Concord area. Thoreau often turned to Minott for advice on questions about the natural world and agriculture, the migrations of local birds, leaving habits of certain trees, and the behaviors of local fauna. In every case Thoreau spoke with the greatest respect for his friend's wisdom. In a journal entry from November 16, 1855, Thoreau writes, "Minott speaks of the last fortnight as good weather to complete the harvesting,—corn, potatoes, turnips, carrots, etc."[13] Minott knew when to harvest because he had an intimate knowledge of the land and the feel of the seasons in one localized area. This knowledge would never be transferrable to a large-scale system or to a report that could be read and applied widely, being too localized to be useful to the majority of farmers. Minott is not the farmer against whom Thoreau must explain his actions in *Walden*. Indeed, Minott is a mentor and guide for him.

Thoreau's agricultural friendships with particular local farmers like Minott were paralleled in his family and in his own experience. Thoreau grew up in a family that had a similar philosophy as his own; they did not serve meat, exotic foods, coffee, or tea at home. The money that would have been spent on such luxurious and unhealthy foods was redirected toward cultural development, like school tuition and lessons in music and art for the children. The Thoreaus were also successful gardeners, locally famous for their melons. Before Henry Thoreau and his brother, John, left on their excursion that would be the basis for *A Week on the Concord and Merrimack Rivers*, they threw a melon party, an event that grew into a town tradition. Indeed, the brothers brought several of these prized melons with them on their journey.[14] These experiences in agricultural and dietary simplification extended beyond Thoreau's immediate family as well. Horace Hosmer, a former student and friend of Thoreau's, writes about his time living with the family: "I never forgot those dinners; the room was shaded and cool, there was no hustle. Mrs. Thoreau's bread, brown and white, was the best I had ever tasted. They had, besides, vegetables and fruit, pies or puddings; but I never saw meat there. Their living was a revelation to me. I think they were twenty years ahead of the times in Concord."[15] The family's modest style of consumption impressed Hosmer enough for him to name it revolutionary. Thoreau's early diet, therefore, already involved a focus on local vegetable foods, and this example from Thoreau's childhood became one of the themes in his diet-focused writings. He justifies his food choices as ways of living simply in order to combat emerging expansionist trends in U.S. agriculture. In this way Thoreau responds to agricultural changes occurring in the nation during the time Emerson named the "age of Revolution."

By making his own agricultural practices more natural, then, Thoreau believed that he could reform a part of society that was becoming increasingly intertwined with global forces. He developed a refined appreciation of simple cuisine—largely based on foodstuffs easily obtained in nature or grown in local plots—in contrast with the over-consuming middle class of this era. An example of Thoreau's practices appears in his personal preference for local fruits throughout his writings. Thoreau's favored festive meal seems to have been a relatively simple pudding, preferably composed of huckleberry or apple, two of Thoreau's favorite wild fruits. Thoreau's culinary choice during visits to cosmopolitan locations like Boston was apple pudding, and "puddings are mentioned oftener than any other article of cooked food in Thoreau's Journal," according to Kenneth Allen Robinson.[16] Even in his most sophisticated dining experiences, then, Thoreau returns to the local, to foods that could be acquired during one of his near-daily excursions. There is a general lack of indoor dining in Thoreau's journal; he favors a more picnic-based lifestyle, one that is paralleled in Harriet Beecher Stowe's descriptions of her Florida picnics in the following chapter. These picnics are Thoreau's feasts.[17] While Thoreau's readers might assume a luxurious feast should be held indoors, with exotic foods and beverages and elegant table settings, the Thoreauvian feast was always outside, with locally harvested foods prepared simply.

In his 1861 essay "Walking," Thoreau describes agri-expansion further. He writes, "It is said to be the task of the American 'to work the virgin soil,' and that 'Agriculture here already assumes proportions unknown everywhere else.'"[18] Thoreau uses quotes around terms already in conversation during his time. The idea of a "virgin soil" that was being theoretically wasted by Native Americans was common during this period of U.S. territorial and agricultural expansion, and this belief was used as a justification for the Indian wars. Thoreau refers to the notion that the United States was to some extent already becoming the breadbasket of the world. The second phrase that Thoreau quotes is about foods grown in "proportions unknown everywhere else" in U.S. agriculture. This statement has become common enough for him to respond to it in his 1861 essay; it connects elements of the nation's agriculture to the larger national mission in the antebellum years. Thoreau continues, "The weapons with which we have gained our most important victories, which should be handed down as heirlooms from father to son, are not the sword and the lance, but the bush-whack— the turf-cutter, the spade, and the bog hoe, rusted with the blood of many a meadow, and begrimed with the dust of many a hard-fought field" (*Ex*, 207). Thoreau uses martial language to describe agriculture here; the national emphasis on production and agriculture had already become intense by the mid-nineteenth century. In these ironic passages, Thoreau correctly describes the connection between national politics and agriculture.

Thoreau's own experiments in agriculture were influenced, not by figures like Colman, but by some of the vegetarian movements of the mid-nineteenth century. Emerson introduced Thoreau to the most influential vegetarian diet reformers in the United States of the time: Bronson Alcott; William Alcott, his cousin; and Sylvester Graham.[19] Graham, for example, was a vegetarian food reformer who wanted to introduce more wheat and vegetable foods into the U.S. diet. He founded his first boarding house experiment in 1838. The inventor of what would become the graham cracker, he believed in a strict diet—one that abstained from meat, coffee, and alcohol—as well as in regular exercise and celibacy.[20] Thoreau could never follow a regimen created by someone else without making it his own, and he criticized Graham's suggestions of reform and dietary practices. Emerson eulogized Thoreau's emphasis on diet as well as his often contrarian attitude; on the one hand, he produced and consumed simply, "yet, when some one urged a vegetable diet, Thoreau thought all diets a very small matter, saying that 'the man who shoots the buffalo lives better than the man who boards at the Graham House.'"[21] Thoreau derided Graham's dietary reforms; however, he had already experimented with similar vegetable-based diets in his own work. In *Walden* he describes his own dietary choices, noting that he has "rarely for many years used animal food, or tea, or coffee."[22]

Thoreau's writing has a distinct pro-vegetable diet emphasis that relates it to contemporary and historical vegetarianism. The history of Western vegetarianism dates back to Pythagoras. At one point theorists speculated on the prelapsarian diet, believing that Adam and Eve must have been vegetarians in Eden. Ideas of vegetarianism grew stronger in the West with the spread of Eastern philosophy in the early nineteenth century, as these writings seemed to support the vegetarians' ideals. The beginnings of Orientalism brought about through expansion also helped to create a backlash against that same development; as the West expanded farther toward the East, it incorporated some of its philosophies. Lawrence Buell observes that Thoreau was acquainted with both the Biblical and the Hindu writings on diet: Leviticus and Manu, respectively. Thoreau appreciates the fact that nothing material "was too trivial" to be elevated (*W*, 221). Moreover, eighteenth- and nineteenth-century scientists dealt with the question of humanity's place in the natural world relative to diet; they attempted to discover what kind of animal a human was, a carnivore or an herbivore.[23] Through his various agricultural and dietary reform activities, Thoreau became one of the most well-known vegetarians in U.S. literature, though he was never strictly vegetarian himself. In his important contribution to U.S. dietary and agricultural reform, Thoreau argues for a diet based on locally grown vegetable foods as a way to live more simply and to free oneself from the attachments of U.S. agri-expansion during the nineteenth century.

However, Thoreau would have had to fight against the established nineteenth-century U.S. food system to promote a diet based on vegetable foods. The excessively meat-based habits of the average U.S. American began as early as the late eighteenth century: U.S. Americans, like their British counterparts, were proud carnivores by the nineteenth century. A national bias existed against vegetable foods and toward the importance of beef, pork, poultry, and lamb. This was especially pronounced in the expanding western frontier, where the course of agriculture's empire was being developed.[24] The expanding ranches of the U.S. West allowed consumers cheaper and easier access to meat, and there was a proportionate increase of such foodstuffs in the national diet, as well as a corresponding decrease of other foods. Reformers like Thoreau confronted a majority of consumers therefore who were hesitant to leave their heavily meat-based diets in order to try more healthy foods like legumes, grains, and produce, a variety of crops that could be grown regionally. This overconsumption of one kind of food, combined with the lessening of vegetable consumption overall in the national diet, became part of Thoreau's focus in his experiments with agriculture.

Thoreau therefore belongs in the spectrum of reform movements of this time through his agricultural and dietary efforts. Cecilia Tichi names *Walden* "Thoreau's own 'Treatise on Domestic Economy,'" referencing a well-known domestic manual written by Catharine Beecher, sister of Harriet Beecher Stowe.[25] Thoreau focuses his attention on the most seemingly mundane aspects of his housekeeping, and this demonstrates the influence of domestic writers on his work. Material and agricultural studies remain rich sites for research on Thoreau; Thoreau is as critical and reform-minded of U.S. agriculture, diet, and expansion as any domestic reformer. Moreover, Gillian Brown compares Thoreau's project at Walden to the Brook Farm community, written about by participant Nathaniel Hawthorne in *The Blithedale Romance*, and Bronson Alcott's consociate family living experiment at Fruitlands, described by Louisa May Alcott in "Transcendental Wild Oats," citing their shared concern with the production and consumption of food.[26] Thoreau is engaged in his own reform community, in a community of one. Though Thoreau takes his reform in a different direction than the domestic manuals of his time, they inform his work in terms of dietary and agricultural experimentation. His simplified living arrangement focuses intently on the production of basic necessities like food and shelter, tending toward the local and domestic. In this way he works to prove the sustainability of the small against expansion.

In *Walden* the first question Thoreau reports the townspeople asking him during his "sojourn" is "what [he] got to eat" (*W*, 3). This comes before questions of loneliness, security, and overall goals. Issues of diet and agriculture are critical to an understanding of Thoreau's work as a whole. *Walden* and *Wild Fruits* present Thoreau's most explicit discussions of agricultural production and consumption. One of Thoreau's primary activities written about at Walden Pond, in addition to the writing and revising of the manuscript of *A Week on the Concord and Merrimack Rivers*, involves the cultivation and sale of a crop of beans. In addition, Thoreau describes a conversation he has with a farmer who tells him that he "cannot live on vegetable food solely, for it furnishes nothing to make bones with," while Thoreau ironically observes the strong oxen with "vegetable-made bones" doing the majority of the farmer's work (*W*, 9). Thoreau extensively discusses both the agricultural and dietary projects developed at Walden Pond as rigorously and as personally as he deals with any other ethical issue. He realizes that he is "glad to hear of experiments of this kind being tried" (*W*, 65). Meanwhile, in *Wild Fruits* Thoreau broadens his conversation on the harvesting of local, vegetable foods to society as a whole. Here, certain wild foods take precedence. He compares the apple to wealth itself: "The apple was early so important, and generally distributed, that its name traced to its root in many languages signifies fruit in general. Μῆλον [Mhlon], in Greek, means an apple, also the fruit of other trees, also a sheep and any cattle, and finally riches in general" (*WF*, 245). For Thoreau wild fruits harvested locally are notably untainted by the agri-expansion prevalent during the nineteenth century. In his eulogy, when Emerson chastises Thoreau for throwing away potential literary greatness in order to gather huckleberries, he fails to understand the depth of Thoreau's agricultural efforts. His greatest experiments are in fact accomplished in his capacity as "captain of a huckleberry party."[27]

RIGHT PRODUCTION IN *WALDEN*

Part of Thoreau's simplification efforts in *Walden* is to earn his living from the land; he becomes a small-scale bean farmer to do so. "The Bean-Field" chapter is important for Thoreau's agricultural reform as an example of both the goals and the dangers involved in producing local foods. Thoreau seeks out an alternative method to grow food while remaining connected to the means of his own consumption. The benefit of farming, he notes, is its connection to nature and to the most basic necessity of life: food. Through his bean field, Thoreau can save on his economic outlay and turn excess harvest into profit to help him buy any other necessities. The beans that Thoreau grows have an economic use, allowing him to trade a large portion of them for rice, a nonlocal crop (*W*, 162). Thoreau shows that he does not want to entirely abandon trade but to trade in a more sustainable fashion. Providing copious charts and records, following the format of other agricultural writers of his time, Thoreau maintains detailed accounts of his expenditures and gains regarding his beans. In *Walden* Thoreau's bean field is the site of useful agricultural praxis. Thoreau's ideas are an alternative to mechanization and intensification in agriculture.[28] Thoreau maintains his theme of self-reliance against an agri-expansionist nation by presenting his experiment at Walden Pond as proof that small-scale farms can maintain their usefulness against the advice of agricultural reformers like Colman, if people simplify their diets to match. Thoreau calls his agricultural venture a success; for Thoreau his bean field counters the intensification of agriculture at this time, which to Thoreau represents great dangers for the physical and spiritual health of the nation. Ultimately, his work is not about economic wealth, but rather sustainability.

Thoreau's agricultural reform through small-scale farming proves that he can survive on a simplified diet working very little land. In *Walden* the themes of simplified consumption and local agriculture work together to fulfill his challenge of agri-expansion.[29]

Thoreau's experiment in growing his own food deals with more than just the issue of consumption. He worries about the expansion of agriculture during this period, aware of the changes brought about through advances in the field. As with all kinds of drastic change, these advances spurred a wave of debate over proper farming methods. In "The Bean-Field" Thoreau engages in a debate with Colman, writing, "This was one field not in Mr. Colman's report" (*W*, 158). In his influential report, Colman had recommended a complete overhaul of Concord agriculture as a way to stay competitive with the new territories of the West. Increasingly, poor soil in the Northeast substantially damaged Concord agriculture between 1840 and 1850. Moreover, the development of the railroad expanded agriculture and trade to greater distances than ever before. In a move to keep Concord agriculture viable in this new food market, Colman advised a change from wheat to corn and hay. Corn and hay could both be advantageously produced as feed for livestock, which was being produced in greater quantities in the West. Hay and corn were transported west, as the cattle—processed into meat—were shipped east. Thus, such specific crop selection replaced the more varied, but less profitable, domestic farm, becoming less self-sustaining but more competitive. Thoreau counters Colman's drive to farm the wild lands around Concord—the woods and swamps—as well as a scientific method of farming completely opposed to Thoreau's own model farm. He avoids any kind of development that adds commercialization to his lessons in simplification. Instead, he attempts a counterexperiment, one in which he earns a living for himself by growing a local crop of beans.[30]

This experiment means that Thoreau has to endure the criticism of neighboring farmers—though not of friends like Minott—who cannot appreciate his deviation from the structure as they understand it. Rather, they think of him as a romantic whose ideas are unfeasible in the new agricultural world. Their comments of "Beans so late! peas so late!" and

"Corn, my boy, for fodder; corn for fodder" show the extent of their distrust of his alternative choices (*W*, 157). Beans, as opposed to the corn or hay grown by his farming neighbors, had never been a very successful economic venture in the region. On the other hand, between 1840 and 1850, corn and hay had boomed as cash crops for Concord farmers.[31] Thoreau relates, "The crop of *English* hay is carefully weighed, the moisture calculated, the silicates and the potash; but in all dells and pond holes in the woods and pastures and swamps grows a rich and various crop only unreaped by man. Mine was, as it were, the connecting link between wild and cultivated fields" (*W*, 158, Thoreau's italics). Thoreau privileges other rewards brought about in his bean crop, though he understands that he will not become wealthy through his choice. However, aesthetically, beans have a greater resonance to Thoreau than hay or corn. Beans were the iconic foodstuff of the region, giving rise to the Boston baked bean.[32] To Thoreau the regional specificity of his choice of crop makes it valuable to him. Like the "limeys," "frogs," and other peoples recognizable by the foods they ate, the Yankee became known as someone who ate these beans. The romance of such a crop appeals to Thoreau, and he embraces his reform efforts to the extent that he establishes his identity as an industrious Yankee, using his own definition of industry through his chosen crop of food. In addition, white beans are a traditional Native American staple food. In planting a crop that has greater historical than economic value, Thoreau is able to engage in an agricultural conversation with the Native Americans of the Concord area. He notes that in this particular field, the Native Americans had already farmed beans: "in the course of the summer it appeared by the arrowheads which I turned up in hoeing, that an extinct nation had anciently dwelt here and planted corn and beans ere white men came to clear the land" (*W*, 156). In a sense Thoreau participates in a cross-cultural historical farming education the way many families educate cross-generationally, using the bean as the subject of his lesson. Thoreau is able to further his simplified undertaking by learning from those whose localized knowledge he values. His regionally specific choice of crop helps cross unnaturally imposed borders within U.S. agri-expansion.

Thoreau is clear about his attitude toward agriculture in "The Bean-Field." Though at one point he disclaims, "Not that I wanted beans to eat, for I am by nature a Pythagorean, so far as beans are concerned" (*W*, 162), and his experiment focuses "rather from an economic than a dietetic point of view" (*W*, 61), the appeal of keeping the connection between economy and diet was important to him. Thoreau's agricultural efforts can, in truth, be considered practical: "This was my curious labor all summer,—to make this portion of the earth's surface, which had yielded only cinquefoil, blackberries, johnswort, and the like, before, sweet wild fruits and pleasant flowers, produce instead this pulse" (*W*, 155). In this exercise Thoreau attempts to navigate the agricultural margin between the "wild fruits" that appear to be his favorite consumables to a modest crop of beans instead. Thoreau implies that there is something deviant about his agricultural experiment—a "curious labor"—at that time. Agriculture is the bridge between nature and industry at its most basic level. Thoreau continues, "It was a singular experience that long acquaintance which I cultivated with beans, what with planting, and hoeing, and harvesting, and threshing, and picking over, and selling them,—the last was the hardest of all,—I might add eating, for I did taste. I was determined to know beans" (*W*, 161). Again, he specifies the "singular," or strange, concept of focusing all of his energy on these beans, as opposed to corn or hay.[33] He lists the various steps involved in even this basic form of agriculture and in his mocking tone claims his role as an unmotivated salesperson. Therefore, there is an interesting duality in Thoreau's work between the idealistic form of simplified production of food exemplified in his harvesting of wild fruits in later writings, and a lessened form of agri-expansion that his experiment at Walden is designed to attempt.

Thoreau comments on what was already becoming the difference between his and the standard farm during this period: "As I had little aid from horses or cattle, or hired men or boys, or improved implements of husbandry, I was much slower, and became much more intimate with my beans than usual" (*W*, 157). He chooses to avoid using the "improved implements" that are to him in terms of agriculture what the Fitchburg train is in terms of transportation. In both cases the technologically advanced method is not necessarily the best; he feels that something is lost rather than gained with these developments. Thoreau maintains that the industrialization and intensification of agriculture is a dangerous practice that must be challenged through his own farming style. He gives an alternate reading of agriculture in which his bean field succeeds against the modern market system, in which "the landscape is deformed, husbandry is degraded with us, and the farmer leads the meanest of lives. He knows Nature but as a robber" (*W*, 165–66). For Thoreau, the farmer has become a "robber" of the natural world in terms of an agri-expansion that leaves the earth "deformed." Thoreau challenges the developments he witnesses in the early years of the U.S. agricultural revolution, which peaked in the years following the Civil War. His beans represent more than his ideas of agricultural reform; they also show his model U.S. farm, where farmers expertly tend smaller fields and grow local crops sustainably.[34] In this Thoreau's judgment against farmers is harsh, but not without justification; Thoreau shows a less-commercial alternative to the agri-expansionist "meanest of lives" through his simplified bean plot.

Thoreau's bean fields accomplished, in effect, the challenge of mid-century U.S. economics and politics that he desired. Thoreau was able to show that a simplified agriculture can support a similarly simple lifestyle in his successful farming project. His bean field experiment is fundamentally in line with his entire Walden experiment and provides a lasting challenge of U.S. agri-expansion.[35] Thoreau's work in agricultural reform, as seen in his bean production, is a key aspect in his larger efforts in simplified living against the expansive materiality of the nineteenth century. The capitalism that was becoming more prevalent in the early stages of this U.S. agricultural revolution was detrimental, Thoreau feared, to the well-being of U.S. citizens. Thoreau criticizes the tendency in agriculture during this time to follow misguided advice, like that of Colman, while observing that the farm remains an ideal place to focus a sustained criticism of consumer culture. The lifestyle of a farm, or even a large garden, is one of continual work that nets—hopefully—an edible, necessary profit; the farm, then, is the intersection of labor and reward. The farmer is often the laborer Thoreau addresses in *Walden*, the iconic quietly desperate figure. Against the developing agricultural philosophies promoted by Colman, then, Thoreau writes *Walden* as his personal idea of agricultural reform.[36]

For Thoreau an alternative relationship to agriculture is a necessary step to combat U.S. agri-expansion during the nineteenth century. The benefit of farming, he believes, is its connection to nature and to life's fundamental necessities. Thoreau expresses the higher nature of his ideological lesson through farming and shows his admiration of the natural flows and rhythms that can and should unite the farmer with the land: "What shall I learn of beans or beans of me? I cherish them, I hoe them, early and late I have an eye to them; and this is my day's work" (*W*, 155). Farming his crop of beans helps to keep Thoreau aware of seasonal fluctuations, reminds him of earlier agrarian poetics, and gives him the satisfaction of being engaged in society's most essential occupation: growing food. At the end of "The Bean-Field," Thoreau returns to an idealized discussion of nature, represented humorously by the woodchuck: "These beans have results which are not harvested by me. Do they not grow for woodchucks partly? . . . How, then, can our harvest fail?" (*W*, 166). In this moment during Thoreau's overall reform, he finds his guide in the figure of the woodchuck, and he eventually adapts his idealization of the wildness for a more hybrid lifestyle, one that the woodchuck maneuvers successfully. The chapters in *Walden* that deal most directly with issues of dietary reform are "The Bean-Field" and "Higher Laws." In each case a woodchuck plays a significant role in Thoreau's development into a simplified consumer adapted to the agrarian reform of *Walden*. Through his experiences in these chapters, Thoreau is able to make a convincing argument for a vegetable-based diet that depends on a small-scale, local agriculture.

RIGHT CONSUMPTION IN *WALDEN*

One of Thoreau's proclaimed goals at Walden Pond was to learn from the natural world around him—to find ways in which the local environment could teach him dietary lessons impossible to learn elsewhere.

As part of that process, *Walden* is replete with examples of plants and animals anthropomorphized by Thoreau into sages and teachers—and scoundrels. While Thoreau would not consider the woodchuck to be imbued with the moral sensibilities required to make it a proper ethical model, the woodchuck does thrive in the liminal space between civilization and wilderness—like Thoreau's bean field—by engaging in a simple, local diet that resonates with Thoreau's larger efforts. Therefore, the figure of the woodchuck guides Thoreau in his movement toward a more vegetable-based diet, in keeping with his agrarian goals. The woodchuck appears in each of the sections of *Walden* in which Thoreau discusses his own diet.[37] A woodchuck helps to introduce "Higher Laws," is Thoreau's great nemesis in "The Bean-Fields," and is discussed early on in "Economy"; it symbolizes both the wildness Thoreau values in nature—as opposed to the agri-expansion of his time—and the simple vegetarian consumer he works toward becoming. Like Thoreau, the woodchuck is a native to the Concord middle landscape; it is familiar with harvesting foods in the land around Concord. However, its status as a local makes the woodchuck less appealing to consumers, who value extravagance and the exotic, especially during this period of economic, territorial, and agricultural expansion. In "Economy" the "cap of woodchuck skin" represents the cheap garment unappealing to fashionable society, which instead makes itself "needlessly poor" in its quest "to buy ... a crown!" (*W*, 35–36). Thoreau desires to escape that "rat race" as the extreme form of the social issues he challenges in his simplified living. The same argument is made in terms of dietary simplicity. The woodchuck represents a consumer of local foods, and to some extent it becomes a guide for Thoreau in his reform project at Walden.[38]

In "Higher Laws," the chapter in which Thoreau spends the most time considering issues of dietary reform, he sees a woodchuck and suddenly feels "a strange thrill of savage delight" in which he is "strongly tempted to seize and devour him raw" (*W*, 210). At this climactic moment, Thoreau's simplified dietary project and his quest for the wildness in nature intersect. He desires to consume the woodchuck as part of his experiment in simplified eating. In this case Thoreau would become, to some extent, a simplified hunter, eating an animal considered base, an agricultural pest as opposed to a romanticized game animal. The fact that this scene opens Thoreau's chapter on "Higher Laws" demonstrates its place in his theme of questioning binaries: wild and developed, natural and artificial, simple and refined.[39] For Thoreau these are not useful distinctions, and the better way of living would embrace the wild, noble, and natural. Like Thoreau's elaborate feasts of apples and berries, or like his bean field, the woodchuck is also useful as a way to challenge the nineteenth-century agri-expansion seen in national consumption habits.[40] Literally and figuratively, Thoreau questions his diet through a discussion of the woodchuck, which is uniquely suited to his reform.

Originally *wuhak* from the Algonquin and also known as the ground-hog, the woodchuck is described in U.S. legends as a savvy survivor, instinctively understanding nature better than civilized humans do. Thoreau applies this understanding of natural patterns when he uses the woodchuck as his own seasonal calendar in *Walden*, as a woodchuck helps to herald in the spring: "I am on the alert for the first signs of spring, to hear the chance note of some arriving bird, or the striped squirrel's chirp . . . or see the woodchuck venture out of his winter quarters" (*W*, 302). The woodchuck communicates seasonal variations to Thoreau by leaving its burrow where it has lived for the winter months in a state of hibernation. As part of his anthropomorphosis of the woodchuck, Thoreau connects the animal and the physically and spiritually hibernating person in U.S. society during this period. Later in the season, however, the trickster nature of the woodchuck returns to terrorize farmers. In the summer and fall, the woodchuck becomes most active. This productivity causes an ongoing battle with the agricultural community, summer and fall being planting and harvest times as well. The woodchuck's twilight feasts on almost anything green and edible, which frustrate Concord farmers, stand as a symbol for Thoreau's own goals. The woodchuck lives outside the accepted agriculture of mid-nineteenth-century Concord. While the popular tongue twister wonders, "How much wood would a woodchuck chuck?" Thoreau's interest seems to be more about how much and what would the woodchuck eat?

Much to Thoreau's consternation, the woodchuck also seems determined to know, and to eat, beans. Thoreau describes his ongoing battle against the woodchuck for his harvest in the chapters "Economy" and "The Bean-Field." As a novice bean-farmer, Thoreau's nemesis was early and often the woodchuck. Thoreau states, "My enemies are the worms, cool days, and most of all woodchucks. The last have nibbled for me a quarter of an acre clean. But what right had I to oust johnswort and the rest, and break up their ancient herb garden?" (*W*, 155). Torn between frustration and his morality, Thoreau ignores his neighbors' advice to set harsh (and often useless) traps for the pest. Rather, he takes this opportunity to test his own methods against this most natural agricultural competition. He tries to humanely rid himself of the nuisance. Walter Harding, Thoreau's biographer, shares an anecdote about Thoreau's humane attempt at ridding himself of the "grandfather of all the woodchucks" by trapping a mature, fat one and moving it miles away.[41] He lectured the creature and released it where he hoped it would be far enough removed from his bean field as not to cause any further damage. However, as is the way with gardens, either this or another woodchuck returned within a few days and resumed its diet of Thoreau's beans. His gentler measures proving useless, Thoreau tried to enlist the aid of the local farming community in a desperate attempt to stop the woodchuck from ruining his bean crop; "shoot 'em, you damn fool" was their experienced reply. Thoreau's "not-too-strongly-held vegetarian principles" and desire to live close to nature without wasting the lives of the woodchuck remained, at that time, too strong for him to follow their time-tested advice.[42] While complicated efforts like this make an entertaining example of Thoreau's challenges during his farming project, they are less feasible for the large-scale farmer. However, they are useful reminders of Thoreau's true goals for his foray into farming, which were ultimately moral. After all, the woodchuck is the perfect bridge between the wild and the domestic, Thoreau's ultimate aim at Walden.

In "Economy" Thoreau shows that his magnanimity regarding the woodchuck does not last forever, though; the pest is also the cause of Thoreau's largest moral lapse, as he would frame it, in *Walden*: "The next year I sometimes caught a mess of fish for my dinner, and once I went so far as to slaughter a woodchuck which ravaged my bean-field,—effect his transmigration, as a Tartar would say,—and devour him, partly for experiment's sake; but though it afforded me a momentary enjoyment, notwithstanding a musky flavor, I saw that the longest use would not make that a good practice, however it might seem to have your wood-chucks ready dressed by the village butcher" (*W*, 59). While Thoreau occasionally eats fish in the course of *Walden* (he eventually reduces this practice as well), this is the only instance of his killing and eating a mam-mal. Though he may have eaten the woodchuck hoping to enact a kind of romanticized primitivism, an ideal simplified diet, he actually seems to feel debased by the act. Thoreau has contradicting attitudes regarding this act of his and of the woodchuck in general. While Thoreau writes that he would not recommend going to a butcher for dressing wood-chucks as a common practice, Harding maintains that Thoreau rather enjoyed the flavor of the meat, something Thoreau did not expect.[43] On the other hand, Thoreau writes that the temporary sensual pleasure and wild gratification that came from killing and eating his longtime enemy was tempered by the "musky flavor" and, more important, his own damaged moral sensibilities. At this point Thoreau has determined the woodchuck-eating diet to be a failure. Instead, the woodchuck becomes Thoreau's dietary guide into the world of local plant consumption. Though farmers and villagers typically depict the woodchuck as a nui-sance, Thoreau decides to emulate it in terms of its eating habits.

Thus, Thoreau begins to observe the eating habits of the woodchuck more closely. In his journal entry for April 16, 1852, he details an encoun-ter with a woodchuck that lasts over half an hour in which he talks to the animal in "quasi forest lingo—baby-talk" and realizes that with "a few fresh bean leaves thus in advance of the season," he "should have tamed him completely." At the end of their communion, Thoreau desires to "learn some wisdom" from this creature who "is more thoroughly acclimated & naturalized" to the woods of Concord even than himself.[44] He observes that the woodchuck's natural food—the bean leaves—would be an ideal tribute to cement their relationship. Knowing the woodchuck's choice in cuisine, he connects it to his bean field, even in this journal entry. At this point in the journal, Thoreau is working on his fourth draft of *Walden*, so although this section about the woodchuck does not appear in the final text, it does give insight into Thoreau's attitude toward the animal as a natural guide while he organizes his book for publication. Thoreau's developing respect for the woodchuck is seen in this passage as he appreciates the "thoroughly acclimated" citizen of the woods around Concord. This appreciation translates into Thoreau's characterizing the woodchuck as something like a dietary guide, following the themes established in *Walden*. This experience may be something Thoreau draws upon when he challenges the agri-expansionism developing among the farmers of the Concord area. He connects the meat-based diet growing dominant in U.S. consumption to larger issues involved in expansion.[45] Meanwhile, the kinds of foods that the woodchuck eats are outside of a market-based economy of agri-expansion. Thoreau does something more radical than challenging his own dietary choices here. He challenges the U.S. way of life, one of an exploitative economics of consumption at a time of drastic territorial and agricultural expansion. In this way Thoreau becomes individually political, if only morally, and his philosophical project becomes more active. He does not call for wide social change, however, but rather a self-reliant, simplified diet as a necessary adjustment to a society that is overconsuming to an extreme degree.

At one other instance in "The Bean-Field," Thoreau brings up wood-chucks as a metaphor for society at that time, specifically a martial society that celebrates wars involving the conquest of lands and peoples. Thoreau listens to the sounds of the marching band coming from town while at his cabin. Bringing society back to him while he is trying to establish his experiment in the reform of the U.S. lifestyle, this militaristic music reminds him of society's intrusive presence even during his Walden sojourn. He observes—not without a touch of irony—"a really noble and inspiring strain that reached these woods, and the trumpet that sings of fame, and I felt as if I could spit a Mexican with a good relish,—for why should we always stand for trifles?—and looked round

for a woodchuck or a skunk to exercise my chivalry upon" (*W*, 160–61).
In this instance he refers to the U.S.-Mexican War, the support of which
he argues against in "Resistance to Civil Government" (1849). His metaphor is well chosen, for the warlike practices of the United States at that
time literally consumed the lands, nations, and even people in the path
of U.S. expansion closely allied with the development of agri-expansion.
Thoreau is forced to process this aggressive U.S. expansionism during his
reform experiment. In this passage, then, he links the human with the
nonhuman as the victims of a martial urge to destroy life. In his moment
of ironic imperial sympathy, he finds himself in one of his most violent
urges, and his time at Walden is connected to the national project. Of
course, Thoreau quickly controls this urge; he returns to his beans.

A self-reliant social reform is one of the ultimate goals for Thoreau's
agricultural and dietary work in *Walden*. In many ways the woodchuck
can be seen as Thoreau's guide to achieve this simplicity. Contemporary critics of *Walden* mocked Thoreau's elevation of the woodchuck
throughout his work. John Greenleaf Whittier, for example, comments,
"Thoreau's *Walden* is capital reading, but very wicked and heathenish.
The practical moral of it seems to be that if a man is willing to sink
himself into a woodchuck he can live as cheaply as that quadruped;
but after all, for me, I prefer walking on two legs."[46] What Whittier
read as impractical, though, has also been read as a representation of
Thoreau's answer to the economics of the antebellum period. Thoreau
tests the possibility of small-scale farming and eating to show a contrast
to the tendency of the U.S. citizen to overconsume. In his experiment,
of course, he has his successes and his lapses, as in the devouring of the
woodchuck in "The Bean-Field" or the passion to do so in "Higher
Laws." Thoreau's successes, then, would be the fact that he manages
to sustain himself on a physical, moral, and philosophical level during
this period by eating only a simple diet. As his own scientific guinea
pig (or woodchuck, to name an alternate rodent), Thoreau realizes that
his simple diet can be seen as a moral and economic success. Through
the wild woodchuck itself, a vegetarian, or Thoreau, an anachronistic "flexivore" and occasional woodchuck eater, issues in agricultural

production and consumption played a crucial role in Thoreau's treatment of the ethical imperative of simplicity during this period of U.S. expansion.[47] The woodchuck truly does consume only a local diet of vegetable foods—it must. In the farmer's suggestion to shoot the "damn" woodchucks, we can see the aggression felt toward a successful wild animal that has learned to thrive within the middle landscape of the farm. In trying to eat locally, and avoiding meat, condiments, tea, and coffee, Thoreau is in some ways imitating the diet of the woodchuck as a way to live outside the U.S. agri-expansion of the nineteenth century. When he does finally succumb to the level of the rest of the practical, consumer-driven farmers whose advice he begs, and kills and eats one of the woodchucks, he fails in his experiment in two ways. First, he consumes something he has spent time naming his equal, even if often as an opponent—he kills something therefore "human." Second, he enters the excessive world of U.S. consumerism he has been trying to avoid. In Thoreau's later reform experiments, namely, in *Wild Fruits*, he will move even further from that consumerist world of agri-expansion, while applying his reform philosophy to society more broadly.

THOREAU'S *WILD FRUITS* OF REFORM

Thoreau hints at his later engagement with simple wild foods, in a highly symbolic manner, at the beginning and the end of *Walden*. In "Economy" Thoreau introduces certain themes that will be developed further in *Wild Fruits*: "I thought often and seriously of picking huckleberries; that surely I could do, and its small profits might suffice. . . . But I have since learned that trade curses every thing it handles; and though you trade in messages from heaven, the whole curse of trade attaches to the business" (*W*, 69–70). Meanwhile, in his "Conclusion" Thoreau links the progress of humanity to the image of a "strong and beautiful bug which came out of the dry leaf of an old table of apple-tree wood" (*W*, 333). The bug, a useful comparison for the individual owing to its process of transformation into a superior entity, becomes "strong and beautiful" through its diet. Thoreau has the bug eat at the same table as people do. In this way the bug has accessed its higher self through a diet of apples, like any person. This scene resonates for Thoreau, as he finds his "faith in a resurrection and immortality strengthened by hearing of this" (*W*, 333). He is not simply making an ironic play on Christian imagery in this scene, though; his choices in this story are deliberate. He earnestly admires the transcendence of the apple tree–consuming creature. As he did with the woodchuck, Thoreau finds a symbolic instructor in the natural world in the form of the resurrected bug. Furthermore, he is not the only author of the time to write a story about a bug growing out of an apple-tree table; Melville published a short story on the subject as well: "The Apple-Tree Table," published in *Harper's* in 1856.[48] Using this common story, then, Thoreau's simplified living project combines the flora and fauna of Concord: the bug and the apple.

Thoreau's goal in *Walden* is to show a self-reliant alternative to consumerism through simple living, focusing particularly on agricultural and dietary reform. By *Wild Fruits* his goals have changed, and the wild apple and huckleberry have become fundamental symbols for his refined reform efforts. In addition to the democratic accessibility of these fruits, Thoreau finds other reasons to promote their agrarian virtue; to Thoreau they are symbolic of ethical and moral ideas that might be transmuted through their harvest and consumption. This has become more complicated, though, as private property forces a-berrying parties off lands that previously were commonly accessible. Thoreau's final reform mission is to convince people to reduce their dependence on an agriculture based on the private ownership of land and instead to become a part of a community of berry pickers. He continues to develop his ideas of the ethics of agriculture in his later sketches, which highlight plants in their natural ripening progression. In *Wild Fruits* the pieces that most directly speak to Thoreau's ideas about agricultural reform on an individual and community level are the long entries "Wild Apples" and "Black Huckleberry."[49]

Thoreau returns to his earlier concerns in his late writings collected in *Wild Fruits*, focusing on the material objects being produced and consumed, idealized wild foods like the apple and huckleberry. Between *Walden* and *Wild Fruits*, Thoreau moves from a more self-reliant system to more active strategies that encourage social endeavors. His goal has gone beyond a self-contained economy; rather, at this point he actively encourages a reform of nineteenth-century agri-expansion through a communal harvesting of local wild foods. This form of social change is significant in that Thoreau emphasizes community harvesting specifically. His material reform in this case connects the production and consumption of food; he realizes that the trend of excessive use of lands by the United States as part of an expanding agricultural, territorial, and political goal has a correlation to the national diet. Therefore, the reform needed to counter this consumption must also relate to agriculture in a healthy and sustainable manner. By this point Thoreau recognizes that reform is no longer a purely individual affair but must be used to encourage change among community members by having them become directly involved with their own food production.[50] This theme is developed in *Wild Fruits* as Thoreau watches the nation intensify its politics following the publication of *Walden*. He must still face the issue of consumption and national agri-expansion—but his political activism and focus on preservation of wilderness has changed the manner by which he communicates this.

In the introduction to *Wild Fruits*, Thoreau lays the groundwork for the rest of his discussion of sustainably harvesting local plants to reform an expanding and intensifying agricultural economy. He compares adventurous voyages of discovery with his daily walks in and around Concord. While both the voyages and the Concord walks have the potential to give the thrill of the novel, the global journey is focused on commodities to the exclusion of all else. As the nation uses greater expanses of land for the purpose of wealth, U.S. consumers quickly devour the fruits of these newly controlled spaces, once again comparing U.S. expansion in terms of agriculture and the nation. Thoreau compares his Concord fields with the fruit trade of the agricultural industries represented in these voyages: "Fruits imported from the East or South and sold in our markets—as oranges, lemons, pine-apples, and bananas—do not concern me so much as many an unnoticed wild berry whose beauty annually lends a new charm to some wild walk or which I have found to be palatable to an outdoor taste" (*WF*, 3). Though exotic fruits are more desirable for a status-driven society as a sign of Thorstein Veblen's "conspicuous consumption," they have an inferior quality substantially. Thoreau argues that local fruit available democratically to rich and poor alike tastes better than these global alternatives, defining "taste" as including, but more than, the physical palate. He goes beyond a mere rationalization of living near the level of poverty; he delineates a goal of a sustainable agrarianism that works to remove the producers and consumers from the path of U.S. expansion. Furthermore, he becomes the adventurer in his local journey, whereas with the market-driven fruits, someone else always has the initial pleasure of adventure. With local fruits, the adventurer and the consumer feel that gratification, as they are in fact the same person. Thoreau engages the reader quickly into his discussion of domestic and international expansion and commercialization, even imperialism, based on and around the market for fruit. The way to oppose this development is to eat local, wild fruits harvested on a small scale.

Apples are some of Thoreau's favorite wild fruits. Not only does the apple lend itself to his ideals of a mostly vegetable diet, it also possesses a transcendent quality that goes beyond mere food. Fruit was traditionally the primary food associated with sweetness, and with pleasure, in a manner like honey. Apples have thus been associated with pleasure and beauty throughout history. The apple has been associated with Greek deities, Genesis morality tales, British scientific discovery, and even U.S. national narratives via the story of Johnny Appleseed.[51] The human connection to eating apples, historically as a dessert food, dates back to 8000 BCE. The apple traveled west from Persia to Rome and was then distributed through the Roman Empire. Finally, the British brought the apple to the United States, where it flourished until it became as wild as a native species. Thoreau feels a direct relationship, almost a kinship, with the apple: "*Our* wild apple is wild only like myself, perchance, who belong not to the aboriginal race here, but have strayed into the woods from the cultivated stock" (*WF*, 79, Thoreau's italics). Like Thoreau, the apple began as "cultivated stock" that at some point left the town for a simpler existence. Growing apart from civilization gives the apple tree its freedom and independence, and Thoreau looks to gain some of that in the consumption of this particular wild fruit. The free and independent apple tree, then, stands in direct contrast with the cultivated crops grown in the market economy. Thoreau's ideal tree and its fruit can transmit their wildness to their harvester as well, as an agriculture that seeks to fulfill itself through nature.

Thoreau contrasts this natural wildness to the cheerless image of a horse-drawn carriage laden with unappealing apples on its way to a central market. To emphasize the unnaturalness of this image, Thoreau shows that nothing goes well for the members involved. The cart is weighed down too heavily, so the horse suffers, and the apples fall off the wagon to be eaten by wild animals, so the farmer must run after them in a seemingly losing battle. The apples that remain in the cart are nothing more than "pulp and skin and core only . . . not apples, but pomace" (*WF*, 75). These apples are not the same item anymore—they have been made artificial by their introduction into the market economy. The apples that do continue on to the market lose their "evanescent and celestial qualities" somehow into the air (*WF*, 75). The apples forced into cultivation suffer the same desperate fate as the people who cultivate them.[52] At this point nothing wild about the apple remains; only the flavorless husk is left to disappoint market consumers. Moreover, Thoreau argues that the few fallen apples have escaped with their spirits intact. Not surprisingly, Thoreau encourages the fallen apples as if they have escaped from servitude. To Thoreau domestication and marketing proportionally diminish the value of an apple. If the apple that was delicious out in the open air becomes almost unpalatable indoors, then the apples driven by horse cart to market would taste like their by-products, even less appealing. Thoreau makes it plain that the quality of wildness is essential for the apple's flavor.

Thoreau raises the status of the apple above other vegetable foods based to a large extent on its adaptability and wildness—its resistance to cultivation. As Thoreau states, "Most fruits which we prize and use depend entirely on our care. Corn and grain, potatoes, peaches, melons, and so on, depend altogether on our planting; but the apple emulates man's independence and enterprise" (*WF*, 78–79). The cultivated foods, products of a human-based economic and social system, are less tempting than their wild cousins. In this way Thoreau goes beyond agriculture entirely, to a system of harvesting that is almost entirely wild. If buyers choose wild over cultivated, they support an independence of spirit and morality that Thoreau associates with the apple. In the wild, Thoreau writes, "even the sourest and crabbedest apple growing in the most unfavorable position suggests such thoughts as these, it is so noble a fruit" (*WF*, 79). Thoreau continues to show the nobility of the fruit through examples of the reverence earlier communities had shown to apple trees. After all, the apple has always been the food of gods and legends. Thoreau writes of festivals and rituals surrounding the harvesting of apples throughout British history. Villagers would offer gifts and "salute the apple trees with much ceremony, in order to make them bear well in the next season" (*WF*, 76). These celebrations, at a time before the mechanization of agriculture, when even cultivated apples were relatively wild, are contrasted with U.S. agriculture, in which the closest the farmer comes to saluting an apple tree is the application of fertilizer around its base. Attitudes toward apples—perhaps toward food in general—have changed in the expanded market society of Thoreau's time. Thoreau would like to return to the earlier time in his relationship with local wild foods. In the former connection between food and reverence, especially in the case of a food so intimately connected with mythology and lore, Thoreau shows his respect to the products of the natural world. He concludes, "Let the most beautiful or the swiftest have it. That should be the 'going' price of apples" (*WF*, 75). Thoreau appreciates the apple more like histories show, and he wants the United States to return to a place where people are more thankful of foods in natural settings like this one.

Thoreau is concerned about the growing commercialization of previously wild lands and foods. He looks to counteract the drive to cultivate and commercialize nature one person at a time. He gives his readers a lasting image to make that case even more strongly; at the end of "Wild Apples," Thoreau warns that large cultivation can come only at the expense of wilderness and local traditions involving communal apple-picking and a-berrying harvesting parties. He writes, "I fear that

he who walks over these fields a century hence will not know the pleasure of knocking off wild apples . . . and the end of it all will be that
we shall be compelled to look for our apples in a barrel" (WF, 92). In
a comment disturbing in its prescience, Thoreau foretells a tragic new
society in which a market economy moves into towns like Concord and
the new territories of the nation alike. In each case food becomes one
more commodity, and apples, in Thoreau's example, are to a large extent
no different than any other barrel-shipped item, food or not. Thoreau
argues that this would reduce the essence of the apple. While the apple
is wild, that wildness can pass on to its consumer; when the apple has
become commercialized, however, the only essence passed through the
consumption of it is further commercialization. As a way to counter
this future, Thoreau attempts to convince his readers to maintain the
importance of wildness in their food as part of his new experiment.

Meanwhile, the local huckleberry, perhaps even more than the wild
apple, represents Thoreau's ideal form of agriculture. In the "Black
Huckleberry" section of *Wild Fruits*, Thoreau writes about the ethical importance of consuming the huckleberries of the Concord area.
Huckleberries played an important part in Thoreau's earlier project;
tellingly, Harding writes that Thoreau is soon picking huckleberries after
spending his night in jail.[53] The huckleberry is local, a plant native to
the U.S. Northeast. Therefore, it gives Thoreau a platform to encourage
a local agrarianism above one that requires foods from ever-expanding
territories.[54] Their harvest can become the improvement Thoreau seeks.
Thoreau long idealizes the huckleberry in his essays, texts like *Walden*,
and his journal. As a native plant, the huckleberry is truly representative; the appreciation of the huckleberry is elevated to a patriotic act.
Thoreau invokes his patriotism as he mocks the naming practice of the
huckleberry. According to European custom, the berry was named after
a man who had never looked upon or eaten one (WF, 37). However,
Thoreau spends several paragraphs methodically cataloguing the differences between European berries and U.S. varieties. This European who
added U.S. berries into the common language placed them in the Heath
family. Thoreau writes that this is because they are "occupying similar

ground with the heaths of the Old World, which we have not" (*WF*, 40). The berry's name is ironic: it is after someone who never observed it, after a kind of ecosystem in which it does not live. The ironic naming of the huckleberry (sometimes called "whortleberry") and its placement proves to Thoreau that it is an underappreciated food in Europe and the United States. Thoreau defends this native food against a culture of exoticism based on agri-expansion by turning the huckleberry's commonness and convenience, supposed flaws, into its greatest attributes.

To Thoreau, the Native Americans of the Concord area appreciate the huckleberry's commonness, so he turns to them for an example of a community that harvested and consumed an appropriately sustainable diet of berries. Thoreau describes their agricultural superiority as he writes, "The Indians made a much greater account of wild fruits than we do, and among the most important of these were huckleberries. They taught us not only the use of corn and how to plant it, but also of whortleberries and how to dry them for winter" (*WF*, 46). Thoreau's curiosity about Native American culture has been well discussed.[55] Native Americans are appropriate teachers in regard to the area's local foods, unlike exploitative U.S. agri-expansionists. Thoreau sees the Native American treatment of local foods and their cultivation as a positive model for an alternative to the U.S. market economy, which overharvests and privatizes the wilderness around Concord, endangering the huckleberry in its wild state. He emphasizes this danger through an anecdotal warning: "The last Indian of Nantucket, who died a few years ago, was very properly represented in a painting which I saw there with a basket full of huckleberries in his hand, as if to hint at the employment of his last days. I trust that I may not outlive the last of the huckleberries" (*WF*, 50). For Thoreau the nature of U.S. agri-expansion seems to be that of destruction and overconsumption. Thoreau writes about local wild fruits as the alternative to that end, interweaving three themes in his work: the local agricultural model of the region's Native American population, the U.S. culture that overconsumes the natural world and other cultures, and the huckleberry in the wild. Thoreau worries that the U.S. drive to expand and consume may cause its people to destroy the wilderness, and the huckleberry, in much the same way that so much Native American land and culture was exploited and destroyed.

Throughout his argument for sustainable forms of agriculture in "Black Huckleberry," Thoreau returns to a market example. He emphasizes the importance of the wild huckleberry to the United States economically: "We do not realize how rich our country is in berries" (*WF*, 41). The huckleberry is something that the United States possesses already without the need for expanding into other territories to obtain. As a natural gift, Thoreau makes a case for the national appreciation of it. Here, the reward is in simplified agriculture as an alternative to U.S. agri-expansion. U.S. citizens in New England are in an enviable position compared to their counterparts in Europe, who have to consider the berry a luxury item. Meanwhile, Thoreau brings an indictment against the U.S. market economy, which might destroy the wilderness outright, as it seems to be in fact destroying much of the natural world on which it depends. Thoreau gives an example of the huckleberry being turned into a product, not a fruit, for sale at the local butcher shop as a sign of an extreme of the current market trends in agriculture:

> What becomes of the true value of country life—what, if you must go to market for it? It has come to this, that the butcher now brings round our huckleberries in his cart. Why, it is as if the hangman were to perform the marriage ceremony. Such is the inevitable tendency of our civilization, to reduce huckleberries to a level with beef-steaks; that is, to blot out four-fifths of it or the going a-huckleberrying, and leave only a pudding, that part which is the fittest accompaniment to a beef-steak. You all know what it is to go a-beef-steaking. It is to knock your old fellow laborer Bright on the head to begin with, or possibly to cut a steak from him running, in the Abyssinian fashion, and wait for another to grow there. The butcher's item in chalk on the door is now "Calf's head and huckleberries." (*WF*, 57)

In this gruesome reading of market economy, Thoreau links the eating of market-bought berries with butchery. He cannot unite the two kinds of food in his understanding—fruit picked in relative innocence in the wilderness as opposed to the ultimate savagery of commodity-based agriculture. He brings his conversation, and his argument, around to a plea for people to harvest mindfully and locally and not to depend on the novel and exotic to please a gross appetite prevalent in this growing market economy.

Thoreau fears for the fate of the wilderness around Concord if people fall into an unsustainable agriculture. This concern causes him to imagine the time when society will have consumed all the wild huckleberries, leaving the future with no comparable culinary or cultural experience. He examines, then, a resistance to such an outcome in the form of a communal wild fruit harvesting alliance that would require people to return to the preserved middle landscapes of local communities. This alliance might counteract the nation's developing consumerism, which corresponds with agri-expansion. Wild fruits are Thoreau's greatest hope for battling the agri-expansion that he feels turns people away from nature and toward a more profit-based relationship to harvesting. In this community spirit, Thoreau's "a-," designates the ritual activities that bind people together: "a-strawberrying, a-huckleberrying, a-nutting" are now part of his reform. Indeed, Thoreau, accompanied by friends like Ellen Emerson and Louisa May Alcott, was the locally acknowledged leader of various nutting and berrying excursions in the woods around Concord.[56] While his bean field at Walden is primarily seen as a solitary experiment, by his later writings, his subversive "a-" parties make for an agriculturally improved society. These community activities act against the capitalism that seeks to subjugate nature. "Black Huckleberry" shows the plight of a culture endangering itself in its insatiability and a possible alternative to destructive practices that involves a simpler kind of consumption, one that does not destroy but rather maintains the wild fruit abundance.

CONCLUSION: HOW TO EAT WELL

In a late passage from *Wild Fruits*, Thoreau looks at four professionals united by their relationship to the huckleberry. There are four distinct levels of separation from the original producer to the final consumer owing to the changes occurring within U.S. society and agriculture at the time:

It has come to this, that A—, a professional huckleberry picker, has hired B—'s field, and, we will suppose, is now gathering the crop with a patent huckleberry horse-rake. C—, a professed cook, is superintending the boiling of a pudding made of some of the berries, while Professor D—, for whom the pudding is intended, sits in his library writing a book—a work on the *Vacciniæ* [berry], of course. . . . I believe in a different kind of division of labor: that Professor D— should be encouraged to divide himself freely between his library and the huckleberry field. (*WF*, 58)

Thoreau carefully distinguishes between the landowner and the worker on the land. The "huckleberry picker" has become a product of large-scale agriculture; "A" must first lease the land on which to work and then buy the "patent" rake with which to pick the huckleberries. After these original financial transactions take place, "A" can then reap whatever profits possible. Meanwhile, "Professor D," a scientist, lacks the actual experience with the huckleberry that Thoreau has. The berry has become merely a commodity for all the people discussed, both as a manner of income and as a consumable good. Thoreau's solution to this dilemma aims at all of U.S. society implicated in this market-based structure: the simplification of agriculture. At a time in U.S. history of destructive food production practices, Thoreau offers useful alternatives: a return to small-scale, community-based agriculture. Thoreau's various agrarian goals in *Walden* and *Wild Fruits* work to elevate the status of a local, mostly vegetable-based diet against an exotic one dependent upon U.S. agri-expansion. Jacques Derrida posits that the issue, the "moral question," is in fact not "should one eat or not eat, eat this and not that, the living or the nonliving, man or animal, but since *one must* eat in any case and since it is and tastes good to eat, and since there's no other definition of the good [*du bien*], *how* for goodness' sake should one *eat well* [*bien manger*]?"[57] Derrida's question echoes Thoreau's own: his agricultural and dietary reform projects are experiments in how to "eat well" by both producing and consuming in a moral, self-sufficient, and socially responsible manner.

3

Fruits of Regionalism

The child scampered, with all his little strength, after the prize, while his master laughed.

"Come here, Jim Crow," said he. The child came up, and the master patted the curly head, and chucked him under the chin.

"Now, Jim, show this gentleman how you can dance and sing." The boy commenced one of those wild, grotesque songs common among the negroes, in a rich, clear voice, accompanying his singing with many comic evolutions of the hands, feet, and whole body, all in perfect time to the music.

"Bravo!" said Haley, throwing him a quarter of an orange.

HARRIET BEECHER STOWE, *Annotated Uncle Tom's Cabin*, 8

Often and often [Eva] walked mournfully round the place where Haley's gang of men and women sat in their chains. She would glide in among them, and look at them with an air of perplexed and sorrowful earnestness; and sometimes she would lift their chains with her slender hands, and then sigh woefully, as she glided away. Several times she appeared suddenly among them, with her hands full of candy, nuts, and oranges, which she would distribute joyfully to them, and then be gone again.

HARRIET BEECHER STOWE, *Annotated Uncle Tom's Cabin*, 156

In two separate scenes from *Uncle Tom's Cabin*, white characters give oranges as gifts to slaves in differing contexts. Mr. Haley is "rewarding" young Harry for his "grotesque" performance by giving him "a quarter of an orange."[1] The orange in this scene becomes more than a simple food source, but rather a form of payment for services. Later, Evangeline St. Clare, an innocent child growing up in the South, hopes in some small way to ease the torments of a "chained gang of men and women." As she witnesses Haley's slave-trading operation in front of her, she "sighs woefully" and is described as "perplexed and sorrowful."[2] Once again the orange taken for granted by a white consumer is held as a treat for the slave. In the antebellum South, oranges were not readily accessible for the U.S. slave population, which was instrumental in their production. Meanwhile, oranges were also relatively rare in the Northeast in the years before revolutions in transportation and preservation greatly expanded U.S. agriculture. Thus, the orange was regionally and politically associated with the South in the first half of the nineteenth century, as much as the North was affiliated with the apple. In *Uncle Tom's Cabin*, Harriet Beecher Stowe draws attention to the orange as a symbol of the South. However, she carefully connects it to diametrically opposite characters: the slave trader Haley and the innocent Eva. The oranges that mark a cruel condescension in the slave trader also show an idealized Christian benevolence in the child. Stowe uses the orange in her writing to show the issues to be faced regarding the South—slavery, the Civil War, and Reconstruction—and the hope for an agricultural solution.

Stowe draws attention to a markedly regional food, the orange, first through its implication in slavery and later through the promotion of regional—as opposed to global—trade as a way to support U.S. agriculture during and following the Civil War. As the United States combined politics with agriculture throughout the nineteenth century, Stowe wrote about the production and consumption of oranges as a way to engage with U.S. policy at the domestic level. She makes note of oranges in her iconic *Uncle Tom's Cabin* (1852), her Civil War pieces collected in 1865 in *House and Home Papers*, and her works written during her time in Florida, *Oldtown Folks* (1869) and *Palmetto Leaves* (1873). As the United States entered a major shift in agricultural production following the Civil War, and as it grew more politically and economically powerful on a global scale, Stowe focused her domestic writings on reuniting the South with the North culturally and economically in part through regional agriculture. During her time in Reconstruction-era Florida, where she wintered from 1867 through 1884, she invested in an orange grove. In *Palmetto Leaves* Stowe shows the orange as a crop that takes advantage of agricultural advances in production and shipping in order to be distributed to expanding markets in the North. By promoting a regional agriculture, she keeps consumption within the nation's borders, as opposed to encouraging reliance on imported foodstuffs. Stowe includes a scene in *Palmetto Leaves* in which she describes former slaves managing an orange grove, showing another aspect of the economic healing potential of this regional foodstuff during the period known as "Radical Reconstruction."[3] Meanwhile, Stowe uses an extended Thanksgiving Day scene as a harvest-related unified national celebration in her regionalist work of the period, *Oldtown Folks*. For Stowe, therefore, a kind of agri-expansion, as it has been defined, became a tool for reforming the Union after the war; she applied the emerging technologies in the agriculture of this period through her own Florida orange production and in her writings. She hoped to help rebuild the South economically through advances in agriculture made possible by maintained borders and freedom from its direct connection to slave labor. I argue that Stowe's orange-based writings perform the domestic side of the national mission put into question by the Civil War. Stowe focuses on the production and consumption of regional foods as an integral element of her larger domestic reform work.

Stowe writes to improve the nation's agricultural trajectory within its physical and cultural borders, demonstrating the significance of domestic agriculture to the nation. Jane Tompkins maintains that Stowe's writing, specifically *Uncle Tom's Cabin*, is an example of the significant power available to ambitious women novelists in the nineteenth century.[4] I expand this reading of Stowe to include her goals in her regionalist writings following the Civil War as well. There, she engages in the political issues of reunification, education, and assistance to emancipated African Americans. Judith Fetterley and Marjorie Pryse connect Stowe to the regionalist tradition, placing her in the position of a necessary challenger to the literary traditions of the nineteenth century and to the culture of expansion that was predominant at that time. Stowe reforms through her literature. Meanwhile, Pierre Bourdieu's work on "taste" pertaining to cuisine as a marker of "class" can be applied to Stowe's work in terms of her ideal of a shared national taste during the nineteenth century as she moves from imported to domestic foods.[5] While Bourdieu notes that the educator in twentieth-century France expresses taste through exotic foods and "culinary populism," Stowe's food-based reform during the nineteenth century, rather, was an attempt to establish a shared national taste uniting North and South.[6]

The Civil War was far from the only U.S. site of change or conflict in Stowe's experience. She came of age during a time that brought revolutions to the United States both physically and agriculturally. The nation was expanding its territory well before the "manifest destiny" speech of John L. O'Sullivan in 1845. Stowe was born less than a decade after the Louisiana Purchase of 1803 drastically increased the nation's physical and economic boundaries, and her childhood was also the era of the 1819 procurement of Florida, where she would later spend her winter months.[7] These acquisitions brought about correspondingly drastic challenges. The Missouri Compromise of 1820 resulted in a wave of abolitionism that would become Stowe's domestic crusade, and the Indian Removal Act of 1830 showed the lengths to which the country was willing to go for land. In addition to territorial expansion, the young Harriet grew up at a time of developing industrialization, exemplified in the establishment of the Lowell Mills in Massachusetts in the 1830s.[8] Meanwhile, a generation of U.S. farmers applied newly available technologies in the lands of the U.S. West to intensify agriculture. Stowe's writings engage in the issues of nation, politics, and the development of agri-expansion as she experienced them during this period along the nation's expanding borders.[9]

For Stowe, the drive to influence the nation's agriculture and diet through her writing came naturally. In the large Beecher clan—Harriet was the sixth of influential minister Lyman Beecher's thirteen children—there was an expectation for Harriet and her siblings to become leading ministers and intellectuals. Young Harriet's childhood prepared her for a life in education as her particular form of ministry. Litchfield, Massachusetts, her birthplace, was home to the nation's first women's school, the Litchfield Female Academy.[10] As an adolescent in Hartford, Connecticut, Harriet taught at her sister Catharine Beecher's Hartford Female Seminary—the elder Beecher being one of the nation's foremost domestic authorities. There, Harriet honed her skills as a "teacher, preacher, and writer," according to biographer Joan Hedrick.[11] In Cincinnati, at sixteen, she was writing literary sketches and helping Catharine once again at the Western Female Institute. In 1834 Harriet's education received a strong abolitionist shift. She attended the influential Lane Seminary debates, during which a group of students clamored for the immediate abolishment of slavery. These "Lane Debates" received national attention and ultimately popularized the abolitionist movement.[12] As the girl who would grow to become Harriet Beecher Stowe wrote in 1829 to her brother George, "I was made for a preacher . . . in a certain sense it is as much my vocation to preach on paper as it is that of my brothers to preach viva voce."[13] Stowe would apply her sense of mission, developing it from an early age, first in her abolitionist work in *Uncle Tom's Cabin* and later in her Reconstructionist work in *Palmetto Leaves* and *Oldtown Folks*, in which she would use the orange as a symbol of perseverance and community.

As Catharine Beecher's domestic writing largely influenced Harriet's own work, so did that of another sibling. The agricultural writing of Henry Ward Beecher was significant for Stowe in terms of venues for her sense of mission. She could turn to a form of agricultural reform in her regional writings following his model. Henry was an avid gardener and gentleman farmer, owning property in the town of Lenox, in the Massachusetts Berkshire region, a five-hour train ride from his primary residence in Brooklyn Heights, New York. The "most famous man in America" would say about himself as a young minister, "I went to bed every Sunday night with a vow registered that I would buy a farm and quit the ministry."[14] He published *Plain and Pleasant Talk about Fruits, Flowers, and Farming* in 1859, placing his work between Henry Colman's 1838 reports on agriculture and the founding of the Grange movement in 1867. In his own work, Beecher advocates the practical use of new technologies to maximize production, while encouraging education and farming, foreshadowing agrarian reform movements like the Grange and the Morrill land-grant college system. He too discusses methods to keep U.S. rural farmers competitive against nineteenth-century urbanization. Promoting common schools for farmers, he chastises the "crafty" politicians who call farmers the "bone and sinew" of the nation without providing them with proportionate respect. He admonishes, "You will never be anything else but bone and sinew without education," which, he believes, would allow farmers to develop more economic and political power at the national level.[15] This attitude is paralleled in Stowe's writing, as she also promotes education—including the education of new Florida farmers—in the South during Reconstruction.

Henry Ward Beecher's passion for farming and reform are such that he includes a section on "Farm and Garden" in his 1870 journal, *Christian Union*. Largely a family affair, the periodical published contributions from siblings Harriet, Edward, Catharine, Thomas, and Eunice, adding to Henry's own work as editor and regular contributor. *Christian Union* first published Stowe's sketches that would be consolidated in book form in 1873 as *Palmetto Leaves*. Furthermore, *Christian Union* published a recommendation of the Grange movement on February 11, 1874, in a piece titled "Patrons of Husbandry." One of the elements of particular interest to the editors of *Christian Union* was the relative equality of gender in the Grange movement. Oliver Hudson Kelley, one of the movement's founders, refers to the issue of gender equality in an 1868 correspondence with Anson Bartlett. Kelley notes that it is "merely a question of time" before the nation in general would "recognize woman as the equal of man, just as surely as the tiller of the soil will be recognized as the peer of any in the land."[16] The connection of the rights of women with the rural farmer makes a representative figure like Stowe useful as both a writer and a manager of an orange grove in Florida. Stowe contributes to the nation's agricultural project through an acceptance of and challenge to reforms in operation at this period. She adapts and maneuvers them to the regional level during her time wintering at her orange grove in Mandarin, Florida.

Oranges were not discussed in Henry Ward Beecher's 1859 work; instead he focused on crops of the U.S. Northeast. As an agricultural reformer and a writer, though, Stowe developed a focus on the U.S. South. The history of oranges was developing independently of the regional fruits of the North during the first half of the nineteenth century. During her abolitionist years, oranges would have been an exotic—perhaps imported—item for Stowe, living as she did in a harsh climate in the U.S. Northeast that was inhospitable to the cultivation of citrus fruit. Oranges were associated with the South's warmer weather, as well as its slavery-based agriculture. Outside of regionally specific climates, oranges had been the exclusive purview of the wealthy into the nineteenth century. For example, European royalty would have maintained "orangeries," or dedicated greenhouses, in order to grow citrus in their own harsh climate.[17] Oranges immigrated to Florida in 1513, most likely, with the help of Ponce de León.[18] Oranges thrived in Florida's sandy soil, becoming an excellent crop for the state, and after the Civil War, oranges came to replace cotton as the predominant crop of certain Florida districts.[19] Particularly connected to oranges ever since this era, Florida named the orange blossom its state flower in the early twentieth century. Stowe spent her later years wintering in a region where oranges literally fell from trees, a genuine treat once she was able to detach the fruit from its ties to slavery. For Stowe, the regional specificity of oranges represented an appealing mirror to the apples of her native New England, where she returned every summer.[20] Stowe's domestic work in agriculture and literature helped make oranges as nationally symbolic as apples.

In addition to the history of the orange, the literary symbolism of oranges must have appealed to Stowe. Oranges and apples are connected through the literature of the Greeks, who used the term "apple" to represent basically any fruit; therefore, as Greek armies found varieties of citrus during their expansionist movements, they named newly discovered fruits after apples, as in the "Median" or the "Persian" apple. In addition, the "golden apple" given to Aphrodite by Paris in order to earn "the heart of Helen" was believed by Roman historians to have been an orange.[21] Stowe often makes classical references about oranges in her writings: "These are the veritable golden apples of the Hesperides,—the apples that Atalanta threw in the famous race; and they are good enough to be run after."[22] In classical myths, then, Stowe unites her "golden apples" with the red and green ones. She continues this theme, adding Biblical allusions: "The orange-tree is, in our view, the best worthy to represent the tree of life of any that grows on our earth. It is the fairest, the noblest, the most generous, it is the most upspringing and abundant, of all trees which the Lord God caused to grow eastward in Eden" (PL, 18). Turning to a cultural reference she would have in common with almost all of her audience, Stowe alludes to Eden to again draw a connection between oranges and apples, South and North. As opposed to a fruit that would be considered exotic to the average northerner, Stowe shows that after the Civil War oranges could grow as familiar, and as nationally representative, as apples. In addition, taking advantage of recent advances in agriculture, oranges could become almost as readily available to northern consumers as apples, without their having to resort to imported foodstuffs. Through her efforts in Reconstruction-era Florida, then, Stowe was part of a movement to help democratize oranges by making them available to a greater number of U.S. Americans. Stowe uses a regional form of agri-expansion to reunite an agriculturally sophisticated "New South" with an orange-eating North.

Moreover, Stowe promotes regional over foreign agricultural consumption. By focusing on the regional as opposed to the exotic and foreign, Stowe's postbellum writings from Florida extend some of the agricultural localization work done in Henry David Thoreau's bean-field and berry-picking adventures. Stowe attempts a kind of Thoreauvian agricultural reform work in *Palmetto Leaves*, as seen in the description of a Thoreau figure in that work. Stowe writes of "a naturalist, who, like Thoreau, has sojourned for months in the Florida forests to study and observe Nature" (PL, 198). This naturalist educates Stowe and her family on local flora and fauna, emphasizing the significance of the region. Stowe returns to this Thoreau figure later: "On the steamboat, coming back, we met the Florida Thoreau of whom we before spoke,—a devoted, enthusiastic lover of Nature as she reveals herself in the most secluded everglades and forests" (PL, 223). Stowe's Florida writings are not only some of the state's earliest tourist propaganda, but also some of its earliest ecotourism pieces. As Thoreau is known for his love of nature, Stowe allies herself with him in her writings about the natural beauty of Florida. She argues against the frivolous killing of alligators and birds native to Florida at several instances in the work, and she devotes several sketches to representations of the natural world around the St. Johns River region. In both cases Stowe and Thoreau make statements about the future of U.S. politics and economics through their experiments in regional farming, though on a decidedly different scale. While Thoreau argues against the intensification of agriculture coming as steadily as the Fitchburg train in the background of *Walden*, Stowe hopes that by applying certain new technologies connected to U.S. agri-expansion, she can use the northern markets to provide a reliable source of income to postbellum farmers. These farmers would increasingly be African Americans owning and managing their own orange groves.

Thus, Stowe works with, as opposed to against, the nation's agri-expansion challenged by Thoreau. She seeks to apply innovations and developing technologies to expand a regional agriculture into northern markets, encouraging the growth of domestic regional markets. Stowe's primary concern is with the lives of the people of the South—black and white. This becomes her primary mission in Florida. Stowe is therefore a strong force for social change through her domestic reform writings. At the same time, her work makes a useful addition to a discussion of various reforms of U.S. agri-expansion. Additionally, as a woman breadwinner, first as a writer and later as the manager of an orange grove, Stowe understood how to delicately navigate public and private spheres in order to smoothly influence both.[23] Stowe's domestic writings effectively encourage the production and consumption of U.S. regional foods, through discussions of northern Thanksgiving holidays and southern orange farmers.

Returning to the epigraph, the two Christian heroes of *Uncle Tom's Cabin* are connected to oranges as well and are thus a significant counterpoint to the slavery motif of oranges in the novel. Eva is connected to—yet untainted by—the problem of southern oranges. Meanwhile,

Tom is a strong Christian character and a slave also connected to oranges in the novel. Tom "would sometimes walk with her [Eva] under the orange-trees in the garden, or, sitting down in some of their old seats, sing to her their favorite old hymns."[24] These Christian model characters sit among orange trees in an Edenic garden. This scene shows on the one hand another regional marker of the South, while on the other hand it shows a "golden apple" with the potential to be a significant part of the nation's cornucopia of foods, depending on the outcome of the Civil War. Likewise, Tom treats Eva with gifts of oranges and peaches, and Stowe inverts her theme of white people gifting slaves with oranges in this scene: "In the market, at morning, his eyes were always on the flower-stalls for rare bouquets for her, and the choicest peach or orange was slipped into his pocket to give to her when he came back" (*UTC*, 271). Stowe adapts a nonnative food, the orange, into her catalogue of regional foods to demonstrate the possible success of regional agriculture following emancipation. She uses the example of her own orange grove to encourage further expansion by northerners into the South, as the South's agricultural production would simultaneously expand into the North. In their biography of Stowe, her son, Charles, and grandson, Lyman, observe that "it was a necessity of her mind to persuade herself that some higher end was being sought in everything she did from raising potatoes to writing a book," referencing a usefully symbolic U.S. crop in their analysis of Stowe's sense of mission.[25] In this way Stowe hopes to unite apples and oranges, North and South, under one nation's agriculture.

SOUTHERN ORANGES AND NORTHERN CORNUCOPIA

In *Uncle Tom's Cabin*, Stowe describes oranges in particular scenes, using their different status, as it were, to draw attention to the troubling element of slavery through the crops associated with it. Throughout the novel slavery and abolitionism correspond with certain foods: oranges are connected with slavery, while apples and peaches are connected with the abolitionist North. In her Civil War sketches collected in 1865 in *House and Home Papers*, Stowe dedicates a section to the "Cookery" of U.S. foods. In this work, Stowe has a complementary plan: she seeks to unite the nation culturally while it remains in conflict politically. Stowe argues that U.S. cuisine is superior to that of the British—or even the French—based on the quality of produce involved. As food is perhaps the most recognizable cultural marker, Stowe uses U.S. crops to draw attention away from the major national conflict and toward a domestic unification. The exotic oranges of the St. Clare plantation in *Uncle Tom's Cabin* and the cornucopia of foods available to the U.S. homemaker described in *House and Home Papers*, then, are symbols of domestic political choices.

Stowe pairs foods in *Uncle Tom's Cabin* in much the same way as she doubles character names throughout the novel. There are two characters named George, Tom, John, and Henry or Henrique.[26] While Stowe gives the same names to key characters—black and white—throughout the novel, she uses other modes of doubling to make a similar commentary with food. Oranges are introduced at pivotal moments, and they are contrasted to other foods like peaches and apples, which are described as emancipatory northern foods. Returning to the epigraph, oranges connect the children Eva and "Jim Crow," whose real name is Harry, as Eva's father at one point also gives her "a quarter of the orange he was eating" as a treat (*UTC*, 171). While Stowe's pairing of names in the novel may be the clearest example of this approach, her pairing and contrasting of food items is also useful as it is more subtly applied. By connecting a southern food like oranges to slavery, Stowe influences a northern readership through their diet, perhaps the most significant site of domestic consumption and thus of reform and praxis.

Stowe describes the St. Clare residence as "an ancient mansion, built in that odd mixture of Spanish and French style, of which there are specimens in some parts of New Orleans. . . . Two large orange-trees, now fragrant with blossoms, threw a delicious shade; and, ranged in a circle round upon the turf, were marble vases of arabesque sculpture, containing the choicest flowering plants of the tropics" (*UTC*, 172). She is conscious to add orange trees to a scene that details the exotic architecture and landscape of the wealthy southerner. This picture may do as little as putting oranges on a par with aloes, jessamines, and other exotic plants—a living equivalent of the "arabesque sculpture" also found in the garden. In fact, Stowe goes as far as to describe the scene as comparable to the "oriental romance in Spain," supporting an "orientalist" reading of this scene (*UTC*, 172). At the same time, the presence of orange trees in the St. Clare garden gives another example of the extravagance that characterizes Augustine St. Clare, Eva's father and a type of southern slave owner: lazy and privileged. This characterization shows the importance of abolitionism in order to discourage this kind of indolence. However, while Stowe uses this scene to set St. Clare apart from a northern audience that would have more in common with his abolitionist cousin, Ophelia, she cannot help but make the orange trees a "delicious" addition to the garden. They give shade in a hot, muggy climate, their blossoms sweetly perfume the air, and their fruit is a tasty treat. Eva and Tom further ameliorate the problems with this exotic, tainted space, a kind of a reversal of the story of Eden. Stowe creates a potentially ideal southern space—one that could become truly pleasant if freed of its connection to slavery. This reading becomes more pronounced once Stowe buys an orange grove in Florida after the Civil War. In the early years of Reconstruction, Stowe allowed herself to believe that Florida could become this idealized space: an orange tree–growing environment with lush plants and an agricultural economy based on greater equality of labor and educational opportunities. During the nation's antebellum period, though, orange trees remained untenable.

As is the case with many of the paired elements of *Uncle Tom's Cabin*, those orange trees that delight Eva are similarly drawn as part of the tragic autobiography of the slave, Cassy. She describes her experiences under similar orange trees to Tom: "The first I remember is, playing about, when I was a child. . . . There was a garden opening from the saloon windows; and there I used to play hide-and-go-seek, under the orange-trees, with my brothers and sisters. I went to a convent, and there I learned music, French and embroidery, and what not" (*UTC*, 381). Once again orange trees are markers of the South and of slavery. The garden of Cassy's childhood is comparable to the garden adjoining the

St. Clare mansion, in which Eva sits in the shade. Cassy has a childhood not unlike Eva's own, used to indulgences like oranges and a quality education. In this instance, however, because Cassy is a slave, she is not allowed to maintain this lifestyle under her orange trees. As often occurs in *Uncle Tom's Cabin*, a death forces a valuation of property among slave owners that breaks up families, in this case ultimately sending Cassy to the brink of insanity, where Tom finds her. While one child under the orange trees is a martyr who dies, going to a Christian heaven, the other child is led down a steadily degrading path into a living hell, where she becomes the broken woman Tom tries to comfort before his own martyrdom. Stowe does not directly duplicate the names of the two girls in this case; however, both characters are connected through a relative named "Henry": Cassy's son is Henry and Eva has a cousin named Henrique. In addition, Stowe connects the girls through orange trees in idyllic gardens in order to emphasize the drastically different endings to childhood possible in the antebellum South.

Furthermore, oranges appear during the philosophical debate regarding slavery between the southern slave owner St. Clare and his northern cousin, Ophelia. In the course of their discussion, Ophelia's racial prejudices are brought to light, as is St. Clare's true understanding of the immorality of slavery. In one of the most sophisticated sections of the novel, Stowe forestalls the arguments of apologists for slavery by using a southerner as her antislavery mouthpiece. She begins the scene with a seemingly lighthearted comment by the southerner: "I will be serious, now; but you must hand me that basket of oranges;—you see, you'll have to 'stay me with flagons and comfort me with apples,' if I'm going to make this effort" (*UTC*, 232).[27] Oranges are compared directly to "apples" as St. Clare quotes from the Song of Solomon, one of the most romantic sections of the Bible. This allusion in a sentimental novel would be significant for Stowe's audience. Following this comment Ophelia stops her cousin, believing him to be using excessive levity to avoid a difficult conversation. However, St. Clare is true to his earlier warning that he would "be serious," and from this point he launches into a bitter diatribe against slavery in the South. That Stowe would choose a joke alluding to a well-known lover's speech to begin her debate on slavery is further evidence that St. Clare finds it ultimately difficult to "be serious." However, Stowe parallels oranges and apples again in this passage—connecting the orange to potentially the most symbolically national fruit and a fruit decidedly associated with the Northeast. Doing this, Stowe draws attention to the differences between the two regions, as well as demonstrates a potential commonality between them, via their fruits. In this scene, then, oranges become already the "golden apples" that Stowe discusses at greater length in her later regional work.

The fact that Stowe chooses oranges in particular to represent slavery in *Uncle Tom's Cabin*, finally, is suggested through her contrasting descriptions of peaches and apples in scenes among abolitionist figures connected to the Underground Railroad. Although Tom and St. Clare give peaches and oranges to Eva, these are the only instances of a slave-connected family associated with peaches. Elsewhere, Eva gathers apples, their only direct presence in the novel in the context of a slave-owning family. In both cases, though, the fruits emphasize Eva's purity in the context of the slave system around her. Other than in connection with the idealized Eva, therefore, peaches and apples are seen in abolitionist spaces alone, like the kitchen of the Quaker Rachel Halliday. As much as oranges are connected to the abuses of slave characters like Harry, Cassy, or the chained slaves where Eva meets Tom, peaches and apples are connected to the Quakers in this novel. Indeed, Rachel is first introduced in the domestic role of preparing food—in this case, peaches: "By [Eliza's] side sat a woman with a bright tin pan in her lap, into which she was carefully sorting some dried peaches. . . . Her face was round and rosy, with a healthful downy softness, suggestive of a ripe peach" (*UTC*, 143–44). Not only is Rachel cooking with peaches, but she herself is a peach. The peach, in this context, is the opposite of the orange in the sense that the North would be the opposite of the South, or Quakers would be the opposite of slave traders. Apples are also connected to the Quakers; Rachel's friend Ruth is as apple-like as Rachel is peach-like: "The door here opened, and a little short, round, pin-cushiony woman stood at the door, with a cheery, blooming face, like a ripe apple" (*UTC*, 145). Oranges are contrasted to peaches and apples throughout *Uncle Tom's Cabin* in almost the same manner that Stowe contrasts paired names, homes, and families—to depict the unnatural aspect of slavery and the fact that people are basically equal, regardless of race, like the fruits they choose to eat.

As Stowe uses oranges in *Uncle Tom's Cabin* to represent a regional southern fruit tainted by its connection to slavery, in *House and Home Papers* (1865), she has a corresponding mission. In a series of domestic sketches, she moves beyond exotic southern foods to establish an ideal U.S. diet that focuses on the regional agriculture of the Northeast. This text deals with supposedly lighter national issues, like material goods and agricultural products, and its goal is to unify the nation as much as possible through its consumption habits during a time of great division. Historically, U.S. Americans had been subsisting on as close to a British diet as possible, often overlooking superior native foods out of a lack of familiarity. Indeed, U.S. diets were considered so poor that during a tour of the United States, Charles Dickens suspects "Americans deserved first prize for a diet sure to destroy teeth, stomach, and health," recommending that the government "undertake an educational program to teach Americans how to eat."[28] Stowe responds to critics like Dickens in *House and Home Papers*. Domestic reformers like Stowe would have taken Dickens's comments seriously, and she uses her writing to teach U.S. Americans to produce and consume foods more healthily, often by incorporating a culinary nationalism into her dietary recommendations and moving away from the cuisines of European nations. For Stowe, the cultivation and preparation of more U.S.-based crops would be the answer to issues of quality in the national cuisine.

Through her narrator, Christopher Crowfield, Stowe argues for her patriotic readers to purchase domestic goods—including agricultural products—as a show of national solidarity during a time of crisis. Stowe first discusses clothing in this manner, and later she makes the same argument in terms of diet. Stowe's narrator notes the startling variety and quality of native U.S. foods, more than would be available either in Britain or in continental Europe:

I recollect how I was once struck with our national plenteousness, on returning from a Continental tour, and going directly from the ship to a New York hotel, in the bounteous season of autumn. For months I had been habituated to my neat little bits of chop or poultry garnished with the inevitable cauliflower or potato, which seemed to be the sole possibility after the reign of green-peas was over; now I sat down all at once to a carnival of vegetables: ripe, juicy tomatoes, raw or cooked; cucumbers in brittle slices; rich, yellow sweet-potatoes; broad Lima-beans, and beans of other and various names; tempting ears of Indian-corn steaming in enormous piles, and great smoking tureens of the savory succotash, an Indian gift to the table for which civilization need not blush; sliced eggplant in delicate fritters; and marrow-squashes, of creamy pulp and sweetness: a rich variety, embarrassing to the appetite, and perplexing to the choice.[29]

Stowe gives her readers an anatomy of agriculture in the Northeast during the nineteenth century. This list of U.S. bounty is directly contrasted with Europe's relative sparseness. With quality ingredients and skilled preparation—of the kind that Stowe describes through the rest of her chapter on "Cookery"—the United States could establish a cuisine of simple crops that, she argues, would rival that of any other nation. While Stowe describes in this passage a particularly rich agricultural time, during the region's harvest season, she implies that this is not the only cause for the superiority of U.S. produce. Having traveled the Continent during its summer and early autumn seasons, her narrator presumably would have encountered elements of their harvest season as well. The fact that the narrator does not, excepting the "green-peas" described, leads to a kind of culinary homesickness. Stowe turns this homesickness into a national pride in the "carnival of vegetables" available to the United States.

As part of her goal to demonstrate national culinary pride, Stowe highlights particular foods in terms of quality. Europeans have seemingly only cauliflower, potatoes, and "green-peas" as vegetable options for their meals. Stowe describes the cauliflower and potatoes as sadly "inevitable," and even the fresh "green-peas" are tainted by a monarchical element through her description of their "reign." At this point Stowe's tone seems to be primarily one of disappointment. The narrator is surprised to find while abroad that Europe, known for its culinary superiority to the United States, did not have better crops as a foundation. To counter the limited extent of European produce available during the summer and early autumn, Stowe spends the next several lines cataloging U.S. vegetables; this list includes eight differently named native vegetables— not to mention "beans" and "squashes" that each have multiple varieties. In fact, Stowe notes that with this abundance, "the vegetarian doctrine preached in America left a man quite as much as he had capacity to eat or enjoy" (*HHP*, 229). Furthermore, Stowe includes qualifiers that emphasize the quality of U.S. foods. Tomatoes are "juicy," and succotash is "savory." More noteworthy, though, are the monetary descriptors she uses for certain foods following the U.S. idea of plenty. She writes of "rich" sweet potatoes and "a rich variety" of squash. These riches become "embarrassing" and "perplexing" to one who has had to deal without such wealth for an extended period of time. Even the "enormous piles" of "steaming corn" are described like stacks of gold bullion "tempting" once more with its richness. Somewhat ironically, Stowe applies the concept of democratic access to wealth to U.S. agriculture, in contrast to an implied European stratified cuisine.

Stowe is concerned that U.S. Americans favor European cuisine because they do not understand proper preparation: "We in America have the raw material of provision in greater abundance than any other nation. There is no country where an ample, well-furnished table is more easily spread, and for that reason, perhaps, none where the bounties of Providence are more generally neglected" (*HHP*, 228). She spends the rest of this chapter discussing the proper forms of "cookery" for her domestic, primarily northern, audience. Through food production and preparation—as seen in Stowe's example of harvest's plenty—the domestic joins the national in terms of agri-expansion. Stowe uses kitchen and hearth scenes like those in *Uncle Tom's Cabin* to show the importance of domestic issues to her overall reform. She connects national and domestic into a "manifest domesticity," to use Amy Kaplan's term. Stowe is not providing an example of early U.S. agrarianism in this scene; rather, she shows an adaptive agriculture influenced by the Industrial Revolution of her childhood and realized through the domestic world of U.S. cookery. Stowe places herself in conversation with U.S. politics and economics through her "domestic" works like *Uncle Tom's Cabin* and *House and Home Papers*, combining politics, economics, and domestic production specifically in certain foods. This focus on both the domestic and the economic became significant again in her postbellum writings on orange cultivation in Florida.[30]

Stowe uses oranges in *Uncle Tom's Cabin* for a number of sentimental reasons. It is striking that the fruit appears in noteworthy moments throughout the novel, and this connection is strengthened during Stowe's later writing while managing an orange grove in Florida. In *House and Home Papers*, meanwhile, Stowe specifically turns her critical gaze toward Europe, making a culinary stand against a foreign entity and helping the warring U.S. regions work toward economic and cultural recovery through domestic consumption. While she concedes that Europe remains culinarily superior to the United States in terms of cooking in general, her chapter on "Cookery" is meant to teach any U.S. American—middle class, immigrant, or newly emancipated African American—how to prepare this "rich" abundance of U.S. agricultural production. In a text that focuses on a community of materiality, from clothes and housewares to foodstuffs and cookery, Stowe encourages the consumption of U.S. goods as an opportunity to find a cultural common ground through food. The themes that appear in these early texts are built upon in Stowe's postbellum agricultural writings in *Palmetto Leaves* and *Oldtown Folks*. In her Florida work, oranges become a conscious symbol of the potential for the hope of an emancipated "New South." In her regional novel, meanwhile, the anatomy of U.S. foodstuffs is demonstrated during a Thanksgiving Day feast. Stowe idealizes the holiday, nationalized in 1863, as part of a developing national ideology based on the production and consumption of regional foods: an autumnal harvest festival with national significance. In these later works, Stowe links domesticity and U.S. politics in much the same way as she does in her most famous novel.

PALMETTO LEAVES AND ORANGE BLOSSOMS

After the Civil War, Stowe considered it her continuing mission—on the domestic and national levels—to help the people of the South. Perhaps surprisingly, then, there has been little critical attention focused on her writings from the South, like *Palmetto Leaves*, the collected sketches describing her experiences in Florida. Applying Lawrence Buell's assessment of *Uncle Tom's Cabin* to her later work, Stowe's mission in Florida is quite an ambitious one, among the more aspiring of the Reconstruction efforts in the state, worthy of a "9.5 out of 10" based on "degree of difficulty attempted."[31] The South as a region, she believed, would need assistance reintegrating into the Union politically and economically; furthermore, the newly freed African-American population would need education and employment opportunities that had been forcibly denied to them during slavery. During her seventeen winters in Florida, Stowe worked to promote the development of a strong regional agriculture, one that would provide opportunities to the emancipated citizens of the state, in addition to founding integrated schools and churches. For Stowe, oranges again represent a personal and national venture to reintroduce the South into the Union. In her work of the postbellum period, she makes oranges more democratically accessible than in her antebellum writings. In *Palmetto Leaves* Stowe uses oranges, her "golden apples," as a regional crop that can help both the North in terms of access and the South in terms of economics in the years following the Civil War.

In choosing to grow oranges in Florida, Stowe gives the fruit a privileged status. She noticeably does not choose sugarcane or cotton to be the crop representing Florida's reformed agriculture. Admittedly, her first investment in Florida, in 1866, involved a cotton plantation to be managed by her son, Frederick. However, this experiment quickly failed. Perhaps, after all, there was too much history involved in this cotton plantation to make it tenable. The plantation had previously been owned by a local, an infamous slave owner named Zephaniah

Kingsley, a possible model for the character of Simon Legree in *Uncle Tom's Cabin*.[32] Also, Stowe's troubled son often abandoned the farm for drinking bouts in Jacksonville. After one year and a dismal two-bale harvest, the $10,000 investment was abandoned. When Stowe arrived in Florida, she was too late to save the plantation or her son from alcoholism.[33] She writes that the one positive of their otherwise resounding failure was that the African-American hands "were all duly paid, scot and lot,—in many cases with the first money they ever earned, and it gave them a start in life."[34] Not admitting defeat, Stowe quickly moved and adapted, finding a cottage nearby that boasted "five large date palms, an olive tree, and an orange grove warranted to produce 75,000 oranges."[35] In Mandarin, Stowe found a crop, adventure, and mission in one location. She took advantage of the fact that oranges remained appealing to northern markets while becoming easier to transport there; oranges could be produced and consumed within the United States in a closed circle. Stowe would come to see the Florida orange as a symbol of what the South could become agriculturally, an economic complement to her educational and religious missions in the state.

Oranges are particularly appropriate to represent this new form of agriculture; in addition to their relative ease growing in warmer weather, orange trees are, in fact, resilient survivors. In an early section in *Palmetto Leaves*, Stowe describes the heartiness of oranges after they survive various trials—including deep freezes and the orange beetle: "Truly we may call them trees of the Lord, full of sap and greenness; full of lessons of perseverance to us who get frosted down and cut off, time and time again, in our lives. Let us hope in the Lord, and be up and at it again" (*PL*, 19). This ode to perseverance in the orange tree is also a commentary on her other objective in Florida—her romanticized goal to help the South economically and politically. Stowe's comment is largely applicable to the African Americans of Florida who must, far more than she, deal with repeated blows as they try to appreciate the rights and equality recently granted to them.[36] In her writing Stowe prepares northern reformers like herself, as well as African Americans living in the South, for the inevitable hindrances in the coming years by giving an example of the persevering orange tree. Shortly after this passage, Stowe describes early setbacks she and the rest of the St. Johns River community meet with in regard to their integrated school and church. At one point the building housing both church and school burns to the ground. Though Stowe quickly reassures her readership that she does not suspect arson, specifically not of a racially motivated kind, she is nevertheless devastated by the loss to the community, particularly the loss of the school. While church meetings can move from home to home, she observes, the school needs a dedicated location. Stowe writes, "Alas for the poor children, black and white, growing up so fast, who have been kept out of school now a year, and who are losing these best months for study! To see people who are willing and anxious to be taught growing up in ignorance is the sorest sight that can afflict one" (PL, 22). Following this, she must apply her lesson of resolve as she again recommends that she and her comrades in Florida "imitate the pluck of the orange-trees" (PL, 21).

Therefore, oranges, Stowe's "golden apples," represent a model food to sustain her economic, educational, and religious missions to assist African Americans in Florida. Though emancipated, African Americans were still discriminated against in the South based on "Black Codes." The U.S. Congress had to become more engaged with the enforcement of emancipation, resulting in the period of "Radical Reconstruction," beginning in 1867, the year Stowe moved to Florida. Republicans in the South, named "scalawags," took on a more active political role during this time. For example, the governor of Florida during Stowe's early years in the state was a moderate Republican from the North named Harrison Reed. Reed and Stowe shared a concern for the education of newly enfranchised African Americans. Stowe's goal in Florida was to create a series of schools and churches to provide opportunities for black and white Floridians. The governor, whose wife was an educator in integrated schools and who appointed Stowe's brother, Charles, to be Florida's superintendent of "public instruction," shared this goal. Ambitious projects like these were rife with controversy, though, and Reed encountered one trial after another during his Florida tenure.[37]

Stowe's educational, literary, and agricultural experiments in Mandarin were some of the most successful examples of reform during Reconstruction. Furthermore, she found a way to work smoothly with white southerners while attempting to reform several of their institutions. The oranges were significant elements of Stowe's reform, as they progress in her work from a symbol of southern slavery to a representation of a hopeful future for Florida, and the South, during this formative period.[38]

In addition to her interest in the political history of Florida in the 1860s, Stowe had particular personal reasons for wanting to establish a residence in the state. Like many snowbirds after her, Stowe no longer wanted to toil against an inhospitable nature; she traveled to the South every winter for physical and mental comfort. She believed the milder climate helped her writing. She looked to Florida's mild winters to ease her sense of what she termed "betweenity," the time between the last falling autumn leaf and the early spring growth, commenting that "cold weather seems to torpify my brain, I write with heavy numbness."[39] When Stowe first visited Florida, she had a revelatory moment in which she "stripped off the woolen garments of my winter captivity put on a thin dress white skirt & white saque & then came & sat down to enjoy the view of the river & the soft summer air . . . feeling quite young & frisky," even gathering orange blossoms for her hair.[40] She further writes, "We have so delicious a spring! I never knew such altogether perfect weather. It is enough to make a saint out of the toughest old Calvinist that ever set his face as a flint. How do you think that New England Theology would have fared if our fathers had landed here instead of on Plymouth Rock?"[41] For Stowe the physical comfort of a winter in the South led her to consider a more comfortable relationship with religion and its connection to education as well. If Calvinism were the prevailing spiritual code in the harsh northern climate, Episcopalianism would be the religion she favored in the mild, orange-bearing Florida. While placing more of her emphasis on education, Stowe preferred an accessible religion as opposed to the strict Calvinism of her forefathers as the spiritual accompaniment to the pleasant weather and correspondingly available orange cultivation of Florida.

Not all in Florida was mild and orange scented, however, even for Stowe's hopeful energy. Referring to the persevering orange trees once more, she writes, "It is certainly quite necessary to have some such example before our eyes in struggling to found a colony here" (PL, 19–20). Stowe notes that the efforts of northern investors in Florida are imperial in nature, as well as a "struggle." She brings imperialism within the U.S. borders—borders recently reestablished through the North's defeat of the South in the Civil War. Stowe compares her experience in Florida with the history of early U.S. globalization: "It is not a joke, by any means, to move to a new country. The first colony in New England lost just half its members in the first six months. The rich bottom-lands around Cincinnati proved graves to many a family before they were brought under cultivation" (PL, 38). Stowe names Florida a "new country" and compares it to the early settlements in New England and to U.S. western expansion. The South has in this instance become a renewed territorial space for the United States. In each situation, moreover, Stowe is connected personally to these examples of U.S. expansion. While her connection to the British settlers is a distant one, she moved to Cincinnati in her adolescence and then, during her middle years, spent her winters in Florida. Her experience followed the course of U.S. expansion to west and south. Instead of criticizing, though, she hopes to amend this expansionist tendency—specifically in regards to agriculture—in order to help Florida citizens achieve success in their own form of agri-expansion.

To help her achieve this domestic agri-expansionist goal, then, Stowe makes an appeal to her northern readers to invest in Florida farms. In addition to presenting a forlorn image of fertile lands "now growing back into forest with a tropical rapidity," the reverse of the early nineteenth-century U.S. agricultural ideal, she describes the ease with which northern investors may recuperate their outlays in Florida oranges and other agricultural products (PL, 243). Along the St. Johns River, she argues, a "ready market might be found for what good farmers might raise. A colony of farmers coming out and settling here together, bringing with them church and schoolhouse, with a minister skilled like St. Bernard both in husbandry and divinity, might soon create a thrifty farming-village" (*PL*, 244). As opposed to agri-expansion, in this passage she condenses the regional production to a culture more like the farming villages of the nation's early history. However, this reading is complicated by Stowe's own practice, as she personally participates in a form of agri-expansion to make her products available to a greater market in the North. Local trade was not enough for her ambitious economic goals. In fact, Stowe became well known for her orange crates bearing the label, "ORANGES FROM HARRIET BEECHER STOWE—MANDARIN, FLA."[42] Her famous name became the brand she used to market her produce. Through her writing and her own example, Stowe combines elements of the revolutionary spirit of potential northern "colonizers" with agriculture in postbellum Florida in order to make the South able to compare agriculturally to the industrial North.[43]

Stowe argues in favor of northern investment in southern orange crops by focusing in some detail on the ease of growing oranges. Florida's oranges take advantage of the development of new technologies like "grow houses," new preservation techniques, and Florida's relative proximity to northern consumers. Contrastingly, she writes, "The oranges that come to us from Malaga and Sicily are green as grass when gathered and packed, and ripen, as much as they do ripen, on the voyage over" (*PL*, 264). In a global orange trade, Stowe makes a case for regionalism and "buying American." By demonstrating the benefits of Florida oranges over their European counterparts, Stowe continues her argument for the consumption of domestic over foreign goods from *House and Home Papers*. She reemphasizes that her northern readership should consume regional products to serve the national work of reunification in the period immediately following the Civil War: "The oranges of Florida might be gathered much nearer ripe in the fall, ripen in the house or on the way, and still be far better than any from the foreign market. On this point fruit-growers are now instituting experiments, which, we trust, will make this delicious crop certain as it is abundant" (*PL*, 264). While her primary object in Florida may have been to establish integrated schools and churches, her work promoting agricultural investments, specifically in the orange industry, became a significant part of her larger domestic reform.[44]

In her writings from both before and after the Civil War, however, Stowe has been justifiably criticized for her treatment of African Americans—the population that she most wanted to aid. In the final two chapters of *Palmetto Leaves*, as in *Uncle Tom's Cabin* before it, Stowe uses questionable—even directly offensive—language to describe African-American characters. At one point, Stowe describes a man named "Cudjo" as both a "baboon" and "the missing link" (*PL*, 269). As shocking as this language is, however, Stowe also describes the man's feelings sympathetically. After struggling through a series of trials that would require him to demonstrate the pluck of an orange tree, Cudjo laments, "He take ebry t'ing, ebry t'ing,—my house I built myself, my fences, and more'n t'ree t'ousand rails I split myself: he take 'em all!" (*PL*, 274). Cudjo speaks in heavy dialect—which makes for a more dramatic scene as he describes his wrongs. Stowe follows his speech immediately with her own reaction to his story: "There is always some bitter spot in a great loss that is sorer than the rest. Those rails evidently cut Cudjo to the heart. The 't'ree t'ousand rails' kept coming in in his narrative as the utter and unbearable aggravation of injustice" (*PL*, 274). Stowe does not mock his pain in this instance; he is not merely a "local color" element of her Florida story. Indeed, this may be her most pointedly critical discussion of the ultimate failings of Reconstruction—and of reformers like herself—in the larger picture. She relates to Cudjo's loss and invites her readers to relate to him as well. Appealing to a largely northern audience, Stowe gives examples of African-American farmers in Florida during the postbellum period.

Stowe explains that this "colony" of African Americans from Georgia and the Carolinas had moved to Florida to invest in agriculture as she had done. She expresses the hardships these newly emancipated families must overcome:

> The native Floridian farmer is a quiet, peaceable being, not at all disposed to infringe the rights of others, and mainly anxious for peace

and quietness. But they supposed that a stampede of negroes from Georgia and Carolina meant trouble for them, meant depredations upon their cattle and poultry, and regarded it with no friendly eye; yet, nevertheless, they made no demonstration against it. Under these circumstances, the new colony had gone to work with untiring industry. They had built log-cabins and barns; they had split rails, and fenced in their land; they had planted orange-trees; they had cleared acres of the scrub-palmetto: and any one that ever has seen what it is to clear up an acre of scrub-palmetto will best appreciate the meaning of that toil. Only those black men, with sinews of steel and nerves of wire,—men who grow stronger and more vigorous under those burning suns that wither the white men,—are competent to the task. (*PL*, 271–72)

This passage is one of Stowe's most direct descriptions in *Palmetto Leaves* of the circumstances of African Americans in Florida during her time there. Her delicacy in the treatment of her white neighbors is evident in her careful elision of the racist treatment against the newcomers. While the locals feared "depredations upon their cattle and poultry," Stowe quickly focuses on the "untiring industry" of the African Americans who work to create their own Florida colony, a more labor-intensive investment than her own orange grove had required. These new investors build barns and fences and plant the orange trees that she merely purchased. Whatever fears the white Florida farmers had, Stowe maintains, were warrantless. Moreover, she continues, the newcomers cleared brush that would have "withered" a white person. Here, undoubtedly, Stowe's language takes on an essentialist tone by asserting that African Americans would be more comfortable laboring in the sun than Euro Americans. However, her goal in this section is to diplomatically commend the efforts of her black neighbors without overtly criticizing the racist behavior of the local white community.[45]

Throughout Stowe's Florida work, she desires to help the newly emancipated African Americans, and one of the ways to do this is through helping them with their own farms. In 1865 Gen. William Tecumseh

Sherman had guaranteed African Americans forty acres and a mule as reparations. One of the goals behind this promise was the reclamation of abandoned lands. In an account given during the time, an ex-slave named Margaret Nickerson puts into perspective the events following emancipation: "Mr Carr got us all together and read a paper to us that didn't none of us understand except that it meant we was free. Then he said that them what would stay and harvest the cotton and corn would be given the net proceeds. Them what did found out the net proceeds wasn't nothing but the stalks."[46] The agricultural promises made to former slaves ended up stalk-like for the most part as well, but these investors remained orange-like in their perseverance. In Florida alone, between August and October 1866, African Americans entered patents on thirty-two thousand acres of public land, according to the Freedmen's Bureau. In the following year, ending October 1867, 2,012 homesteads and 160,960 acres were entered in Florida alone.[47]

However, white southerners almost instantly attacked this progress; in the version of the bill that was eventually passed through Congress, the opportunity for African Americans to own land had been greatly reduced. Labor contracts remained unjustly distributed and enforced through the 1860s. Congress largely gave lands back to the previous white owners through the Amnesty Act of 1872.[48] At the same time, racist laws as well as the development of the Ku Klux Klan prevented African Americans from taking advantage of new opportunities. Nevertheless, African-American farmers remained in Florida and the rest of the South following Reconstruction, growing oranges as well as cotton, corn, and garden vegetables. By 1910 census data would show that "nonwhite farm operators"—renters, owners, or a combination—made up 49.5 percent of the farmers in Florida.[49] When Stowe advises her readers to imitate the pluck of the orange tree and persevere through adversity, she describes the African-American community of Florida to a large extent. In that case northerners purchasing Florida oranges would, in some small measure, be supporting their efforts at building farms and communities in Florida during the Reconstruction era.

The importance of Stowe to Florida's postbellum history is such that she warrants an extended discussion in studies of the state, including in John McPhee's *Oranges*. McPhee remarks, "Florida accepted her warmly, partly because she was quoted in the northern press, soon after her arrival, as having said that people in Florida were 'no more inclined to resist the laws or foster the spirit of rebellion' than people in a state like Vermont."[50] Stowe's advertisement of orange groves as a profitable investment brought together northerners and southerners from other states; these entrepreneurs were soon working together after having been fighting a few years earlier. Stowe's diplomacy toward the South throughout her tenure in Florida was appreciated by her neighbors and aided in tourism—often focusing on Stowe herself as a tourist object. During her residence in the state, tour boats regularly cruised past her cottage, tourists hoping to catch a glimpse of the famous author.[51] While in 1873 fourteen thousand tourists visited Florida, that number jumped to thirty-three thousand by 1874, following Stowe's publication of *Palmetto Leaves*, and Stowe "was proud to take credit" for such a surge of visitors in a letter to her friend Annie Fields. Unfortunately, the citrus boom of the St. Johns River region did not long outlive Stowe's time there. After a harsh freeze during the 1894 through 1895 season, the oranges of that region were permanently abandoned. Tourism, on the other hand, has remained a strong source of income in Florida ever since.

Stowe's *Palmetto Leaves* includes descriptions of agriculture, pleas for her educational and religious mission, ecotouristic descriptions of Florida's flora and fauna, and sketches about her daily life. In this perhaps she attempts too much; part travel narrative, part memoir, and part social tract, the book never truly excels at any of these genres. Again, reading Buell's comment about *Uncle Tom's Cabin* onto Stowe's later efforts to help improve the lives of the African Americans she was credited with having in large part helped to emancipate, her execution was never ultimately as satisfying as her original goals.[52] In spite of its shortcomings, though, *Palmetto Leaves* was a best seller during Stowe's time, and it has remained a significant regional text in Florida owing to its historical relevance. With her orange grove in Florida,

Stowe became the owner and manager of a successful farm. The farm's orange crates are, after all, stamped with her name.[53] In her agricultural experiment and in her writing, she shows an ideal domestic lifestyle in Florida while challenging ideas of domesticity. Stowe is an important figure in feminism in terms of property rights and political power for women.[54] Following the phenomenon of *Uncle Tom's Cabin*, *Palmetto Leaves* makes the most directly feminist argument regarding national agriculture and politics. In this case Stowe is not only a writer wintering in Florida, but also an agri-expansionist and a feminist sustaining herself and her family through her writing and farming, while trying to reform Florida's education and religious systems. Stowe's work in Florida is a national reform effort based on agriculture, education, and religion in addition to being fundamentally feminist. Stowe's multivalenced project in Florida is symbolized by the image of the orange; once oranges have been adopted as a national food, they become a sign of a unified nation. Meanwhile, Stowe continued her work on national unification through agriculture in her depiction of a Thanksgiving dinner in her regional novel *Oldtown Folks*.

A RECONSTRUCTION CORNUCOPIA

While growing oranges in Florida, Stowe wrote what she considered to be her magnum opus, *Oldtown Folks*. There is a temporal connection between *Palmetto Leaves* and *Oldtown Folks*: the one a series of Reconstruction-era sketches set in Mandarin, Florida, and the other a post–Revolutionary War novel set in Natick, Massachusetts. Stowe ultimately published *Oldtown Folks* in 1869, having completed it while dividing her time between New England and Florida; it was one of only two of her books to be published without previous serialization.[55] Stowe found that she had a great deal of "resistance" writing this regional novel, and biographer Joan Hedrick posits that one explanation for this is her continuing political activism during Reconstruction. Stowe consciously works through these problems as well, combining her utopian vision of a reformed postbellum nation with remembered stories of Calvin Stowe's childhood in small-town Massachusetts.[56] *Oldtown Folks* is therefore both a regionalist work promoting unification following the Civil War and a nostalgic look at the nation's revolutionary past. With this ultimate end in mind, Stowe describes the prototypical U.S. American holiday, Thanksgiving, at a pivotal moment in the novel. Though Stowe does not describe oranges in *Oldtown Folks* in any detail—indeed, it would have been anachronistic to have done so—her Florida reform venture is recognizable in the novel through another food-connected scene: the production and consumption of a Thanksgiving Day feast. It is useful to study Stowe's domestic arrangements: the food itself from farm to kitchen to table. If one of the most pronounced cultural markers is its cuisine, then Stowe makes a significant national commentary during U.S. agri-expansion and Reconstruction by describing a national Thanksgiving feast that brings together families and friends through a festive shared meal.

Stowe's description of an elaborate Thanksgiving feast is politically important given the charged history of the holiday. George Washington pronounced the nation's first official Thanksgiving Day in 1789; however, it was not regularized as a national holiday until 1863, when Abraham Lincoln declared it to be the final Thursday of November.[57] Lincoln's declaration followed two Union Civil War victories, Vicksburg and Gettysburg, and it brought together food and politics once more.[58] Before Lincoln's declaration, Thanksgivings had been celebrated regionally on a variety of days, with little cohesion in terms of the nation as a whole.[59] Bridging the roles that Washington and Lincoln played in the formation of the holiday, Stowe manages to span two defining U.S. wars in one feast. Symbolism is key for Stowe in this description, as she would have already been in Florida over Thanksgiving. The regional crops of the Northeast during harvest season would not have been her primary foods there. Rather than the turkey-and-pumpkin meal traditionally associated with the holiday, hers would have been more in keeping with her "picnicky kind of life" described in *Palmetto Leaves*. This geographical distance resonates in her descriptions of the meal, as her foods are a somewhat generalized version of northern U.S. foods traditionally associated with the holiday. This ritualized meal based on regional foods was symbolic of a shared nationality. Stowe continues Lincoln's efforts in naming Thanksgiving a national—as opposed to a regional—holiday by giving it prominent placement in her Reconstructionist writings.

In her chapter "How We Kept Thanksgiving at Oldtown," Stowe describes feast-day preparations through the voice of her child narrator, Horace Holyoke. First, Horace asks, "Are there any of my readers who do not know what Thanksgiving day is to a child? Then let them go back with me, and recall the image of it as we kept it in Oldtown."[60] This straightforward, simple style is in keeping with a child narrator, as well as with Stowe's nostalgic tone, which allows her to navigate issues pertaining to both the federalism following the American Revolution as well as Reconstruction following the Civil War. Furthermore, she connects the time of the feast to the work involved in harvesting the crops prepared. Thanksgiving is reconnected with the autumnal harvest—a truly global festival with localized specificity. In Oldtown, this festival occurs "when the apples were all gathered and the cider was all made, and the yellow pumpkins were rolled in from many a hill in billows of gold, and the corn was husked, and the labors of the season were done . . . there came over the community a sort of genial repose of spirit,—a sense of something accomplished" (*OF*, 283). Stowe focuses on specific foods of U.S. regional history; apples, pumpkins, and corn are all identified with the northeastern United States. These are the foods that had given the United States its distinct culinary culture. Furthermore, the feast must come after "the labors of the season" have been completed. In this way Stowe makes a moral judgment regarding the feast. The labors of the harvest itself give the community of Oldtown a sense of something "accomplished," and this causes a general and communal "repose of spirit." This community feast day is an earned indulgence, as opposed to the relaxed picnics of Florida, where oranges and other foods are available to consumers for a longer period. Stowe advances this as the "natural feeling" appropriate following the labors of the divisive war between the U.S. regions. Stowe attempts to return the nation to a single family unit again, a reposeful body that shares an agricultural holiday through the consumption of regional foods.

As Horace Holyoke describes the varieties of regional foods eaten on Thanksgiving, Stowe has an opportunity to illustrate the importance of this symbolic holiday during a time when the nation remains in a state of political and cultural upheaval:

> But who shall do justice to the dinner, and describe the turkey, and chickens, and chicken pies, with all that endless variety of vegetables which the American soil and climate have contributed to the table, and which, without regard to the French doctrine of courses, were all piled together in jovial abundance upon the smoking board? There was much carving and laughing and talking and eating, and all showed that cheerful ability to despatch the provisions which was the ruling spirit of the hour. After the meat came the plum-puddings, and then the endless array of pies, till human nature was actually bewildered and overpowered by the tempting variety; and even we children turned from the profusion offered to us, and wondered what was the matter that we could eat no more. (*OF*, 291–92)

Stowe describes an "endless variety of vegetables" unique to the "American soil and climate" but leaves the specifics of that variety for her audience to imagine based on their various regional identities.[61] Other than specific poultry listed, everything is described generally and could be eaten in any U.S. region. Even the "pies" and "puddings," generalized as "plum-puddings," are used to represent a variety of desserts. In modern discussions of Thanksgiving, people are quick to observe the regional specificity of the usual holiday foods. Stowe, however, does not fall into that normalizing role describing the foods in this scene. Instead she describes a common food cornucopia, contrasted against her detailed list of foods in *House and Home Papers*.[62] Indeed, while the earlier list, compiled during the Civil War, reads like a harvest inventory in the U.S. Northeast, in this later scene such an anatomy is not Stowe's focus. She rather hopes to reconcile North and South in a shared food culture.

To help reunite the U.S. North and South, Stowe finds it helpful to describe a common culinary enemy as well. The "French doctrine" is the antithesis of the celebration of abundance inherent in the U.S.

Thanksgiving feast. As in *House and Home Papers*, the United States sets itself against European nations in this scene. The French, Stowe notes, eat several courses served with rigid formality. In the United States, however, as opposed to courses and stages, there is a "jovial abundance." The food itself is full of good spirits in celebration of this agricultural feast day, and the time is spent equally on "laughing and talking and eating." In *House and Home Papers*, Stowe argues for a new U.S. method of preparing the superior produce to compete against European nations, specifically France and Britain. In the earlier work, she describes a custom in Paris: "Each family has one evening in the week when it stays at home and receives friends. Tea, with a little bread and butter and cake, served in the most informal way, is the only refreshment. The rooms are full, busy, bright" (*HHP*, 190). Stowe notes that the absence of a formal dinner in favor of a light meal keeps the party "bright" without the fear of overconsumption and regret. This scene demonstrates a casual attitude she later celebrates in *Oldtown Folks*, though with a different attitude toward the foods themselves. In the later work, the informality and jollity of the scene makes it comparable to the "bright" Parisian custom of the earlier piece, while at the same time showing some of the excesses she would have warned against previously. So, while at first she uses the Parisian example as a model for U.S. cookery, by the time she describes her national Thanksgiving holiday, the "informal" French tradition has become a rigid "doctrine" revolutionized by the United States as part of its "jovial" attitude during this day. Stowe changes her attitudes toward French cuisine in order to make French stiffness a common foil for both the North and the South on this U.S. holiday.

Stowe also returns to her theme of the abundance of quality U.S. regional crops as described in *House and Home Papers*. Her narrator Horace observes that charity, like food, is abundant in his region in part because the quantity of "*food* in our New England life is one subject quite worthy of reflection . . . good, plain food was everywhere in New England so plentiful, that at the day I write of nobody could really suffer for the want of it . . . no one ever thought of refusing food to any that appeared to need it" (*OF*, 223–24, Stowe's italics). Though Stowe does not show a categorical list of the foods available to the U.S. consumer in this passage, she emphasizes the fact that food is abundant enough to warrant special attention. The foods in this scene are described expansively. Stowe writes that the idle Sam Lawson is given, in addition to a Thanksgiving turkey, "a mince and a pumpkin pie" for his family's Thanksgiving enjoyment and that "a multitude of similar dispensations during the course of the week" kept Horace's Grandmother Badger busy cooking (*OF*, 290). During these parallel periods—Revolution and Reconstruction—there is enough food grown across the nation that people should not have to "suffer for the want of it." Stowe highlights her political goal for *Oldtown Folks* in this scene: "no one ever thought of refusing food" to another during this time. The United States is seen as a nation of plenty, and there is indeed plenty to share with a neighbor— whether that neighbor is a regionalist folk figure like Sam Lawson in *Oldtown Folks* or African Americans looking for opportunities in the postbellum South as described in *Palmetto Leaves*. In either case, and in every region, Stowe encourages a basic benevolence. Furthermore, as if to hint between the two works and regions, Stowe does bring an element of her Florida experiences into her Revolution-period novel through the description of the "candied orange-peel" that young Horace samples in the excitement of Thanksgiving-feast preparations (*OF*, 285). The "folks" are not eating whole oranges per se, but preserved orange peels, and only as a holiday treat. Through material insertions like this one, connecting the two eras and locations, Stowe is able to communicate her ongoing agricultural, educational, and religious programs in Florida through her regionalist fiction set in the U.S. Northeast as part of her overall goal of cultural unification through a shared food identity.

Stowe uses her depiction of a Thanksgiving Day feast to encourage an empathetic attitude toward the people of the South from her audience.[63] She wants her readers to laugh with, as opposed to at, regional characters. Even in her writings based in the North, Stowe attempts to make a statement of unification, working always toward reforming the national project. Throughout Stowe's writing, the sharing of food in domestic settings is one of her dominant themes.[64] *Oldtown Folks* gives a specific example of this kind of scene. Stowe continues to show that the sharing of food—especially in the ritualized context of a newly nationalized Thanksgiving feast—is also understood in the sense of communion, in the religious sense, demonstrating an element of Christian benevolence and sacrifice via cuisine. Stowe combines her depth of feeling about religion with her commitment to improve the conditions of African Americans after emancipation and to reestablish a successful agricultural economy in the South overall. There can be nothing more domestic than Thanksgiving, a time specifically apportioned for sharing with friends and family over a ritualized meal. Therefore, Stowe chooses it as the ultimate domestic space in which to set her mission during the abolitionist period, one that is translated into a similarly large undertaking during the postbellum period. The Thanksgiving feast is for Stowe a festive meal in which the domestic becomes political (and even economic) and the regional becomes truly national.

In *Oldtown Folks* Stowe again attempts to reconcile the nation in the postbellum years. While ostensibly a regionalist text set in Massachusetts, much of the work was written in Florida, and the politics of the era are represented in the novel. The Revolution and Reconstruction became twinned themes for Stowe as she sought to reimagine the nation in the midst of agricultural revolution and a failing Reconstruction. Part of Stowe's enduring influence is the fact that she was one of the most successful women authors of the nineteenth century—mostly working in the genre of sentimental and regional fiction. Already a woman working in a male-dominated field, she made the field of authorship—specifically in regionalism—more accessible for women and minority writers following her.[65] Stowe's focus on regional agriculture during this period was directly connected to her work influencing the nation in terms of taste. Stowe's work on domestic agriculture and celebrations of national Thanksgiving feasts is not a pronounced revolt against the nation's agriexpansion; rather, it is a sympathetic reform of that mission from within. As the figure of Grandmother Badger in *Oldtown Folks* observes, "*We* musn't reap the corner of our fields, nor beat off all our olive-berries, but leave 'em for the poor, the fatherless, and the widow, Scripture says"

(*OF*, 150, Stowe's italics). Grandmother Badger uses a Christian maxim to describe acts of basic charity. Stowe uses this theme throughout her novel, as it concerns the most basic domestic materiality of food.[66] In this way she gives her readers—regardless of their region—examples of how to help those in need on a larger scale. The United States should give a portion of its time, energy, even domestic goods, to the symbolically poor, orphaned, and widowed "folks" represented by the newly freed African Americans of the South. This ameliorating effort through shared food-based traditions would make the nation stronger than it was before the Civil War and a more successful force on the global stage.

CONCLUSION: A MISSION UNFULFILLED

If Grandmother Badger is a generalized figure of Christian benevolence in *Oldtown Folks*, Ophelia St. Clare is another generalized example of Christian moral development for Stowe. In *Uncle Tom's Cabin*, Ophelia represents an example of Stowe's northern abolitionist figure and to some extent Stowe herself. Ophelia develops as a character from a hypocritical northerner, a nominal abolitionist who harbors racist thoughts against African Americans, into a legitimate abolitionist. In addition, Stowe foreshadows her own projects, including her Restoration agricultural endeavors, and potentially some of her own issues with race, through Ophelia. In a scene between Evangeline's death and his own, one punctuated by a walk underneath orange trees, Augustine asks Ophelia, "If we emancipate, are you willing to educate?" (*UTC*, 331). This critical question about the North's motivation toward abolitionism remains important to Stowe even after the publication of *Uncle Tom's Cabin*, and it is one that she continues to struggle with on a personal level in her Reconstruction work in Florida, as seen in the final chapters of *Palmetto Leaves*. Throughout her writings on domestic production, both ante- and postbellum, Stowe privileges the regional above the foreign in terms of material goods and foods. In *House and Home Papers*, Stowe challenges a national trend in consumption that might keep the United States dependent upon a foreign nation like Britain, its one-time colonizer. Stowe also shows examples of this work through direct cultural and economic influence via her orange production as well as her corresponding educational and religious missions in *Palmetto Leaves*. Furthermore, her symbolic cultural production in *Oldtown Folks* shows the possibility of a shared national cuisine based upon a food-based holiday like Thanksgiving. As Stowe creates Ophelia St. Clare to represent the potential failings of northern abolitionists and how it is possible to overcome such failings, she is determined to show an example of positive praxis in her own efforts in the postbellum South as well.[67]

Stowe was fundamentally committed to educating African Americans in Florida and fighting for their rights through her writings and activism. However, like most Reconstruction-era goals in the South, Stowe's educational, religious, and agricultural works did not long outlive her direct presence. How much of what Stowe missed during these later years was owing to her self-confessed need to write about the world with the "couleur de rose" and how much was owing to her "nomadic" mental faculties—as she termed them—in her final years cannot ultimately be known.[68] Stowe is remembered as saying, "Why should we not be friends? What earthly interest have we now to separate us?"[69] During the years of Reconstruction, she hoped to use diet and agriculture, the production and consumption of regional U.S. foods, to make the South and the North "friends" once again. It is interesting that she did not write specifically about the failure of Reconstruction, especially considering that her own project in Florida was impermanent and she eventually retreated to Nook Farm, Connecticut, after her husband's poor health made travel impossible. She spent the remaining years of her life in the North. It fell upon her neighbor and friend, Samuel Clemens—or Mark Twain—to write more critically about the issues of race and the failure of Reconstruction in his essays, travel narratives, and children's novels.[70] Specifically in his travel narratives, he brings these issues to U.S. agriexpansion. Twain connects imperialism, agriculture, and the U.S. sugar trade as it relates to the regions of the South and the Pacific Islands.

Sweet Empires of Labor

I know the taste of maple sap, and when to gather it, and how to arrange the troughs and the delivery-tubes, and how to boil down the juice, and how to hook the sugar after it is made; also how much better hooked sugar tastes than any that is honestly come by, let bigots say what they will.
MARK TWAIN, *Autobiography*, 1:216

All through supper [Tom's] spirits were so high that his aunt wondered "what had got into the child." He took a good scolding about clodding Sid, and did not seem to mind it in the least. He tried to steal sugar under his aunt's very nose, and got his knuckles rapped for it. He said:
  "Aunt, you don't whack Sid when he takes it."
  "Well, Sid don't torment a body the way you do. You'd be always into that sugar if I warn't watching you."
MARK TWAIN, *The Adventures of Tom Sawyer*, 37

In passages from his *Autobiography* (2010) and most famous novel, *The Adventures of Tom Sawyer* (1876), Samuel Clemens—better known as Mark Twain—introduces the themes of sweetness, theft, and desire through his descriptions of sugar. In his youth Clemens spent summers on his uncle's farm. There he acquired firsthand knowledge about the production of sugar from maple trees in a model of local agriculture; this experience for him included stealing choice samples of the sweet treat during the process. As opposed to "New Orleans sugar," which was produced from cane grown on southern plantations, Clemens's memories of the production of a family's stock of maple sugar are not contingent on plantation labor or large-scale production. Sugar appears again in a similar, semiautobiographical scene from *Tom Sawyer*. In a related event, young Sam Clemens was blamed for breaking a treasured heirloom sugar bowl that was in fact broken by Sid's inspiration, Henry Clemens, and Sam was "whacked" for it in much the same way that Aunt Polly punishes Tom in the fictionalized account. The young Tom is drawn to sugar as a forbidden treat in much the same way that the real Sam stole tastes of maple sugar by "hooking" them. For both the author and the fictionalized character, eating sugar was one of the choice—in part because forbidden—treats of youth, and anecdotal instances of sugar eating are given prominence in some of Mark Twain's best-known writings.

Meanwhile, the Louisiana sugar industry of the antebellum period had intensified to the point that a barrel known as a "sugar hogshead" was so common—and so large—that Huckleberry Finn would sleep inside one in *The Adventures of Tom Sawyer* and *Adventures of Huckleberry Finn* (1884).[1] Twain is known as the author of beloved children's novels. In addition, Twain was one of the most prolific and popular U.S. travel writers of the nineteenth century. Furthermore, he became known as one of the most passionate anti-imperialists in U.S. literature. Twain himself declares in a 1900 *New York Herald* article that he had changed from a "red hot imperialist" to someone "oppose[d] to having the eagle put its talons on any other land."[2] I track Twain's development as an anti-imperialist following his theme of sugar—looking at a text that may be his most imperialistic piece of writing, his 1866 Hawaiian letters written for the *Sacramento Union*, against a foundational work of his anti-imperialism, *Following the Equator* (1897). In both writings sugar plays a prominent part; Twain focuses on sugar production in Hawaii in the earlier piece and visits several sugar-producing nations within the British Empire in *Following the Equator*. Comparing these works that bookend his writing career, I suggest that Twain's experience with the global sugar industry allowed him ultimately to grow from the "red hot imperialist" to a writer who eloquently criticized the U.S. eagle's talons clawing at other territories. The path of sugar parallels westward expansion; sugar is also noteworthy as one of the commodities implicated in Western imperialism. In his travel writings, Twain analyzes the ways in which the global sugar trade affects a diasporic labor force compelled to produce the commodity for industrializing Western nations, specifically Britain and the United States. One of the commonalities between the African Americans, Hawaiians, Australians, and Mauritians in Twain's writings—one that is compounded by the Cubans and Filipinos of U.S. imperialism following the Spanish-American War—is that their labor is exploited in sugar plantations across the sites of Western agri-expansion.

Twain wrote at a time when the United States was growing into a global force, and the country's ambitions were connected to its agriculture. Current theories of globalization, particularly concerning food, are therefore useful to apply to nineteenth-century travel narratives. While globalization commonly refers to a time around the end of the twentieth century, it can also signify the technological, political, and cultural developments of the nineteenth century. David Held emphasizes the transcontinental flows and networks as key elements of globalization, and these were similarly present during the second half of the nineteenth century in the United States, as seen in Twain's work on travel, imperialism, and sugar. Moreover, globalization is interestingly connected to food production and distribution, which changes at times of drastic advancements in technology and communication.[3] Food is dependent on global currents at the same time as it helps to form and reform those currents. U.S. agri-expansion in the late nineteenth century—as seen in Twain's writings on global sugar production—must be considered alongside the development of the United States via globalization during the same period. Twain's perspective on the global sugar trade was in conversation therefore with reformers of domestic agricultural production. As Harriet Beecher Stowe argued for a regional agricultural expansion in her descriptions of Florida's orange industry, Twain framed issues of sugar production in terms of the global.[4]

Sugar has long been implicated in Western imperialism. The connection between large-scale production in agriculture, industrialization, and diasporic labor patterns dominated the nineteenth century. Originally, the sugar industry relied on the labor of slaves; however, following emancipation this system of diasporic labor transitioned into a form of wage slavery based on "coolie" labor.[5] The relationship between a "nonwhite labor" force and Western nations remained virtually unchanged after the abolition of slavery—in 1838 in Britain, 1865 in the United States, and 1884 in Cuba. There was a direct relationship between struggles against emancipation in the British Empire—in addition to other imperialist nations—and the interests of sugar plantations.[6] Sidney Mintz, discussing sugar production and consumption during Britain's Industrial Revolution, analyzes the history of the global sugar trade in a way that applies to Twain's discussion of U.S. sugar interests and agri-expansion. The British sugar trade began as a slavery-based industry, primarily located in the Caribbean and forming part of the slave triangle of Barbados, Britain, and West Africa. The sugar trade, in fact, aided the British Industrial Revolution by providing cheap calories to an increasingly nonagrarian working population. As demand grew, an increasing number of nations, or "sugar islands" to use Mintz's term, were colonized to fill that need.[7] Eventually, the British Empire spanned the globe—and the majority of Britain's colonies were involved in the production of sugar to fuel the urbanizing labor force within Britain's borders at the height of its expanding economy. The colonies of Jamaica, Trinidad, and British Guiana were joined by new colonies in Fiji and Mauritius, nations Twain would visit during his 1895 through 1896 tour of the British Commonwealth.[8] The need for sugar among Euro-American nations created a series of diasporas that were related directly to sugar plantation labor; consequently, Mintz names sugar "one of the major demographic forces in world history."[9]

The United States quickly followed the British in its development of a national sweet tooth. In the United States, as in Britain, there was an increased demand for a cheap stimulant to increase productivity in an industrializing work force. By the 1880s the United States was consuming more sugar than any nation other than Britain, and by the time of the Spanish-American War, it had almost doubled even that rate of consumption. Following the perceived demand for this foodstuff, what Mintz calls a "drug food," the United States would develop an interest in acquiring global territories, specifically sugar-producing nations, in order to satisfy that demand.[10] The United States pushed beyond its territorial borders, turning to a global model of imperialism contrasted against its earlier territorial and agricultural development. Britain and the United States are paralleled in terms of the expansion of their sugar industries across the world: "Instead of Barbados the United States had Puerto Rico; instead of Jamaica, Cuba; for the Pacific areas, there were Hawaii and the Philippines."[11] As Britain had, the United States developed protectorate nations in sugar-producing regions following the Spanish-American War, another episode of U.S. imperialism. Sugar bridges the global issues of imperialism, expansion, and agriculture, and the United States followed the British model of imperialism to the point of mirroring locations of sugar-rich lands in various parts of the global tropics.

Meanwhile, the trajectory of sugar and imperialism is also the trajectory of some of the major turning points in Twain's personal and professional career. The diasporic global laborers engaged in the sugar trade included enslaved Africans, who were taken mostly to the U.S. South and the Caribbean, and coolie laborers from China, India, and eventually the Pacific Islands, who worked in the tropical sugar fields across the world. As a young man, Twain traveled along the Mississippi River, seeing firsthand the plantation labor of African Americans. He then wrote a series of expansionist letters for U.S. business interests in Hawaii, his first major assignment as a journalist. Finally, in almost every country Twain visited in his life-changing lecture tour that resulted in *Following the Equator*, he witnessed and heard descriptions of coolie labor practices, which resembled the slave labor he remembered from his youth. Part of what brought Twain to Hawaii in 1866 was the changing state of southern sugar production, and he followed his nostalgic sweet tooth in his travel narrative, *Life on the Mississippi* (1883). Based on Twain's youthful employment as a riverboat pilot in the U.S. South, *Life on the Mississippi* was published between *The Adventures of Tom Sawyer* and *Adventures of Huckleberry Finn*. In this narrative Twain returns to his childhood haunts at the time of his greatest literary success. This was, after all, his first return to the beloved river of his childhood since leaving it for the Nevada Territory in 1861 with his brother, Orion. Twain describes various industries he visits along the river, making a particular note of the cotton and sugar plantations. He goes so far as to visit a sugar plantation as part of his reflective journey, attempting to bridge the antebellum South of his memories to the New South of his present. With Horace Bixby, his childhood mentor, Twain visits "ex-Governor Warmouth's sugar plantation" to see for himself what these new farms looked like in the U.S. South of the 1880s. Twain notes that the intensification of sugar production had managed to bring about "a yield of a ton and a half, and from that to two tons, to the acre; which is three or four times what the yield of an acre was in my time."[12] This plantation, with its elements of modern technology combined with wage-based labor, is described as representative of the industry during this period. In *Life on the Mississippi*, Twain shows the agri-expansion of the second half of the nineteenth century, following emancipation and agricultural revolutions.

At the Warmouth plantation, Twain writes about the sugar-milling process; this colorful anecdote serves to educate his readers about sugar production. He observes, "The great sugar-house was a wilderness of tubs and tanks and vats and filters, pumps, pipes, and machinery" (*LM*, 479). This laboratory-styled building is complete with "centrifugals," an "evaporating pan," an eerie-sounding "bone-filter," a "clarifying tank," and finally a "vacuum pan." These terms represent various stages involved in processing sugar from the cane to the final foodstuff to be distributed across the nation and the globe. In some ways these descriptors are reminiscent of Twain's own experiences in the California and Nevada gold and silver mines. Much like panning for precious metals, this sugar-milling process—and agriculture in general—is a speculative, mechanized industry and more complicated than it seems at first. Twain concludes, "It is now ready for market. I have jotted these particulars down from memory. The thing looks simple and easy. Do not deceive yourself. To make sugar is really one of the most difficult things in the world. And to make it right, is next to impossible" (LM, 479). Twain is noticeably ironic as he observes that processing sugar "looks simple and easy." This episode represents a different scene than the maple-sap gathering of his childhood. Sugar production has expanded well beyond the family-sized quantities produced at his uncle's farm. Technology has to some extent helped intensify agricultural production, yet the human labor on the plantation is still performed by African Americans. While Twain describes a system of production more like contemporary factories than previous plantations, these advances do not prevent the majority of the labor—difficult and menial—from being performed by African Americans. Though he later notes that this technologically advanced site of agricultural production still lost $40,000 the previous year, he winkingly assures his readers that "this year's crop will reach ten or twelve hundred tons of sugar, consequently last year's loss will not matter" (LM, 476). The U.S. South was losing money in the sugar industry—while plantations around the globe were growing. Sugar became part of a global agricultural system, and the southern producers were feeling the strain of greater competition—a strain literalized in the bodies of the laborers.

Twain's narrative of the southern sugar-milling process helps to show how these technologies developed. But a more complete account of the work involved in the production of cane comes in the anthropological writings of Sidney Mintz as he describes a twentieth-century cane field—one that sounds eerily similar to the nineteenth-century iteration. He writes, "The lowing of the animals, the shouts of the *mayordomo*, the grunting of the men as they swung their machetes, the sweat and dust and din easily conjured up an earlier island era. Only the sound of the whip was missing."[13] Laborers—in either the nineteenth or twentieth century—manually planted and cultivated the cane, dug irrigation ditches for the fields, harvested the cane, and carted away loads of the raw material to be processed. The machines were often reserved for the milling process, and as Twain's descriptions likewise reveal, laborers continued to shoulder the brunt of the actual fieldwork. Sugarcane is here shown to be one of the most grueling and labor-intensive of crops—and the expansion of "sugar islands" during the nineteenth century involved the drastic increase of a subjugated labor force around the globe. The fact that the global sugar industry felt the need to use coolie labor, that the work in the cane fields was forced upon slaves and later the wage-slave system of coolies, demonstrates the brutality involved in its labor process. When itemized tasks like these are imagined in the heat of the tropics, and with the pressure of a foreman forcing laborers to move quickly, they give a counternarrative to Twain's descriptions of the small-scale maple sugar works of his youth.

While Twain's writing career paralleled the nation's history, his attitudes toward U.S. agri-expansion and imperialism moved in the opposite direction from the national mission. The "manifest destiny" movement of the United States extended through most of the nineteenth century. During his life Twain witnessed the United States consume land more aggressively than at any other time in its history, through territorial expansion, annexation, and economic globalization. The United States appropriated land following the annexation of Texas in 1845; the U.S.-Mexican War, which ended in 1848; and the purchase of Alaska from Russia in 1867. The spirit of expansion turned global at the end of the nineteenth century, following the closing of the frontier of the western U.S. territory. Presidents William McKinley and Theodore Roosevelt brought the nation into an era of global consequence with the Spanish-American War in 1898 and the Philippine-American War that followed (1899–1902).[14] The prevailing image by the end of the nineteenth century was one in which U.S. pioneers continued to expand the nation's borders beyond the West Coast, into the Pacific Ocean. This fervor led the United States to Guam, the Philippines, and Hawaii.[15] The nation ultimately controlled territories in both the Caribbean and the Pacific, two key sugar-producing regions. No longer satisfied with the territorial expansion that differentiated the United States from its European counterparts, the United States looked to become a world power in its own right, and that ambition was reflected in its participation in agri-expansion on the global stage.

The global sugar trade—as part of the larger food trade—assisted the nation's economic expansion in anticipation of the closing of the physical western frontier. Nineteenth-century U.S. politicians actively searched for new markets for U.S. foods. In 1874 the secretary of state under President Ulysses S. Grant, James G. Blaine, described "the twin economic pillars of America's unrivaled agricultural and industrial production" as key elements of U.S. economic expansion and increased global influence.[16] While secretary of state under President Benjamin Harrison, Blaine added, "It would not be an ambitious destiny for so great a country as ours to manufacture only what we consume, or to produce only what we eat."[17] Using signal phrases like "destiny" and "so great a country as ours"—Blaine and policy makers like him sought to use agriculture to drive U.S. influence beyond the national borders. Blaine argued for the United States to become the breadbasket of the world, associating agriculture and U.S. political expansion in the second half of the nineteenth century. He argued for maximizing crop selection, monoculture, and intensive growth for the greatest profit—pushing beyond even the farms of the West and into the Pacific. Agricultural globalization became the next logical stage for agri-expansion, as in the sugar industry, in much the same way that global expansion replaced the territorial version at the end of the nineteenth century.

In his late sugar-based work, Twain argues against the U.S. imperialism of the late nineteenth century that involves the oppression of people of color around the world, such as African Americans and Pacific Islanders. In his earlier letters from Hawaii, however, Twain suggests the importation of Chinese coolie labor to the Hawaiian Islands as a potential asset for sugar producers. While arguing on behalf of business and agri-expansion, Twain acknowledges the labor issues at stake. Twain's time spent meandering around Hawaiian sugar plantations is mirrored in his later experiences in Mauritius and the South Pacific. There he learns of the Australian coolie trade. Twain applies his deepening concern for the world's victims of imperialism in his later meditations on coolie labor. While describing his experiences witnessing Western imperialism in *Following the Equator*, Twain links the United States to the global sugar trade and to its abuses of labor within that system. He applies his skill with writing and the common knowledge of the sugar industry to make a commentary against U.S. imperialism.[18] Twain would have been at least as well acquainted with the issues regarding sugar-producing countries and their connection to Euro-American imperialism as any concerned U.S. citizen of his time. In his *Autobiography* he attaches a newspaper article about a woman attacked by White House staffers as she attempted to meet the president. In this clipping there is also a discussion of a Philippine Tariff bill opening for debate in Congress. Regarding tariffs on imported sugar, the bill questioned how foreign production would affect other sugar-producing areas within the nation's physical borders, like Louisiana and Hawaii.[19] These sugar-related connections ultimately prompted Twain's growing anti-imperialist sentiments—and he brings the issue back to the laborers themselves.

Though the British abolished the slave trade in their colonies beginning in the 1830s, and U.S. emancipation followed with the result of the Civil War, the practice of bringing workers to sugar plantations as indentured servants occurred almost immediately thereafter. Coolie laborers quickly became another exploited labor force. Following the Civil War, the United States grew interested in the global sugar trade, and the nation found itself engaged in the slavery debate once more—this time regarding its role in the global coolie trade. As the United States grew more like European nations by expanding across the globe to Hawaii, Cuba, Puerto Rico, Guam, and the Philippines, it became equally embroiled in issues of labor and trade. The U.S. official in China in 1856, Peter Parker, framed the debate as being "replete with illegalities, immoralities, and revolting and inhuman atrocities, strongly resembling those of the African slave trade in former years, some of them exceeding the horrors of the 'middle passage.'"[20] Even before the emancipation of U.S. slaves, coolie labor was one of the primary methods of international human trafficking, most often involving labor in the dangerous cane fields of the Euro-American controlled sugar-producing regions. Sugar became one of the primary crops of a continuing slavery discourse, possibly more than comparable crops like coffee, tea, or cotton. W. E. B. Du Bois connects U.S. imperialism and the lands that produce cheap sugar: "Imperialism, despite Cleveland's opposition, spread to America, and the Hawaiian sugar fields were annexed. The Spanish war brought Cuban sugar fields under control and annexed Puerto Rico and the Philippines."[21] Du Bois specifically comments on the sugar-producing nations of the Caribbean and South Pacific that the United States obtained as a result of winning the war against Spain—a war that he sees as an example of imperialism in its most basic form. The sugar industry in particular was involved in the exploitation of Du Bois's "dark proletariat" on a global scale. Twain writes about the subjugation of this racialized labor force in global sugar production and its connection to the United States throughout his travel narratives.

Twain's capacity to write sympathetically about people of other races and ethnicities has been the subject of much literary criticism.[22] Raised in a family of Missouri slaveholders, Twain was indoctrinated in the institutionalized racism of slavery from an early age. According to Shelley Fisher Fishkin, Twain was forced to familiarize himself with the violence and savage cruelty of slave owners toward African slaves. He once witnessed the murder of a slave by a white man "for some trifling offense" without consequence; he realized that his father, who would not collect on his debts, "had no qualms about selling Charley [a slave] down the river for about forty dollars' worth of tar"; and he always remembered Benson Blankenship, who found a runaway slave and "brought him scraps of food instead of giving him up for a reward."[23] Twain's childhood, steeped in this background of slavery and racism, laid the groundwork for his reactions to the racialized nature of U.S. imperialism, including how it played out in agri-expansion and the global sugar trade. In the period between the Civil War and the Spanish-American War—a period of drastic change in U.S. agriculture—issues of civilization and race along the expanding borders of the United States became even more troubled for Twain. Fishkin asks how Twain could grow from a "knee-jerk racist" to one of the nation's most critical thinkers on the subject of race and quotes Twain himself in her answer: "What is the most rigorous law of our being? Growth. . . . In other words, we change—and *must* change, constantly, and keep on changing as long as we live."[24] For Twain this growth is to some extent a broadening of the conception of racial subjugation from a black-white binary to a more nuanced awareness of the racial power dynamics involved in Western imperialism. Twain's later writings, following a sweetened path of empire, incorporate issues of race and labor perhaps more fully than any of his earlier texts. First, though, Twain's assignment to write about sugar in Hawaii provides him with the opportunity to enter into the discussion of U.S. agri-expansion. In "Letter 23" Twain appears through his promotion of the expansion of U.S. sugar to be as imperialistic as any of the businesspeople or politicians he will later lambast in his anti-imperialist writings.

LETTERS FROM THE SUGAR ISLANDS

During the antebellum period, the nation's sugar primarily came from the sugar-growing region of Louisiana and along the Mississippi River. The laborers in these sugar plantations were almost exclusively slaves. During the Civil War, though, this source was cut off from the rest of the nation, which then sought another supplier for cheap sugar. At this time the United States developed a stronger economic presence in the Hawaiian Islands. By the close of the Civil War, Hawaiian sugar had become one of the potential alternatives for what was seen as a dwindling southern sugar industry. Twain received his first sizable assignment as a journalist to visit the Hawaiian Islands and promote that nation as a suitable alternative sugar-growing region for U.S. investors. In the four months that Twain spent there, he wrote a series of letters that would include the source of a popular news piece about the shipwreck of the *Hornet*, material for a successful lecture tour across the West and eventually the East and Britain, and the final chapters of his second travel narrative, *Roughing It* (1872). The letter that most particularly deals with the sugar industry in Hawaii, however, was never reproduced in these outlets. "Letter 23" is one of Twain's most pro-imperialist pieces. In this particular letter, Twain promotes the production of sugar in

Hawaii, gives an example from a specific Hawaiian plantation, suggests the importation of Chinese coolie labor, and finally presents a manifesto encouraging U.S. agri-expansion in the Pacific.[25] In "Letter 23" Twain is not the passionate force against imperialism that he would become after *Following the Equator*. Therefore, reviewing this text reveals Twain's earlier attitudes toward the development of U.S. globalization, race, and labor—viewed through the lens of sugar—and how they contrast with his later writings.

Hawaii was a strong example of agri-expansion in the United States, specifically in terms of the production of sugar and pineapples. Waverly Root and Richard de Rochemont suggest Hawaii might be the only U.S. state to have entered the nation "primarily because of food." Hawaii was useful to the United States for the most part economically, particularly because of its agriculture; food was the "economic drift" that eventually led to Hawaii's annexation into the United States by the end of the nineteenth century.[26] The significance of the aggressive promotion of Hawaiian agriculture—the push toward its global agricultural presence—is vital to the development of both the continuing expansion of the United States into the Pacific as well as the agricultural causes for that growth. As an extension of the westward expansion movement of the first half of the nineteenth century, the United States ventured beyond California and into the Pacific. The country developed economic interests in Hawaii during this period, to the point where the nation controlled much of Hawaii's land and capital by midcentury.[27] The United States was primed to take advantage of situations within the Hawaiian government for its own agricultural business interests, and King Kamehameha III was already in talks with the United States regarding annexation as early as 1851.[28] In the early nineteenth century, Britain, France, and the United States competed over control of Hawaii. Twain argues for investment in trade between Hawaii and the United States. As a result of increased traffic between the two nations, the United States "would soon populate these islands with Americans, and loosen that French and English grip which is gradually closing around them."[29] Sugar's significance in the development of U.S. interest in Hawaii in the nineteenth century mirrors that in other Pacific sites that were pursued by Western imperialist nations. By the 1860s the physical presence of U.S. citizens in Hawaii overpowered the presence of the British and French there and made Hawaii a viable focus for U.S. agri-expansion, specifically in the sugar industry. Sugar is not a native foodstuff in Hawaii, though it began to be grown in plantations there as early as 1835. In addition, the first cargo to pass through the Panama Canal, upon completion, was a shipment of Hawaiian sugar.[30] Becoming economically invested in Hawaii—and in Hawaiian sugar—was "of interest to American businessmen of the time," and trade with Hawaii in general would bring the promise of import taxes to California (*LH*, vii).

The movement of U.S. agriculture into Hawaii in the 1860s provided material benefits to both U.S. businesses and to Twain himself, as he began a thriving writing and lecturing career based upon his wildly successful show, "Our Fellow Savages of the Sandwich Islands." Twain performed this lecture nearly a hundred times in the United States and Britain between the years of 1867 and 1873.[31] Before Twain had this breakthrough in his career, though, his audience was U.S. businesses. In his letters he encourages entrepreneurs to expand into Hawaiian agriculture, "which, in its importance to America, surpasses them all [other business interests]" (*LH*, 257). In "Letter 19" Twain briefly describes the usefulness of developing U.S. control of Hawaiian sugar: "In Kona, the average yield of an acre of ground is two tons of sugar, they say. This is only a moderate yield for these islands, but would be extraordinary for Louisiana and most other sugar-growing countries" (*LH*, 209–10). Twain frames sugar as one aspect of Hawaiian culture and part of the larger narrative of Twain's experiences there, possibly of less interest to a lay reader than his descriptions of the lush landscape of the Big Island. Still, Twain's general statement about Hawaiian sugar production in "Letter 19" is the only segment of his original argument on the growing sugar trade to be repurposed as part of his lecture or in the Hawaiian chapters of *Roughing It*, both of which were addressed to a general audience. In addition, this comment is in itself a pro-expansion statement for U.S. agricultural interests. Twain recommends the intensification of sugar production in Hawaii as an alternative to the southern sugar industry. While Twain does not go into detail about the expansion of the sugar industry as much as he does in "Letter 23," this earlier letter already demonstrates Twain's willingness to exploit a region like Hawaii for the sake of U.S. agri-expansion.

In "Letter 23," then, Twain becomes yet more focused in his recommendations to U.S. agribusinesses interested in investing in Hawaiian sugar—his primary audience. He brings statistics and figures into his discussion of the industry, using terms like "aggregate yield" and the "Patent Office" and naming various levels of sugar quality "good, bad, and indifferent" (*LH*, 258). Though Louisiana could produce only 25 million pounds of sugar after more than a century of development and a hundred plantations, in four years and only "*twenty-nine* small plantations," Hawaii had produced 27 million pounds (*LH*, 258, Twain's italics). The agricultural investment in sugar plantations would eventually produce more sugar per acre in Hawaii than the United States had ever been able to produce in the South. By "Letter 23" Twain's language had become an attempt to be both salesperson and business investor. As Twain writes his ode to U.S. globalization interests in the Pacific, his voice is nearly unrecognizable as the witty reporter of life on the "Rainbow Islands." He lyricizes, "To America it has been vouchsafed to materialize the vision, and realize the dream of centuries, of the enthusiasts of the Old World. We have found the true Northwest Passage—we have found the true and only direct route to the bursting coffers of 'Ormus and Ind'" (*LH*, 274).[32] In a statement aggressively pursuing the Euro-American ideal of imperialism, Twain challenges the United States to more or less "play the European game," which he would lambast in a later essay. Twain is apparently out of character from his later writing self in this passage. However, in the sense that he encourages a U.S. venture into other territories, he remains the westward-bound adventurer, a character that he adopted at this time and that would become one of his trademark personae. Twain's challenge also connects his idea of the individual adventurer to a spirit of agri-expansion—the domestic agricultural project has become global.

Twain's early pro-imperialist statements regarding agri-expansion in Hawaii begin at a Hawaiian sugar plantation. In the early pages of "Letter 23," Twain describes the plantation more in terms of the constitution of its labor force than the technological aspects of its milling process, in contrast to the way he writes about the Louisiana plantation in *Life on the Mississippi*. In Hawaii's cane fields, Twain's focus is on presenting an image of a familiar plantation experience to U.S. investors. He describes Lewers plantation as "the model in the Islands, in the matter of cost, extent, completeness, and efficiency" (*LH*, 265). Compared favorably to Louisiana plantations, this is "peopled with coolies spreading 'trash' to dry; half a dozen Kanakas feeding cane to the whirling cylinders of the mill and a noisy procession of their countrymen driving cartloads of the material to their vicinity and dumping it." Twain adds, "These things give the place a businesslike aspect which is novel in the slumbering Sandwich Islands" (*LH*, 265). He carefully differentiates the communities of the Chinese, Hawaiians, and whites, observing a tiered system based on race and nationality in Hawaii's sugar industry. He continues to establish these racial and national divisions on Lewers plantation based on the labor performed. He observes that the native Hawaiians are involved in the earlier aspects of milling the sugar, first by bringing cartloads of cane to be processed and then by feeding the cane into the mill itself; meanwhile, the Chinese are responsible for processing the waste product, named "trash," at the end of the milling process. In either case the labor was intense, and one could easily imagine slave laborers performing similar tasks on Louisiana plantations.

Furthermore, the two communities are separated both by labor and by living arrangements. In the "village" of highly segregated communities at Lewers plantation, the environment bore a strong resemblance to slave quarter "villages" on Louisiana plantations before the Civil War. Twain describes, "The neighboring offices of the proprietor, the dwelling of the superintendent, the store, blacksmith shop, quarters for white employes [*sic*], native huts and a row of frame quarters for Chinese coolies, make Waihee a village of very respectable pretensions" that might "number 350 persons, perhaps" (*LH*, 265). Indeed, even the projected census of the plantation, with a population of 350, makes it sound like a large southern sugar plantation with a community of slaves laboring on site. According to the levels of living arrangements, the Chinese are viewed as performing the lowest form of labor. To use Du Bois's term, the "dark proletariat" is doing the labor for a white capitalist—this time for the United States rather than for a European nation. It is relatively startling for Twain to call this comparison "businesslike" as he does, in opposition to the assumed "slumbering" aspect of the islands, where natives and other workers were not being driven in a manner akin to the treatment of African slaves anywhere "between Baton Rouge and New Orleans" (*LH*, 265.) In Twain's analysis the Louisiana plantation—based on the use of slave labor—is the model by which the Hawaiian establishment should be judged. In consequence, the Hawaiian plantation that most closely resembles an earlier Louisiana plantation becomes the "model" for future Hawaiian cane fields in terms of "cost, extent, completeness, and efficiency."

Of course, a notable difference between the Louisiana and Hawaiian plantations is the ethnicity of the laborer being described. Here, Hawaiian and Chinese replace African. With U.S. agri-expansion, though, came tragedy. Twain notes, "The sugar product is rapidly augmenting every year, and day by day the Kanaka race is passing away" (*LH*, 270). Hawaiians are romanticized as part of a "vanishing nation" trope at the expense of the Chinese coolie laborer, who Twain recommends as a viable, cheap alternative for the developing sugar plantations. In both cases, though, a subjugated race is exploited as part of the necessary labor of the sugar industry, and Western capital is created through the bodies of a nonwhite labor force. Hawaii enriched the United States by bringing coolie labor from China and allowing the nation to some extent to colonize the islands through a form of economic control based on agriculture.[33] By the 1860s the Chinese had developed a complicated relationship with Western imperialism in terms of immigration, specifically connected to the coolie trade, usually to the cane fields of the Caribbean and the Pacific. Even in the years before the Civil War, Chinese labor was being imported for work in the Caribbean sugar plantations of the British Empire, where the slave trade had been banned since 1838, as well as for work on Louisiana sugar plantations. Hawaiian sugar producers quickly engaged Chinese labor as well. Thus, the coolie trade was incorporated into the global debate over slavery. The struggle for human rights that was part of the antislavery platform, specifically in terms of domestic agriculture, was applied to a broader context here.[34] After the Civil War, coolieism was exploited as other forms of cheap labor were lost to U.S. plantation owners. Although Chinese anti-immigration laws of the second half of the nineteenth century were some of the most severe in U.S. history, they began as part of a debate on human rights issues involving Chinese coolie labor. On the one hand, U.S. politicians promoted the Chinese Exclusion Act as a move against slavery; on the other, white laborers were economically motivated to also call for exclusion.[35] Republicans and Democrats alike pursued Chinese exclusion laws for a number of racist political and economic considerations. Furthermore, the paternalistic theories behind these exclusion acts provided the U.S. government with the motivation to engage in imperialistic actions in Asia and the Pacific Islands during the nineteenth century, motivated by the concept of freeing the Chinese in China from the threat of coolie labor. Some of these issues are evident in Twain's early writings and show an early aspect of U.S. globalizing economics vis-à-vis agriculture, as Asian labor in the Pacific Islands helped to define the economic project of the nation.

Thus, in "Letter 23" Twain promotes Chinese coolieism. As contrasted to his sympathetic portrayals of the Chinese in his later writings, in this letter Twain uses negative stereotypes in order to quickly describe the Chinese as a cheap labor force in the Hawaiian cane fields.

> The Hawaiian agent fell into the hands of Chinese sharpers, who showed him some superb coolie samples and then loaded his ships with the scurviest lot of pirates that ever went unhung. Some of them were cripples, some were lunatics, some afflicted with incurable diseases, and nearly all were intractable, full of fight, and animated by the spirit of the very devil. However, the planters managed to tone

them down and now they like them very well. Their former trade of cutting throats on the China seas has made them uncommonly handy at cutting cane. They are steady, industrious workers when properly watched. If the Hawaiian agent had been possessed of a reasonable amount of business tact, he could have got experienced rice and sugar cultivators—peaceable, obedient men and women— for the same salaries that must be paid to these villains, and done them a real service by giving them good homes and kind treatment in place of the wretchedness and brutality they experience in their native land. (*LH*, 271)

Twain's language in describing the Chinese in this passage is neither as romanticized nor as sympathetic as that used for the native Hawaiians. In this negative depiction of Chinese laborers, they actually victimize "the Hawaiian agent." While the Chinese are being abducted and transported for their labor, this Hawaiian speculator falls "into the hands" of these villains owing to a lack of "business sense." The Chinese figures are "sharpers" and "pirates" who Twain thinks should be hanged. In fact, he makes a joke about how well suited they would be to cut the cane because of their villainous history of piracy, noting that they had been formerly "cutting throats on the China seas." He describes the objectionable trade of coolie-catching as something more akin to his tall tales from the West. For Twain, the true victim in this story is not the Chinese indentured laborer, but rather the Hawaiian agent who resembles the dupe in Twain's humorous western tale, "The Celebrated Jumping Frog of Calaveras County."

Certainly, the reason that the fraudulently rebellious Chinese workers are tricking the Hawaiians is that they appear to be such "superb specimens." Beyond the obvious correlation with scenes of slaves on auction blocks such a phrase must evoke, Twain's choice of words here also shows a positive description of the Chinese. Indeed, they are originally described as impressive. In the final sentences of this passage, Twain returns to the tone he assumes in the course of the rest of this letter. Hawaiian employment would be a positive change for Chinese used to "wretchedness and brutality" in their homeland, as Twain supposes. Further, he describes most Chinese workers as "peaceable, obedient men and women" who are an ideal labor force to replace the newly emancipated African Americans in the global sugar industry and the native Hawaiians, who, Twain writes, are "passing away." In addition, the Hawaiian plantation owners and overseers would be doing the Chinese "a real service by giving them good homes and kind treatment." Twain's potential investors are represented as condescending to provide new homes for the Chinese who would not be able to provide for themselves—either at home or abroad—as well as they could in the cane fields of Hawaii.

Twain's description of the Chinese relationship with plantation owners in Hawaii must necessarily—even in these early writings—include a touch of his trademark irony. Twain notes that "the planters managed to tone them down and now they like them very well." The plantation owners have treated the Chinese in many of the same brutal ways that Louisiana plantation owners treated their African counterparts, in taking the "spirit" out of them through abuse. This sentence is meant ironically, and that makes it all the more interesting when located within Twain's pro-imperialistic "Letter 23." Even amid his promotion of a Chinese labor force to Hawaiian sugar plantations, he inserts a touch of his bitter satire, developed further in his later writings. Indeed, in another passage Twain makes a satirical comment about labor and abuse on the Hawaiian sugar plantations: "The contract with the laborer is in writing, and the law rigidly compels compliance with it; if the man shirks a day's work and absents himself, he has to work two days for it when his time is out. If he gets unmanageable and disobedient, he is condemned to work on the reef for a season, at twenty-five cents a day" (LH, 270). While this seems intended as a sympathetically satirical comment on the brutal laws in favor of plantation owners, Twain challenges this reading by adding, "If he [the laborer] is in debt to the planter for such purchases as clothing and provisions, however, when his time expires, the obligation is canceled—the planter has no recourse at law" (LH, 270). Again, Twain leaves the reader with a sense of ambiguity regarding his attitudes toward these practices. The contract is described not in terms of economics, but rather in terms of temporality. If a worker owes money, this is somewhat unrecoverable; however, if that laborer owes time on a contract, that time can be repaid with interest and an increasingly intense assignment. Twain forces his readers to decide for themselves where to draw the line between business efficiency and cruelty during this period of U.S. agri-expansion.

While maintaining his pro-expansion tone, then, Twain enumerates parts of the industry that may remind his audience of African slavery in the United States. His project in Hawaii encourages some of the work of the slaveholding antebellum South in the postbellum Pacific. After emancipation an imperialistic subjugation of a labor force remains in the sugar plantations of Hawaii.[36] Twain writes that "in Louisiana, sugar planters paid from $20 to $200 an acre for land, $500 to $1,000 apiece for Negroes," while in the islands, "the hire of each laborer is $100 a year—just about what it used to cost to board and clothe and doctor a Negro—but there is no original outlay of $500 to $1,000 for the purchase of the laborer, or $50 to $100 annual interest to be paid on the sum so laid out" (*LH*, 260). Labor for use in the Hawaiian sugar plantations was being exported from places as disparate as the Caribbean, northern Europe, Asia, and the South Pacific.[37] In the early years of Twain's writing career, he is already implicated in national issues of race and agri-expansion at the global level, particularly involving the transportation of a diasporic labor force from the continent of Asia to sugar plantations in the Pacific.

Race plays a significant role in Twain's "Letter 23." Another U.S. author likewise described race and imperialism in Hawaii during the nineteenth century. Like Twain, Herman Melville writes about the United States in the Pacific, romanticizing a diasporic skilled laborer from the Pacific Islands in the character of the Polynesian, Queequeg, in *Moby-Dick*. Further, Melville gives another perspective on King Kamehameha III's collusion with the United States in *Omoo*. Unlike Melville in his description of Queequeg, Twain writes to promote the importation of Chinese unskilled labor for Hawaii's cane fields. Twain suggests that the Chinese could potentially replace Hawaiians and Africans on sugar plantations beyond Hawaii and suggests bringing Chinese laborers to California for a variety of menial jobs.[38] The Chinese, as opposed to Queequeg's "Pacific man," are seen as an ideal replacement for the now-emancipated African populations in terms of an exploitable global labor force.[39] Furthermore, in the racialized narrative of his Hawaiian letters, Twain discovers a new source of treasure out of the "bursting coffers" of Asia: Chinese coolie laborers who can help U.S. agribusinesses increase their wealth. Twain enthusiastically promotes the exploitation of the Chinese both in Hawaii and in California as laborers to ease the work of Euro Americans in the West. However, Twain's analysis of these "contracts" against the Chinese can be read more ambiguously, as he observes that the Chinese are punished beyond their degree if they attempt to subvert their labor contracts. In other words Twain's opinion of the Chinese and the concept of the coolie trade cannot be as easily determined as critics may believe. Not the idealized Pacific Islanders of the rest of his letters—or Melville's Queequeg—the Chinese in Twain's writings are recommended as a necessary investment in the Hawaiian sugar industry. While Twain does write far more sympathetically about Chinese immigrants in his California writings, he remains imperialistic in terms of agri-expansion during this period of his career. "Letter 23" is an artifact of perhaps Twain's most imperialist statement.

Twain's Hawaiian letters, like his later full-length travel narratives, demonstrate his skill as a humorist and travel writer. Furthermore, Hawaii remains a significant symbol in Twain's imagination, even after he returns to the mainland, and he attempts to return both physically and narratively to the islands throughout his writing career. Twain comments finally about the Hawaiian sugar plantation, "I have frequently seen this whole process gone through with in two days, and yet I do not consider myself competent to make sugar" (LH, 268). In some areas Twain cannot claim a high degree of expertise. This includes his analysis of the sugar industry in Hawaii. In the 1880s, between working on *Adventures of Huckleberry Finn* (1884) and *A Connecticut Yankee in King Arthur's Court* (1889), Twain began work on a novel set in the

Hawaiian Islands. This book was eventually set aside, and only a few pages of manuscript remain. In these pages, though, Twain attempted to give a voice to the native Hawaiians as he had previously attempted for African-American characters in *Adventures of Huckleberry Finn*, "True Story, Repeated Word for Word as I Heard It" (1874), and "Sociable Jimmy" (1874). In his earlier writing, Twain did not make that effort. He makes declarations in "Letter 23"; he does not provide an analysis of conditions in the manner of *Following the Equator*, written three decades later. In this way the later text is a far more developed work than Twain's letters from Hawaii. However, there are certain aspects of his earlier writing that appear again in the later work. Twain relates the figure of the coolie and the sugarcane industry, and he describes their relationship as a form of U.S. agri-expansion into the Pacific during the second half of the nineteenth century. President William McKinley once declared, "We need Hawai'i just as much and a good deal more than we need California. It is manifest destiny."[40] However, in the course of writing about Hawaii, Twain begins to see the connection between imperialism and the racism inherent in it. This ambiguity in Twain's tone when writing about the benefits of agri-expansion in Hawaii returns to haunt him when he tours the British Empire and its sugar islands and faces the results of the global economic imperialism that he had once promoted. Thus, Twain's sugar-related writings in Hawaii are a necessary first step in his path toward becoming an internationally recognized anti-imperialist.

FOLLOWING THE SUGAR

Later in his writing career, during his 1895–96 lecture tour among the colonies of the British Empire, which would become the basis for his last full-length work, *Following the Equator* (1897), Twain returned to the relationship between imperialism across sugar-producing nations and the exploitation of a diasporic labor population. In two key sections of *Following the Equator*, Twain describes sugar plantations and the people who work in them. In his descriptions of the sugar production in Australia and Mauritius and the labor of Pacific Islanders and Indians,

Twain brings his trademark satire against the "coolie-catchers" paid to bring indentured servants to Australia from the Pacific Islands as part of the global sugar industry. Though this occurs in one of the earlier sections in the narrative, it demonstrates Twain's developing concerns about British imperialism—and its relation to U.S. agri-expansion and late nineteenth-century globalization—that would be more fully developed in his later chapters and that have received more attention in Twain criticism. This burgeoning anti-imperialism would become more pronounced following the Spanish-American War of 1898. Furthermore, one of the nations the United States would acquire around that time was Hawaii, the site of Twain's first international sugar-based writings. Hawaii is likewise a link to Twain's global tour; his first visit beyond the American continent was to have been in Hawaii, though a cholera scare prevented him from disembarking once in port. This missed opportunity for a nostalgic return to a remembered paradise creates a tone of longing that remains throughout his narrative, seen in Twain's sugar-related considerations. The sugar plantations on the island of Mauritius in some ways reminded Twain of his time in Hawaii, and the stories of coolie-catchers in Queensland are reminders of his earlier suggestions to his readers to similarly "catch" Chinese people for their labor in Hawaii. In both cases Twain would have had to face his earlier imperialistic attitudes in the face of the cruelties of British imperialism. Therefore, the parallels between British and U.S. sugar-based expansion become pronounced for Twain during this lecture tour, and these connections suggest some motivating forces behind his sea change to anti-imperialism.

To recover financially from a decade that brought him failed business ventures and bankruptcy, Twain was persuaded by family and friends that a return to the lecture circuit was the best way for him to recoup his money. Twain was one of the most recognized individuals in the world as well as a charismatic performer.[41] Indeed, Twain's career in large part had been established by a successful lecture tour following his time in Hawaii in 1866. So, Twain's return to the lecture circuit, and the publication of a book based on those experiences, in many ways carried his career full circle.[42] He returned to his creative roots by agreeing to perform again—this time across the nations of the British Empire. Fred Kaplan notes that during his "literary gold" world tour, Twain gave around a hundred performances in "Australia, New Zealand, Ceylon, India, and South Africa"; this is around the same number of performances as his Hawaiian lecture, though over a far shorter period.[43] Twain repaid his debts in full over the course of the tour, and he added to his income with the publication of *Following the Equator*.

However, Twain wrote *Following the Equator* differently than his previous travel narratives.[44] *Following the Equator* is one of his most anti-imperialistic texts, more focused on cultural commentary and criticisms of imperialism than on a familiar travel-narrative style. His observations on the cruelties enacted by one nation upon others are visible throughout the text, as he witnesses it along the contact zones of Western imperialism. Twain makes observations like this in his Hawaiian letters, but in his later work, he establishes them more as a constant than as the exception. In one commonly cited reference, for example, Twain witnesses a German hotel manager hit an Indian servant. This experience makes the writer remember a moment in his childhood when he observed a white man hitting a slave, killing him. In Twain's memory nothing was done to the white man, and similarly nothing happens in the India of Twain's present. However, Twain has made a dramatic empathetic connection between the two witnessed encounters, and the victims of U.S. slavery and British imperialism have been united through Twain's subconscious reaction. He observes, "It is curious—the space-annihilating power of thought. For just one second, all that goes to make the *me* in me was in a Missourian village, on the other side of the globe, vividly seeing again these forgotten pictures of fifty years ago, and wholly unconscious of all things but just those; and in the next second I was back in Bombay, and that kneeling native's smitten cheek was not done tingling yet!"[45] An emphatic connection of this kind occurs as well in Twain's descriptions of the coolie trade, though he does not directly witness the process and he cannot describe it in a visual manner. Rather, in this instance Twain engages in a form of literary empathy, returning to the topic of sugar plantations and the coolie trade in his readings about Australia, researching the topic, and including excerpts from other texts in his narrative. In a sense, then, though the size of his readership is entirely different in these two instances, Twain returns his readers to the earlier Hawaiian letters and to his discussion of the coolie trade there, while refuting his earlier statements. Moreover, Twain makes these connections himself; his reaction to the sugar industry and its shared imperial connection with Britain and the United States performs in a literary manner what Twain's observation of the abuse of an Indian servant does for him in a visual sense. Such a fundamental realization about his own culpability in British or U.S. imperialism through the global sugar trade is a noteworthy moment for Twain and is one of the early stages in his development into a passionate anti-imperialist.

Traveling to Australia from Fiji, Twain makes one of his earliest statements about the sugar industry and its intimate ties with both slavery and imperialism. He discusses issues of the theft of South Pacific Islanders for their labor in the sugar-growing nations of the British Empire along the Pacific:

> From the multitudinous islands in these regions the "recruits" for the Queensland plantations were formerly drawn; are still drawn from them, I believe. Vessels fitted up like old-time slavers came here and carried off the natives to serve as laborers in the great Australian province. In the beginning it was plain, simple man-stealing, as per testimony of the missionaries. This has been denied, but not disproven. Afterward it was forbidden by law to "recruit" a native without his consent, and governmental agents were sent in all recruiting vessels to see that the law was obeyed—which they did, according to the recruiting people; and which they sometimes didn't, according to the missionaries. (FE, 81)

Twain uses the language of the slave trade, part of his historical memory, in this description of the coolie trade for the cane fields of Australia. The ships transporting the laborers are "fitted up like old-time slavers," and the practice is "plain, simple man-stealing," in which people are "carried off " as indentured servants to Queensland. Almost as soon as Twain has left the continent of America, he finds himself forced to confront his past and the manner in which slavery still exists at the turn of the twentieth century. Not only does Twain begin to contemplate certain issues that become visual to him while he is in India, but he also must see the connections between his own nation and the British Empire, a nation that he admires but that is culpable for human rights violations throughout the sugar-growing regions of its empire.

Twain also focuses on the discrepancies in various reports on the coolie trade itself in this passage. The missionaries—formerly Twain's narrative villains—have become his concerned citizens by this time, as they contradict the "recruiters" at every point. These recruiters, in turn, have become Twain's true villains. In each case there is an assumed story that contradicts the direct narrative of the "law." Things are "denied" by the recruiters but presumed true through Twain's tone. When laws are enacted to extend a level of protection to Pacific Islanders, Twain questions the response to these laws as well. The recruiters claim to have obeyed the law, which deprives them of greater profit, though the missionaries state that they "sometimes didn't." Twain's tone becomes ironic here, and it remains so as he continues to observe that laws were also put into place to assist the Pacific Islanders' return home. Twain writes that "when his time was up he [the Pacific Islander] could return to his island. And would also have the means to do it; for the government required the employer to put money in its hands for this purpose before the recruit was delivered to him" (FE, 81). A statement like this, in which the government is going to some lengths to protect the Pacific Islander laborer from abuse at the hands of the recruiter or plantation overseer, is intended to be read satirically. The government is corrupt, leaving the Pacific Islander trapped with no means to return home and in servitude while performing the most arduous tasks involved in the production of sugar for Western consumers.

Twain further lists the costs and expenditures for Pacific Islanders to work in the Queensland cane fields and comes up with "a hundred dollars a year," the laborer being considered as an investment in much the same manner as a slave or the coolies of Twain's Hawaiian letters. Twain takes into account the position of the "recruiter" of Pacific Islander laborers: "One can understand why the recruiter is fond of the business; the recruit costs him a few cheap presents (given to the recruit's relatives, not to the recruit himself), and the recruit is worth £20 to the recruiter when delivered in Queensland" (FE, 84). Twain turns this narrative around, though, when he tries to imagine the situation from the perspective of the natives being coerced to go to Queensland for a brutal life in the cane fields. From, in Twain's words, the "one lazy, long holiday" of their home on a tropical island—which Twain has already established as paradisiacal—a "caught" young man travels to an uncomfortable situation in a foreign country where he must "get up at dawn and work from eight to twelve hours a day in the canefields—in a much hotter climate than he is used to—and get less than four shillings a week for it" (FE, 84). Twain lays out the primary issue with human trafficking involved in the sugar industry in the Pacific islands, using satire to imply that the native Pacific Islander is not choosing to travel to Queensland for these reasons. These individuals—usually young men—are being stolen from their homelands and driven into slavery in almost the same way that Africans had been stolen previously. Though there is some discussion of payment in this case, the pay is negligible compared to the work conditions, and in many cases the laborer is in fact never actually paid—often having incurred debts or died from exhaustion and disease during the first three-year period of indenture. After establishing the shocking ratio of European to Pacific Islander deaths in Queensland, numbers based on the labor in sugar plantations, Twain discusses the comparatively low death rate for Pacific Islanders at home—including during times of war. For the Pacific Islander, working in Queensland "is twelve times as deadly for him as war" (FE, 88). Twain concludes, "Common Christian charity, common humanity, does seem to require, not only that these people be returned to their homes, but that war, pestilence, and famine be introduced among them for their preservation" (FE, 88–89). This entire segment, placed in the text before Twain actually lands in Australia, describes one of the dominant themes of the narrative that remains through Twain's experiences in South Africa: the brutal system of imperialism as experienced by subjugated labor populations vis-à-vis agri-expansion.

Twain goes so far as to introduce the reader to an example of a coolie-catcher, Captain Wawn, in order to refute possible apologist statements about the coolie trade: "Captain Wawn furnishes such a crowd of instances of fatal encounters between natives and French and British recruiting-crews (for the French are in the business for the plantations of New Caledonia), that one is almost persuaded that recruiting is not thoroughly popular among the islanders." In response Wawn apparently maintains, "But for the meddling philanthropists, the native fathers and mothers would be fond of seeing their children carted into exile and now and then the grave, instead of weeping about it and trying to kill the kind recruiters" (*FE*, 82). Twain employs his now-familiar caustic tone to show the disturbing instances of abuses that occur during colonization—within the framework of the global sugar trade. These statements are easily as bitter as the much-discussed "Puddn'head Wilson's New Calendar" epigraphs that begin each chapter of *Following the Equator*. It is worthy to note that this tone begins, not in the scenes in India, where Twain is strongly reminded of the treatment of black slaves by U.S. slaveholders, but much earlier, while he is still traveling among the sugar-producing Pacific Islands.

Sugar makes one more appearance in Twain's discussion of imperialistic cruelties in Australia during British imperialism. This time his narrative involves not just the sugar trade and the cane fields, but rather the cruel uses that the finished product was sometimes put to. In another inserted quotation, Twain cites a passage from Mrs. Campbell Praed's *Sketches of Australian Life* describing her childhood in Queensland and an instance of cruelty against the Aborigines by British settlers, or "squatters." In this instance the squatter bribes Aborigines living near him with a Christmas feast: "There were flour, sugar-plums, good things in plenty in the store, and that he would make for them such a pudding as they had never dreamed of. . . . Next morning there was howling in the camp, for it had been sweetened with sugar and arsenic!"

(*FE*, 211). In this case sugar is displayed as an inducement, something that can hide the poison that is also part of this particular Christmas pudding. This scene plays on several instances of Twain's early usage of sugar imagery—both his childhood thefts of sugar and the cruelty of the British plantation owners to their coolie laborers. This sugar is not stolen, but rather the giver of the sugar is the guilty party, and the punishment is felt entirely by the victim. This gruesome scene in the Australian outback describes yet another instance of the connection between European—and later U.S.—imperialism, the subjugation of native populations, and the sugar industry.[46]

Later in *Following the Equator*, Twain spends nearly two weeks visiting the sugar-producing island nation of Mauritius, located in the Indian Ocean between India and South Africa—five hundred miles from Madagascar. This nation is not as isolated as Hawaii in terms of proximity to a larger landmass, but it is small enough to be considered a relatively insignificant colony compared to India or South Africa. After an extended period of travel and performance through Oceania and India, Twain was in need of a period of rest, especially considering that he was no longer young and his health had not been ideal through much of his tour. Moreover, this tropical island with its lush sugar fields reminds Twain of a Hawaii-like tropical paradise. In a letter to Henry Rogers, Twain describes being "surrounded by sugar plantations and the greenest and brightest and richest of tropical vegetation."[47] Twain is able to spend time leisurely visiting sites of natural beauty that might have satisfied a nostalgic longing for Hawaii: "You have undulating wide expanses of sugar-cane—a fine, fresh green and very pleasant to the eye" (*FE*, 629). In a sense, then, Mauritius is a reminder of an earlier period of recuperation that Twain spent in the Hawaiian sugar fields. To add to the relaxed atmosphere, there is no record of Twain actually performing his lecture while in Mauritius; his time spent there was of an entirely recuperative capacity. Like the Hawaiian sugar fields where Twain spent his restorative periods in between writing assignments, Mauritius becomes a restful tropical paradise outside of his tour responsibilities.

The sugarcane fields must not have been his only reminder of Hawaii, though. Another volcanic, tropical island, Mauritius is described as possessing "a ragged luxuriance of tropic vegetation of vivid greens of varying shades, a wild tangle of underbrush, with graceful tall palms lifting their crippled plumes high above it; and you have stretches of shady dense forest with limpid streams frolicking through them . . . and here and there and now and then a strip of sea with a white ruffle of surf breaks into view" (FE, 629). These references bear some resemblance to Twain's early attempts at a manuscript for a novel set in Hawaii, in which he portrays the nation as the "peacefulest, restfulest, sunniest, balmiest, dreamiest haven of refuge" and describes the landscape as containing "sinuous mountain gorges, floored with flowers & ferns, & shut in on either side by walls of shining verdure" of the island itself, which is, like Mauritius, "a bloomy, fragrant paradise, where the troubled may go & find peace, & the sick & tired find strength & rest."[48] In his Hawaiian letters, Twain describes the land as "the refuge for the weary" and "the sleepiest, quietest, Sundayest looking place you can imagine" (LH, 202). He himself makes this comparison of the two nations, concluding, "The Sandwich Islands remain my ideal of the perfect thing in the matter of tropical islands," compared to Mauritius, though he does also suggest how to make his ideal even more pleasant (FE, 629). In both cases the tropical islands become near-perfect places for Twain to recuperate, and he makes the agricultural industry into something idyllic. Though the two "sugar islands" are not connected geographically—one being in the Pacific Ocean and the other in the Indian Ocean—the tropical lushness of the two countries is described in companionable terms. As Mauritius is a sugar-producing nation foremost, Twain can be understood for first describing the nation's beauty as not solely natural but also agricultural. This pleasant greenness he admires is productive economically while being lovely to look upon.

Once again Twain includes supplementary materials into his section on Mauritius, providing information from "An English citizen" on the history of Mauritius sugar production. This British perspective is introduced with Twain's ironic tone, as if the "citizen" may be Twain himself.

He is informed about the global sugar trade and its key producers: "Sugar is the life of Mauritius, and it is losing its grip" (*FE*, 621). The nation has earned an earlier reprieve, he continues, through "the depreciation of the rupee . . . and the insurrection in Cuba and paralyzation of the sugar industry there have given our prices here a life-saving lift; but the outlook has nothing permanently favorable about it" (*FE*, 621). Twain includes an economic discussion of current issues involved in the British sugar interests in Mauritius in a similar manner as in "Letter 23" of his Hawaiian letters, where he documents the state of Hawaiian sugar for potential U.S. investors. In "Letter 23," Twain argues that Hawaii has become "the king of the sugar world, as far as astonishing productiveness is concerned. Heretofore the Mauritius has held this high place" (*LH*, 257). In "Letter 23," Twain has presented Mauritius as a rival for Hawaiian sugar production; in *Following the Equator*, he discusses Cuba's significance in the global sugar trade—and for certain aspects of British agri-imperialism. Twain cannot have known this in 1897, but the United States would soon be acquiring the large sugar-producing nation of Cuba, among other "sugar islands." Though Twain does not discuss the Philippines or Cuba directly in terms of sugar and its connection to imperialism in his late anti-imperialist writings, he was familiar with the issues at stake involving agri-expansion interests in the United States and Britain. Mauritius was economically important to European imperialism. This explains to some extent the variety of exchanges in colonization in the nation's history, as Mauritius passed from the British to the French and back again to the point where the nation's people did not understand their own official language and their politics did not match that of their colonizing nation. Following this description of sugar and Mauritius's place on the world's sugar stage, Twain philosophizes about the nature of imperialism in general, giving an assessment of globalization that applies even to the modern day: "All the territorial possessions of all the political establishments in the earth—including America, of course—consist of pilferings from other people's wash" (*FE*, 623). Twain's description of sugar on Mauritius flows directly into issues of nineteenth-century global imperialism.

Perhaps the most interesting aspect of Twain's sojourn among the sugar districts of Mauritius, in addition to its connection to the global sugar industry, is the diversity of the nation's citizenry, especially when connected to his earlier sugar-related experiences in Hawaii. Twain notices that the town of Port Louis has "the largest variety of nationalities and complexions we have encountered yet. French, English, Chinese, Arabs, Africans with wool, blacks with straight hair, East Indians, half-whites, quadroons, and great varieties in costumes and colors" (*FE*, 617). This much diversity in a remote locale illustrates the impact of the sugar industry on global diasporas—all of these populations have been connected directly with sugar production, either on the labor or imperial side of the industry. The population explosion, from 185,000 to 375,000 in half a century, he observes, "is due mainly to the introduction of Indian coolies. They now apparently form the great majority of the population" (*FE*, 626). In the multinational space of the Mauritian sugar industry, the coolie laborer has accounted for more than half of its labor and population. Twain goes on to comment that the Indians now control the democratic government based on their larger numbers—an intriguing statement of cosmopolitanism.[49] This is an idealized version of the recommendations from Twain's earlier work, an example of what is possible in a small tropical island nation. Therefore, Twain can observe, again quoting his helpful "English citizen," that regarding this sugar island, "You wouldn't expect a person to be proud of being a Mauritian. . . . But it is so" (*FE*, 620).

Mauritius was a competitor for the growing Hawaiian sugar industry in 1866. By the end of the nineteenth century, sugar was still one of Mauritius's primary crops. In addition, Twain's experiences in this nation were idyllic in a way comparable to his experiences in Hawaii. When these various sugar-related experiences in the two nations are compared, then, Twain's trajectory toward anti-imperialism grows to be as much about his recognition of the connection between sugar and imperialism in idyllic tropical nations as it is about his experiences in South Africa preceding his journey back to Britain. Twain delivers a "blistering criticism" of imperialism, as John Carlos Rowe names it, well before the events he witnesses in India and South Africa.[50] He does in fact undergo a sea change during this journey owing to his repeated encounters with the brutalities of Western imperialism throughout his tour. Meanwhile, Twain's additional research during the writing of the narrative is as significant in many ways as his lived experiences in terms of his developing awareness of this imperialism. These experiences as well are connected directly to Twain's own complicated history involving U.S. imperialism and sugar interests.

Any discussion of Twain's later writings must acknowledge that much of Twain's bitterness is personal rather than political. The emotional strain resulting from the death of his daughter, Susy, in 1896, upon the conclusion of Twain's tour, did much to influence the tone of his later writings in addition to and beyond his coming into direct contact with the effects of the most brutal forms of British imperialism. However, Twain's criticisms are no less powerful for being personal—indeed, they are significantly more so. They represent his efforts to resolve to some extent his residual guilt from his early connection to slavery.[51] The combination of these forces during Twain's final decades brings about a change in him as a writer and as a person. Twain's late anti-imperialist and other writings show more than a surprising depression in an otherwise optimistic person; rather, Twain writes as though he recognizes his association with an imperialistic body of the United States through his early experience with slavery and the promotion of near-slave, coolie Chinese labor in his Hawaiian letters.[52] Twain's development into an anti-imperialist was necessarily brought about through experiences in the agri-expansion of the national project as much as for any other reason. In this case the commercialism of sugar would be of primary importance in Euro-American imperialism. In addition, Twain's ability to understand the suffering of the victims of imperialism increased as a result of his personal suffering.[53]

There is a consensus among critics that the lecture tour of 1895 through 1896 that led to *Following the Equator* is one of the events that made Twain opposed to U.S. imperialism. His various experiences witnessing the actions of the British against their subjugated peoples during this voyage could not change Twain from a racist to a racially enlightened person overnight, of course. He dealt with his issues with race throughout his life, perhaps never completely understanding the nuances of his own beliefs. This becomes significant in *Following the Equator*, as Twain discusses imperialism, the coolie trade, and "the white man's notion that he is less savage than the other savages," which he satirically sees as one of the "many humorous things in the world" (*FE*, 213). Twain's discussion of his experiences with the global sugar industry, one of the harshest forms of agricultural labor, is particularly useful. He was sympathetic to the people subjugated within global agri-expansion, having more knowledge about the industry than some of his contemporaries. Because he describes the cruelty involved in the expansion of the sugar industry through several stages of his writing, his work continues to expand the U.S. imagination in terms of the exploitation of African, Pacific Islander, Chinese, and ultimately Filipino laborers in agri-expansion.

CONCLUSION: THE UNITED STATES IN THE PHILIPPINES

After the publication of *Following the Equator*, the United States went almost directly into what was the most imperialistic war of the nation's history, the Spanish-American War of 1898. After this war, the annexation of Hawaii, and the Philippine-American War, Twain considered himself to be wholly an anti-imperialist. His political writings of this time were controversial; some of them were not published during his life out of fear of public reaction. In his writings about the United States in the Philippines, Twain returns to his concerns about the United States occupying other nations for its own material benefit; however, he has exactly the opposite opinion about imperial conquest than he had in his early letters on the Hawaiian Islands. Twain attempts to give a Pacific Islander a voice in his review of the biography of Emilio Aguinaldo, the president of the Philippines. Without quoting Aguinaldo himself, Twain walks his readers through the life of this Filipino "George Washington," at one point observing his early connection to agriculture as the "son of a peasant vegetable-peddler."[54] Twain makes comparisons to the difficulties presented to other victims of global imperialism during this time. By this point he recognizes the actions of the United States as a form of brutality that he compares to butchery.[55] Although Twain is recognized around the United States and the world for his stories involving rafts, boys, and frogs, rather than nations and their peoples, Jim Zwick writes that Twain has been honored with a monument in the José Martí Anti-Imperialist Square in Havana, Cuba, alongside Abraham Lincoln and Martin Luther King Jr.[56] Twain's anti-imperialist writings have proved to be culturally significant on a global scale, and his place as one of the nation's most profound social critics has now been memorialized.

Twain's life is an extended metaphor of his attempt to obtain the stolen sugar from his childhood. Of his various careers and business ventures, the only success Twain found was as a writer and lecturer. In this he could not fail. Through his adult attempts to obtain the sweetness of money as opposed to the literal sugar of his childhood, Twain ironically turned to sugar in various forms to achieve the results he desired. In the actual version of Tom Sawyer's sugar-bowl story, described in his *Autobiography*, the young Sam Clemens is actually punished unfairly by his mother for something his brother Henry had done. When she discovers this, Sam's mother says only, "It isn't any matter. You deserve it for something you've done that I didn't know about; and if you haven't done it, why then you deserve it for something you are going to do, that I shan't hear about" (*A*, 351). This idea of cause and effect, a punishment out of sync with the crime, and a lingering feeling of potential guilt is something that permeates Twain's work—especially his later writings. An early version of this connection, a hand dipped illicitly into the sugar bowl of imperialism, is seen the earliest in Twain's letters from Hawaii and is most pronounced in his experiences in *Following the Equator*. Twain writes about U.S. imperialism in this piece in terms of the guilt regarding the subjugation of a nonwhite labor force around the world's sugar plantations. After the Spanish-American War, Twain came to realize that global sugar-based imperialism had at this point grown to include the United States. As Twain writes about U.S. practices in the

Hawaiian Islands, learns the pains of imperialism in his experiences in *Following the Equator*, and relates them back to U.S. practices as the nation spreads across the globe following the empires of sugar, he repeatedly sympathizes with those people who are most directly harmed within that system. The abuse of Du Bois's "dark proletariat" within the sugar plantations of the world so that Western nations, specifically the United States, could sweeten their food and drink is an inherently unjust operation directly connected to imperialism, and Twain would spend the remaining years of his life arguing against that injustice. Around the same time, Frank Norris also gave a startling account of agri-expansion in his work on the global wheat industry. In his work Norris pushes Twain's argument further; he suggests potential consequences of agri-expansion on workers, farmers, and capitalists brought about by the wheat itself.

5

The Wheat Strikes Back

Yes, the Railroad had prevailed. . . . *But the* WHEAT *remained.* Untouched, unassailable, undefiled, that mighty world-force, that nourisher of nations, wrapped in Nirvanic calm, indifferent to the human swarm, gigantic, resistless, moved onward in its appointed grooves.
FRANK NORRIS, *The Octopus*, 2:359, 360

He had laid his puny human grasp upon Creation and the very earth itself, the great mother, feeling the touch of the cobweb that the human insect had spun, had stirred at last in her sleep and sent her omnipotence moving through the grooves of the world, to find and crush the disturber of her appointed courses.
FRANK NORRIS, *The Pit*, 374

In *The Octopus* (1901) and *The Pit* (1903), Frank Norris romantically describes the natural world as symbolized by him in the wheat, naming it the "great mother": "unassailable," "mighty," and "Nirvanic" in "her omnipotence." Upon closer analysis, though, certain aspects of Norris's descriptions of wheat destabilize this romantic reading. Norris has gone outside familiar natural landscape models in these passages; he has romanticized a hybrid human-nature entity, wheat, which is more a representative of agriculture and the control of nature than a human-free space. Norris expands the reader's view of what a force of nature looks like in this reading. As an example of interspecies interconnectedness, the wheat and the producers of the wheat are allied in their fulfillment of the wheat's "appointed grooves." Norris repeats the idea of "grooves" in both selections, and this term can be applied to both the grooves of expansionism, like intercontinental railroad tracks or global shipping routes, and the physical furrows in the domestic farms where the wheat is grown. In this way Norris's description of grooves represents agri-expansion, the combination of domestic and global projects. This layered reading of Norris is precarious, however, and when the forces of the railroad or the market exploit farms, farmers, and the wheat itself, Norris shows that the wheat in due course becomes an unstoppable corrective against such exploitation. At this point the wheat becomes a powerful force of nature with the ability to "crush" anyone who would disturb its purpose. The humans who live and die above this "world-force" are rendered comparatively insignificant, seen as "swarms" of "insects." Wheat is therefore located in Norris's work as the highest force, and it acts in several instances as a curative role against excessive agri-expansion. Though his novels are named after capitalist forces, like the fictional Pacific and Southwestern Railroad or the Chicago Board of Trade, Norris's larger epic is named after the natural substance of wheat.

Norris intended his "epic of the wheat" to explore the course of that crop from California, the producer, to Chicago, the distributer, to Europe, the consumer, as was his plan for *The Wolf*, the text that he had not begun researching upon his death from peritonitis at thirty-two. In the two extant works, *The Octopus* and *The Pit*, Norris describes the expanding economic frontier of the U.S. wheat market, both to the East and West, to markets in Europe and Asia. For Norris, this global trajectory of expansion, following a cereal grain like wheat, fulfills his idea of a twentieth-century U.S. frontier, upon the closing of the territorial frontier described by Frederick Jackson Turner in 1893. Norris is not explicitly writing to reform early twentieth-century U.S.-based globalization in his epic; on the contrary, he appears optimistic about U.S. economic growth into international markets in the years following the Spanish-American War. However, Norris also develops wheat throughout these novels as a corrective power against the excesses that might result from that growth. He makes a domestic commentary, as he uses the U.S. wheat trade as a cautionary tale against excessive global agri-expansion. As he anthropomorphizes the Pacific and Southwestern Railroad and Chicago Board of Trade—or represents them as grotesque hybrid bodies in a kind of Harawayan nightmare—he develops wheat as an even stronger being because it is a representative of the natural world. Therefore, while Norris is not against early twentieth-century agri-expansion, he does give specific examples of potential consequences of capitalist forces becoming exploitative of the natural world and those people who work the land most directly, the domestic wheat producers. In both novels, once greed has reached a tragic level, involving the death of people connected to wheat production, the wheat itself takes action against those human characters most associated with the forces of the railroad and the market. This alternative eco-critical reading makes wheat a character that works against an exploitation of agri-expansion at a critical point of the developing U.S. wheat trade.

Norris responds to a developing state of U.S. agri-expansion at the turn of the twentieth century in his epic of the wheat. His depiction at this time of wheat as a corrective agent against individuals associated with the railroad or the market, like the characters S. Behrman or Curtis Jadwin, is, I argue, an early form of what Lawrence Buell describes as second-wave eco-criticism.[1] In Norris's epic the railroad and the market are corrupting the ethics of basic economics within agriculture. While readers have focused mainly on the battle between humans and the forces of capitalism, there is also an eco-critical battle occurring in these texts between exploitative capitalism and nature itself, including the negative potentialities of economic expansion via the global wheat trade.[2] In describing wheat as a corrective natural force, Norris responds to both critics and apologists alike who believe that the force of economics is directly connected to production and demand. The United States and its business concerns were connected in their global expansion. During this time businesses expanded their influence across larger territories than at any other point, and as agri-businesses spread, so did the United States. Agri-expansion during Norris's time, as discussed in the previous chapter about Mark Twain's sugar-related writings, worked to negotiate the growth of the wheat trade with the lives of the farmers and the consumers of the wheat. At the turn of the twentieth century, that growth focused on economics rather than land. In other words, even when dealing with natural forces, Norris recognizes the sentiment of the time in which he writes when he observes "the great word of our century is no longer War but Trade."[3]

U.S. farmers had realized—perhaps too late—that their concerns were not being met in an age of expansion, industrialization, and capitalism, so they formed a number of farming reform communities over the second half of the nineteenth century. The earliest, and perhaps most influential, of these was the Order of the Patrons of Husbandry, known as the Grange. The Grange movement came into being following the Civil War, as President Andrew Johnson sent Oliver Hudson Kelley to collect agricultural data in the South. Kelley returned with the idea of creating an organization to help farmers through social, educational, and political support systems. The Granger Laws helped regulate the railroads, grain elevators, mills, and other key elements of agricultural infrastructure in ways designed to help the domestic farmer. By the 1880s, though, many of these laws had been repealed, and farmers were once again suffering following the Panic of 1873. The next major agricultural reform movement was the Farmers' Alliance. Founded in Texas in 1875 and made official in 1880, following the decline of the Grange, it focused on business monopolies and government corruption. Once more this organization established cooperative agencies to assist farmers with infrastructure concerns, like grain elevators and mills. Though the alliance eventually also declined in popularity, it joined with larger labor unions and organizations to form the Populist Party in 1890. The Populist Party as a unit was able to take on issues against government and industry corruption, making some of the greatest reforms of the second half of the nineteenth century. The Populist Party was at its height around the time that Norris wrote his epic of the wheat. While Norris's farmers are hardly Populists—more like miners of the soil in the West in line with *The Pit*'s Curtis Jadwin—the concerns facing wheat farmers at the end of the nineteenth century are very much at play in *The Octopus* and *The Pit*.

The U.S. wheat trade of Norris's epic was a significant part of the developing U.S. economy in the years between the Civil War and the Spanish-American War, a time both of great U.S. territorial expansion and agricultural revolution. Norris's work shows the existence of an early twentieth-century global "appetite for American wheat," as Walter Benn Michaels has observed.[4] Taking advantage of this hunger, agri-expansionists hoped to reap financial rewards through the excessive production and trade in wheat. They developed a new form of agriculture, one that re-created farming based on the nation's developing industrialism. In terms of work and production, by the 1880s and 1890s, farmers worked against, rather than with, nature.[5] Indeed, the western farms of the late nineteenth century shared much in common with farms in the twenty-first century. They encompassed vast amounts of land, were dependent on large amounts of capital, and were technologically advanced in comparison with their predecessors.[6] Norris's writings depict some of the key elements of this new agriculture, through the original ranchers in *The Octopus* and the speculators of *The Pit*. This economic revolution based on surplus crops was not created in a vacuum, however. Nineteenth-century politicians encouraged trade in surplus foodstuffs. James G. Blaine, secretary of state under Presidents Ulysses S. Grant and Benjamin Harrison, stressed that "overseas markets were not only necessary but essential" as a way to distribute agricultural and manufacturing surpluses.[7] Blaine aggressively promoted expanding beyond domestic markets for excessive U.S. production—most notably in agriculture. In the years between 1870 and the turn of the century, the United States aggressively promoted itself as the breadbasket of the world—using the wheat crops it grew in surplus to do so. In fact, the national importance of the wheat trade was so great that U.S. production and distribution of wheat was second only to Britain's, and it significantly influenced the U.S. economy well into the twentieth century.[8] Thus, the U.S. wheat trade that Norris makes the primary subject of his epic developed into a fundamental part of the U.S. economy in the years between the U.S. Civil War and the Spanish-American War.

Moreover, the issues surrounding the wheat industry during Norris's time were also historically significant. Developments in transportation and communication allowed western grain farmers to cultivate enormous tracts of land. These "bonanza" farmers could make their fortune by growing large quantities of wheat to be sold in a metropolitan center like Chicago, a city designed around agri-expansion. Thanks to the telegraph, wheat farmers no longer had to wait for harvest before selling their crops. In addition, they could move their product over greater distances than ever before—even across the globe. All of these advantages allowed western famers to find yet another way to "strike it rich" on the frontier. Not concerned with the sustainability of their crops, they mined the soil like an ore, expecting to have made their fortunes by the time wheat prices fell or the land failed.[9] Moreover, they were different from the small farmers who were their counterparts because of the distance they were able to maintain from the land itself. According to William Conlogue, "abstraction replaces experience" for these farmers.[10] It is noteworthy that farms in the West during U.S. expansion came to resemble the factories of the urban centers. In addition, a system of public land-grant colleges and universities that specifically focused on agriculture and engineering was initiated during this period. In cooperation with federal and state governments, in lands made available through territorial expansion over the nineteenth century, the land-grant college system expanded throughout the second half of the nineteenth century. In its own language, the Morrill Act asked that each state establish "at least one college where the leading object shall be, without excluding other scientific and classical studies, and including military tactics, to teach such branches of learning as are related to agriculture and the mechanical arts."[11] At a time when agriculture was changing drastically—in large part owing to U.S. expansion—the land-grant colleges worked to prepare an educated farming society to become economically competitive with eastern business models. These farmers who applied new agricultural ideas brought the technological advances of the mechanical age to their farms, while remaining entrenched in the land itself. Norris gives an example of this type of educated farmer in the character of Annixter in *The Octopus*, and this type of new agriculture is highlighted as characters in the novel argue about key points of the system. These educated wheat farmers see themselves as a hopeful combination of farmer and speculator.

Norris too educated himself about the particular symbolism of wheat in U.S. agri-expansion. His choice to write about wheat was not an arbitrary one; his own biography paralleled the history of wheat. Born in Chicago, he moved as a young man to California and as an adult traveled widely in Europe. In this way Norris's life followed the course of wheat's empire, in much the same way that Mark Twain's career followed that of sugar production. In his eulogy to Norris, William Dean Howells observed, "The story of the Wheat was for [Norris] the allegory of the industrial and financial America which is the real America."[12] Wheat held a genuine symbolic significance for Norris and became his "allegory" for this agri-expansion. Furthermore, Norris became aware of global food systems during his time as a news correspondent in Cuba during the Spanish-American War. In an article published in the *Atlantic Monthly*, Norris describes the Cuban people in terms of food security as they entreat U.S. soldiers for "Comida! Comida!"[13] He argues that the United States could essentially be a beneficial presence for the people of Cuba based on the nation's food surpluses.[14] Continuing his arguments for U.S. globalization at the turn of the twentieth century, Norris wrote an article for *World's Work* titled "The Frontier Gone at Last," in which he positively discusses the U.S. presence in the Pacific: "The Anglo-Saxon in his course of empire had circled the globe and had brought the new civilization to the old civilization, had reached the starting point of history."[15] Emphasizing the "civilization" of the United States entering foreign spaces, Norris writes enthusiastically about U.S. expansion and the reopening of the closed western frontier by "circling the globe." Norris's epic connects twinned concepts: global wheat markets and U.S. economic expansion. He comes to see newly opened world markets as vital to extending the twentieth-century U.S. frontier through a new form of economic activity in agriculture.

Moreover, Norris may have chosen wheat as a symbol of the possibilities of agri-expansion owing to its own biologically imperialist nature. Wheat is able to adapt quickly to a variety of environments. In this it is rare among the world's great grasses, making wheat a successful grain that has become one of the most dominant crops, spanning vast geographical regions of the globe. This ability to adapt and dominate a nonnative space is a trait that wheat bears in common with human beings. Wheat is not native to the United States, and early attempts to introduce it, along with several other crops, by both Spanish and British settlers failed. However, once successfully cultivated, wheat thrived, even to the point of becoming an imperial grain. Wheat succeeded globally to such a dramatic extent in part because of its close relationship with humanity through agriculture. Wheat offers people gluten, which makes it a useful energy source as a key ingredient in bread; this association with bread has made wheat one of the most important cereal grains, on a par with rice or corn in terms of global significance.[16] Therefore, in the United States, people involved in agri-expansion would have an interest in the success of wheat—and the two entities would become inextricably linked.

Meanwhile, the complementary aspect of wheat, its connection to nature, is also a major theme in Norris's epic. Like Emile Zola, Norris has a melancholic vision of nature.[17] While such a depiction of nature is romantic, it is at the same time not benign or entirely pleasant. Rather, this vision is more consistent with the evolutionary thesis described by Norris's former professor at University of California–Berkeley, Joseph LeConte.[18] Thus, nature is a potentially greater world force than the economic expansion exemplified by the railroad or the Chicago Board of Trade. It extends almost beyond the romantic to the sublime or the grotesque with its emphasis on the insignificance of humanity. For Norris, wheat has the potential to become "apocalyptic or redemptive."[19] Norris was not alone among naturalists in using agriculture as his symbol for natural forces. Zola's *La Terre*, a potential influence on Norris's work, also uses agriculture as a motif.[20] In this case Zola's naturalist influence over Norris expands beyond the idea of class struggle to that of a natural symbol like wheat that expresses specific characteristics. In his work nature ultimately emerges victorious. Attempts to exploit the wheat for economic reasons ultimately fail, and the wheat destroys representative attempts at such exploitation. While critics argue that wheat's very distance and abstraction cause it to represent a victory for agri-expansion, Norris's ambivalence to new developments in agriculture also foreshadows arguments against modern-day agribusiness.

In 1903 Norris published a short story collection that included a study of themes he would develop more fully in his epic of the wheat. "A Deal in Wheat" focuses on a Kansas farmer, Sam Lewiston, as he struggles to survive within the wheat market that is being manipulated in a similar manner as Norris's character, Curtis Jadwin, attempts in *The Pit*. Norris's short story falls into three main parts: Lewiston's failure as a farmer, which forces him to move to Chicago to look for work; an interlude in which various Chicago speculators discuss their underhanded business tactics; and a return to an impoverished Lewiston standing among Chicago's charity breadlines. An early pivotal scene sets the plot in motion: the bank tells Lewiston that wheat is going for a shockingly low "sixty-two" cents a bushel, a price decided on in faraway Chicago. Lewiston laments, "That—that ruins me. I *can't* carry my grain any longer—what with storage charges and—and—Bridges, I don't see just how I'm going to make out. Sixty-two cents a bushel! Why, man, what with this and with that it's cost me nearly a dollar a bushel to raise that wheat." He follows this with a "quick gesture of infinite discouragement."[21] Norris presents the reader with something missing from the story of the Jadwins in *The Pit*, and to a lesser extent in *The Octopus*. He shows the farmer himself as he is forced to deal with the consequences of the malleable global wheat market. As some people amass great wealth manipulating the market, others like Lewiston are driven into bankruptcy. Norris continues, "Thrown out of work, Lewiston drifted aimlessly about Chicago, from pillar to post, working a little, earning here a dollar, there a dime, but always sinking, sinking, till at last . . . a park bench became his home and the 'bread line' his chief makeshift of subsistence" (D, 22–23). Lewiston has now been driven to homelessness, Norris repeating the image of his "sinking" for emphasis. Lewiston is an example of the western farmer who invested capital in a monoculture in order to turn a better profit—as opposed to the garden farmers of the agrarian-style system of the earlier period. However, he has come to the opposite extreme. When one crop fails, based on natural disasters or the manipulation of a global wheat market in Chicago, farmers who have overspecialized to meet a global demand no longer have alternate resources to sustain themselves. In some ways, then, the situation for small-scale farmers had not changed a great deal since the time of the anti-rent movement of the early nineteenth century in the U.S. Northeast, described by Herman Melville. Driven from their land, these unsuccessful farmers found their situations unimproved once they moved to the larger cities.

By the end of "A Deal in Wheat," Lewiston has ironically been forced out of the breadlines he had come to depend upon, owing to an artificial inflation of the price of wheat, one that has made it impossible for bakers to produce the loaves used for charity. There is a sign on the door outside which a long line of desperate figures has already formed: "Owing to the fact that the price of grain has been increased to two dollars a bushel, there will be no distribution of bread from this bakery until further notice" (D, 24–25). In the course of this brief story, Norris has shown the price of wheat fluctuate between sixty cents and two dollars a bushel. Moreover, he follows a farmer whose livelihood is directly connected to these prices. Seemingly against his naturalist tendencies, Norris allows Lewiston ultimately to survive these experiences, older and wiser for his hardships. However, Norris's ultimate point has been made: the speculators in Chicago exert a dangerous influence over the lives of producers and consumers in the United States and around the globe. This theme continues through his epic of the wheat, specifically in *The Pit*. One of Norris's main points, though, is that unstable prices make a farmer's life profoundly unstable as well. Farmers no longer have a support system to sustain themselves if they struggle.[22] Moreover, Lewiston's story is particularly relevant because wheat is a staple crop for the United States, and the primary ingredient for the bread that is feeding increasingly large portions of the world's workers.[23]

In his novels Norris broadens his focus from the lone western farmers to numerous characters whose lives are interwoven based on their connection to the U.S. wheat trade. Several of Norris's human characters, not only his villains, attempt to exploit wheat for their own material gain. In *The Octopus* wheat growers act like gamblers trying to cultivate their lands in the same manner that they would have mined for gold; Norris considers California agriculture to be another kind of intrusive mining—this time of the soil. As an example, he notes that one of his ranchers, Magnus Derrick, "remained the Forty-niner" in his use of the land for gaining wealth: "It was the true California spirit that found expression through him, the spirit of the West . . . the miner's instinct of wealth acquired in a single night prevailed, in spite of all."[24] Norris makes even his heroic characters tragically flawed, and their destruction toward the end of the novel is foreshadowed in their desire to exploit the wheat and the land, "to squeeze it dry, to exhaust it" (*Oc* 2:14). He gives further examples of the dangers of exploiting the natural world represented by the wheat in his follow-up novel, *The Pit*. Speculators like Curtis Jadwin attempt to control both the national and global wheat markets. Jadwin becomes a "bull" trader in the Chicago Board of Trade, and at his peak "the whole market hung upon his horns" as he manipulated the U.S. wheat supply for his own benefit.[25] Human characters like Jadwin force an ultimately unsustainable level of agri-expansion. Wheat, as a representative of nature, must necessarily crush forces of capitalism once they reach beyond even flawed heroes like Annixter or Derrick, toward the extreme exploitation of villains and antiheroes like S. Behrman or Curtis Jadwin. Norris's work supports an eco-critical reading as wheat triumphs repeatedly over representatives of human forces like the railroad and the market.

In this eco-critical reading of Norris, the "mighty world-force" of wheat shows both the potential and the consequence of turn-of-the-twentieth-century U.S. agri-expansion. In Norris's work, the wheat always flourishes, expanding itself to feed the greatest number of people. It is, after all, a "nourisher of nations," practicing its own form of expansion. Though Norris's attitude toward U.S. globalization through agriculture is ambivalent, and his naturalism relies on a deterministic view of class struggles—seen in *The Octopus* via his portrayal of the

Hooven family's tragedy—his depictions of wheat are ultimately useful warnings against the potential excesses of agri-expansion. The energies of the human and naturalist forces combined to bring the largest agricultural yields that the world had yet witnessed. However, the farmer's control over the land is always tenuous, and sometimes nature strikes out against farmers and speculators. Throughout his epic Norris's characters are eventually punished when they try to come between the wheat and the people who need it to survive: both the domestic producers and global consumers. This is shown first in *The Octopus*, as the wheat strikes out against the railroad representative after the ranchers responsible for farming the wheat have been destroyed—even killed—and the railroad looks to take its expanding business even further into agriculture.

WHEATWARD THE COURSE OF EMPIRE

In *The Octopus* Norris describes wheat growing in California using an ostensibly familiar sublime theme, with one fundamental distinction. Unlike a mountain or body of water, for example, a wheat field is connected to humanity—it is "second nature," to use Lawrence Buell's phrase.[26] The wheat is the primary object of conflict between the ranchers and the forces of capitalism represented by the Pacific and Southwestern Railroad. While the wheat originally seems only peripherally involved in that battle—the purpose behind the struggle as opposed to an actor within it—as the plot of the novel develops, the relationship of wheat to the human actors becomes more complicated. Progressively, the wheat becomes more of a subject of the action rather than merely an object. After the railroad destroys the lives of almost all of the ranchers and farmers, the wheat seems to awaken to the drama unfolding around it. At this point it takes aggressive action, killing the novel's primary villain and rewarding a few of the surviving heroes. These actions potentially show an ethical standard in Norris's work: the wheat, representative of the natural world, acts as a curative entity against the excesses of the expanding U.S. wheat trade. In *The Octopus*, although Norris writes of the inevitability of economic forces like the railroad, the actions of wheat show that a natural force can help to mediate them.

Norris bases his descriptions of the ranches of California on research performed during a visit to the Santa Anita Ranch near Tres Pinos, California, east of Monterey and south of Gilroy. There he stayed for around six weeks as the guest of Gaston and Dulce Bolando Ashe. At the time Tres Pinos was a shipping and storage hub for the railroad, the site for transferring the cattle, hogs, hay, and wheat that Norris would make a central element of his epic. During this research period, Norris experienced the operations of the Santa Anita Ranch, as well as interviewed several people connected to it. Elements of their stories, perhaps particularly Dulce Ashe's stories, appear throughout Norris's novel. He enjoyed his time at the ranch as well and was described by Gaston as "a most delightful comrade and full of personality and magnetism" as he spent his leisure time "in conversation and observations."[27] At this time Norris also visited the San Joaquin Valley, the region in which he sets his novel—having moved his setting east over the Gabilan Mountains into the Central Valley. He writes of his work there to a friend: "I helped run and work a harvester in the San Joaquin—that is I helped on the sacking-platform—but of course you don't know where that is."[28] Norris's real-life experiences became some of the research for his novel of farmers and the wheat.

The agricultural story in *The Octopus* is set during a crucial period of agri-expansion in U.S. history, and Norris focuses on a battle between the railroad and California wheat growers in 1880 that came to be known as the "Mussel Slough Tragedy." These events were so powerful that Norris had little to change for dramatic purposes. The tragedy itself occurred when local ranchers were killed in a fight against the Southern Pacific Railroad over land ownership. The railroad did in fact raise the asking price of land leased to ranchers who had already made improvements to it based on an understanding of the eventual transfers of ownership to themselves. As the ranchers expected to be able to purchase their leased land for less than five dollars an acre, the verbally contracted price, they were stunned to find it raised to as much as forty dollars an acre and opened for public sale. At that point they chose to fight the railroad bodily, and they lost. When the railroad personnel came to physically remove them from the contested land around Mussel Slough, those who stood in the way were killed. Although the railroad was never punished for the killings, public outcry was so great that after years of struggle, eventual policy changes were passed against such corruption. Even the name of the novel, *The Octopus*, would have been a familiar term for Norris's readership as a pejorative name for the Southern Pacific Railroad.[29] The ways in which Norris does fictionalize *The Octopus*, then, are telling in terms of the issues behind his concept of U.S. agri-expansion. Norris sets his story twenty years later than the actual events, moving the period of his climactic battle to a time following the Spanish-American War. This move places the action of the novel around the development of a U.S. global economic supremacy, which shifts the focus of events from the corruption of big business during the robber baron era of the 1870s to a similar period of economic corruption after a war based almost exclusively on U.S. imperialist and economic interests in the late nineteenth century.[30] In addition, Norris develops the wheat into a character in its own right, symbolically giving a voice to nature. Through this characterization Norris demonstrates the corrective powers of the wheat against the forces of the railroad.

Norris is known for representing the railroad in *The Octopus* as a sentient entity, but there is less discussion of how he similarly animates the wheat into a being that can act as a force in its own right. His novel, though, is suffused with images of fecund wheat whose innate purpose is to feed others, a dominant presence throughout the novel. Norris anthropomorphizes the wheat as he writes, "After the harvest, small though that harvest had been, the ranches seemed asleep. It was as though the earth, after its period of reproduction, its pains of labor, had been delivered of the fruit of its loins, and now slept the sleep of exhaustion" (*Oc*, 1:11–12). Norris connects agriculture to a kind of birth, as it literally gives life. Sheep graze on wheat stubble; Presley, the main character, rides his bike through wheat fields; and the novel itself spans one full cycle of the wheat harvest.[31] In an idealized agriculture, humans work with certain plants to make a better environment for both species. This relationship between humanity and the natural world, ideally a mutually beneficial one, exists especially in agriculture, and Norris refers to these romanticized images throughout the novel.

Furthermore, to develop wheat into a potential character able to act out its own desires, Norris must first describe it as one. The farmer Harran Derrick inspects his crop of wheat, and Norris uses this opportunity to give a sensual description. Harran is seen "taking handfuls of wheat from each [sack] and allowing it to run through his fingers, or nipping the grains between his nails, testing their hardness. The seed was all of the white varieties of wheat and of a very high grade, the berries hard and heavy, rigid and swollen with starch" (*Oc*, 1:52). Norris links the businesslike examination of the grain with a sensual description of heavy wheat berries running through Harran's fingers. In this passage the wheat becomes the focal point, described in greater detail than the human figure performing the action. Early on in the novel, then, wheat is being described as a significant entity. Meanwhile, Norris also shows the wheat taking a more active role in events over the course of the novel in later scenes.[32]

For the wheat to awaken to the drama in the later scenes, Norris returns to the humans in their connection with agri-expansion. The story behind the Pacific and Southwestern Railroad, or "octopus," remains important throughout the novel, and it eventually motivates the wheat into action. The significance of the development of the wheat trade is described in a discussion between Presley and his capitalist friend, Cedarquist, who declares, "The great word of this nineteenth century has been Production. The great word of the twentieth century will be—listen to me, you youngsters—Markets" (*Oc*, 2:21). He then explains his idea for expanding the U.S. wheat trade internationally: "As a market for our *Wheat*, Europe is played out. Population in Europe is not increasing fast enough to keep up with the rapidity of production. . . . *We*, however, have gone on producing wheat at a tremendous rate. The result is over-production. We supply more than Europe can eat, and down go the prices. The remedy is *not* in curtailing our wheat areas, but in this, we *must have new markets, greater markets*. . . . We must march with the course of empire, not against it. I mean, we must look to

China" (*Oc*, 2:21–22, Norris's italics). Cedarquist describes the increase of markets for wheat as a direct parallel of the expansion of the U.S. economy in the early twentieth century, and wheat becomes a symbol of this growth. Norris's character takes the "course of empire" farther west than California, as wheat travels with U.S. economic interests to Asia, connecting agriculture and globalization. Cedarquist shows that the wheat is implicit in U.S. capitalism. If wheat represents the U.S. economic empire by conquering the markets of the United States and of Europe, then it may also conquer Asia's markets through trade.[33]

Before the empire of wheat can accomplish what Cedarquist foresees, though, a generation of educated farmers must first come into being. Norris gives what may be his ideal example of a western wheat farmer in the character of Annixter, an educated man who applies theories learned at college, where he majored in "finance, political economy, and scientific agriculture" (*Oc*, 1:23). Norris adds that Annixter also ranked among the highest in his class at the college, validating his intelligence as well as his being a "ferocious worker" (*Oc*, 1:22). Applying the techniques he learned at school at his own farm, Annixter "sold his wheat stubble on the ground to the sheep raisers. . . . He gets a price for his stubble, which else he would have to burn, and also manures his land as the sheep move from place to place" (*Oc*, 1:21). Annixter layers his profits by selling his stubble while saving on manure and the labor for burning. While the local townspeople commenting on Annixter's unorthodox farming practices admire him primarily for the fact that he makes a greater profit than do others who do not sell their wheat stubble, he also demonstrates an early depiction of a sustainable form of agriculture. Norris goes further to show Annixter as a representative of a hopeful, sustainable farmer when he marries a dairy maid, Hilma Tree, a character closely connected with nature to the point of being named "Tree." This union connects Annxiter more strongly to the natural world and to the wheat. The opposite of Behrman, Annixter knows his land as well as any farmer in the novel. He farms a large tract for profit, but he still thinks of the future and wants to replenish the soil for future crops. He represents Norris's example of the appropriate method for farming in the new, post-Spanish-American-War era of U.S. agri-expansion.[34]

Whereas Annixter represents the ideal character through his blend of economics and nature in his farming techniques, the wheat is not much like an active character at this point. Indeed, the wheat does not begin to act, in the sense that it does act, before the climax of the novel at the gunfight in the wheat fields. Wheat has not yet truly interacted in the lives of the human characters before the point where several of the novel's main characters are brought to some form of ruin—financially, emotionally, or physically—in this final fight. The survivors of the fight are also casualties, as they miscarry, go insane, become homeless, and are driven into prostitution. Most tragically described in the novel is the Hooven family, German immigrants who have no support system after Mr. Hooven is killed by the railroad's men. Indeed, Norris gives Hooven an important place in this final battle, as the siege occurs at Hooven's farm itself. The fight can be heard at a distance: "From far away across the rustling wheat came the faint rattle of rifles and revolvers" (*Oc*, 2:234). Furthermore, it is Hooven who fires the first shot, calling out, "*Hoch der Kaiser! Hoch der Vaterland!*" (*Oc*, 2:232, Norris's italics). In his war cry, Hooven's new "fatherland" is California, and his home is his wheat farm. After Hooven is shot and killed, however, the rest of his family is left in destitution. His wife and two daughters, Minna and Hilda, are described later as living on the streets of San Francisco. In an extended scene, Norris intercalates an extravagant dinner party at the Cedarquist house with scenes of Mrs. Hooven starving to death on the street, Minna having already fallen into prostitution, and Hilda, the youngest, being assimilated into the state's foster-care system. Mrs. Hooven's final moments are described poignantly: "Her eyes were open. A grateful numbness had begun to creep over her, a pleasing semi-insensibility. She no longer felt the pain and cramps of her stomach, even the hunger was ceasing to bite" as she tells her daughter "Go to schleep . . . Sick . . . Noddings to eat" (*Oc*, 2:319–320). As is the case for Herman Melville's struggling farmers in chapter 1, the Hoovens are destroyed by the system of capital and manipulation of the wheat trade that does not take into account the workers themselves. In this sentimentalized scene, the Hooven women are starving even as they attempt to beg for "bread'n milk" (*Oc*, 2:318). At this stage, if wheat is an actor in the novel, then it has failed many of the characters.[35]

Though this climactic battle results in a litany of casualties, there remains one notable exception: "Dabney dead, Hooven dead, Harran dead, Annixter dead, Broderson dead, Osterman dying, S. Behrman alive, successful" (*Oc*, 2:248). The successful villain, Behrman, is poised to take over the wheat ranches from the ruined farmers. The wheat seemingly remains an uninvolved natural substance, an inhuman force interested solely in its own growth. Unable to contain his rage at these developments, Presley imagines taking an illegal and violent form of justice against Behrman. He desires "to sink his fingers deep into the white, fat throat of the man, to clutch like iron into the great puffed jowl of him, to wrench out the life, to batter it out, strangle it out" (*Oc*, 2:253). Of course, Presley does nothing of the sort. His attempted bombing of Behrman's home is a failure. Instead, he demonstrates the division of power that will continue for the remainder of the novel, as he does not have the force of the natural world behind him. Rather, only the wheat has the ability to avenge these fallen characters, and it comes into its power incrementally. First, the wheat leads the survivors of the battle to where one of the villains hides. This character, Delaney, is found thanks to a blood trail that leads into the wheat, where he has escaped. He is "deep in the wheat, his knees drawn up, his eyes wide open, his lips brown. Rigidly gripped in one hand was his empty revolver" (*Oc*, 2:241). Delaney has tried to save himself by escaping into the wheat fields, possibly even lying in wait for an opportunity to cause more destruction from there. However, he never gets that chance. He dies within the wheat itself, which then provides a convenient opening trail for the remaining ranchers to find his corpse. Through a series of circumstantial events such as this one, the wheat slowly begins to come into its own as an actor in the novel.

The next act in wheat's awakening is equally subdued. In the novel's time line, the wheat harvest ripens on schedule for Behrman to reap the rewards of the crop brought about by the work of the producers whose lives he helped destroy. The wheat grows for the villain as well—or even better—than it does for the heroes, which leads to questions about the wheat's intention. If wheat is meant to be a curative force, it should punish the railroad representative, not reward him. Behrman sees his newly acquired wheat fields as "'bonanza,' and all that division of the great ranch was thick with just such wonderful wheat. Never had Los Muertos been more generous." He sees himself as "the Master of the Wheat" (*Oc*, 2:324). He takes the credit for the success of the wheat crop, though he does not deserve it. This "bonanza" crop of wheat grows for Behrman as indiscriminately as for the Derricks, and at first this appears to be evidence of the wheat's indifference to the human lives around it. However, the wheat is apparently not as amoral as it at first seems. Behrman makes a fatal error when he calls himself wheat's "Master." He does not realize, as Presley does, that "Men were naught"; it is "FORCE that made the wheat grow" (*Oc*, 2:343). This world force of the wheat, as part of the larger cyclical natural world, works to grow itself, and humans are just its conduit. Once Behrman claims his mastery over the wheat—over the natural world itself—the wheat finally rouses and becomes a corrective entity that can punish him for his hubris.

In one of the most memorable scenes of the novel, Behrman is killed ostensibly by the wheat itself, as it becomes an actor to its full extent: "The Wheat, leaping continuously from the chute, poured around him. It filled the pockets of the coat, it crept up the sleeves and trouser legs, it covered the great, protuberant stomach, it ran at last in rivulets into the distended, gaping mouth. It covered the face" (*Oc*, 2:354). In this scene Norris uses only active verbs to describe the wheat, making it syntactically the subject of the passage. The wheat leaps, fills, covers, runs, and creeps as it kills the novel's most visible villain. Meanwhile, Behrman is described as the object being acted upon—either stripped of his humanity outright or represented as a grotesque subhuman entity. Only at one point is Behrman humanized through Norris's use of pronouns, described as a "him" instead of as an "it." Otherwise, Norris focuses on certain elements of Behrman's physical body and clothes, equating the two as material items represented with a "the"; he uses "the" for coat, sleeves, stomach, mouth, and face. Behrman is allowed to be a "him," but he is not allowed possession of himself. Using such descriptors, Norris shows the wheat act directly against this villain in a way fantasized by Presley earlier. The wheat does to Behrman in effect what the railroad had done to the wheat ranchers; it balances the scale of forces. Throughout *The Octopus*, while exploitation can destroy the lives of the humans most directly affected by it, natural forces can ultimately destroy their destroyer, to the point of taking on the agent of the Octopus itself.[36]

While it is impossible to know Norris's true motivation behind his making wheat such a significant actor in the novel, one clue comes in the form of a newspaper clipping Norris kept that is now at the Bancroft Library in Berkeley, California. The article, "Sinks to Death in a Grain Pit," details the plight of two workers, Patrick Dolan and Petro Amazlo, who fell into a grain elevator in Brooklyn, New York. Dolan, the foreman, died there, while Amazlo, another worker who attempted to save him, survived. This article describes the "little kernels, rolling against one another like myriad cogs of a great machine" as they "drew him down."[37] Such descriptors show some of the language Norris went on to use in his novel. First, the grain was machinelike, each piece a cog. Then, it almost acted of its own volition, as Norris would show, when it drew the men into the pit. Further, the foreman of the workers was the figure who died in the elevator—not the laborer. This is the fact of the article, and one that Norris takes to an extreme by selecting the villain of the novel to suffer. The article is doing its job, which is to dramatize a newsworthy event. Norris, though, finds significant inspiration in this scene and the potential for dramatic effect in his writing. As in the Mussel Slough revisioning earlier in the novel, the ways in which he changes the story are telling. He kills his villain—playing up the drama of the scene further by extending it—and hides the humanity of the figure while making the wheat simultaneously an actor. Moreover, the article seems to unite the natural world with the artificial, as the wheat becomes a machine; Norris, though, maintains a distinction between the two entities: the Octopus remains machine, while the wheat is the great mother, nature.

Once the wheat has become an actor by the end of the novel, it takes an opportunity to reward certain characters, like the mystic Vanamee, whose character exemplifies the regenerative power of the natural world. In the secondary story line, Vanamee mourns his beloved, Angéle, who had died after an assault years before the events of the story take place. Vanamee sleeps outdoors in the wheat fields in an effort to be closer to what he believes to be her spirit. Instead of using wheat for economic gain, he communes with it at a mystical level. By the end of the novel, the wheat seemingly gifts him with a return of Angéle: "In the wheat he waited for her. . . . It was no longer an ephemeral illusion of the night, evanescent, mystic, but a simple country girl coming to meet her lover. The vision of the night had been beautiful, but what was it compared to this? Reality was better than Romance" (*Oc*, 2:347). In truth the woman is not Angéle, but rather her grown daughter; however, in the symbolism of the wheat, she is a mystic resurrection of Vanamee's beloved. Though Norris names this event "Reality," it is perhaps the most "Romantic" scene in a novel of naturalistic forces. Norris shows that the wheat is more powerful than the railroad in yet another way; while the railroad only has the strength to destroy people, the wheat can create life. The wheat survives and acts for and against certain characters. As it kills Behrman, it grants Vanamee his greatest wish.

Additionally, the wheat rewards Presley for his attempted heroism in the novel. As the wheat leaves on its Huckleberry Finn–like journey west on the *Swanhilda* after its own experiment with civilization, it travels with two human characters from the novel. It has killed Behrman, showing in fact that there is ultimately a limit to the amount of exploitation it would tolerate, trapping his body on board the ship. At the same time, the wheat has spared the narrator, Presley, even rewarded him. Presley is one of the few primary characters of the novel to survive the wrath of both the railroad and the wheat, being only peripherally connected to the exploitation plot. However, he has also been changed by the wheat, to the point where Cedarquist suggests that Presley is also in need of relief, like the unseen citizens of India, and he hopes that this trip will "fat" Presley up—especially since there presumably would be bread enough on a ship filled with wheat (*Oc*, 2:357).[38] This is a final commentary of the wheat as a character: that there will always be bread enough for the people in need, regardless of the forces who seek to prevent it. Presley succeeds where other characters in the novel have been made to suffer. He survives and has allied himself with the greatest force of the novel: the wheat. The novel's concluding image shows Presley looking toward the wheat fields of Central California one last time. After assessing the utter destruction of the other primary characters, besides himself and Vanamee, beneath the force of the railroad, Presley wonders, "Was good to be thus overthrown? Was evil thus to be strong and to prevail? Was nothing left? . . . *But the* WHEAT *remained*" (*Oc*, 2:360, Norris's italics). Norris concludes *The Octopus* with a controversial optimistic passage in which his narrator is able to find meaning amid the human tragedy. Because the wheat remains, and continues to feed people, the fate of the human actors has somehow been judged and avenged. The wheat tolerates some kinds of agri-expansion—especially as concerns its own drives. However, once the railroad tries to exploit it and stop it from feeding people, to the point even of allowing them to starve, it becomes a violent world force.

The wheat becomes the "master-symbol" of *The Octopus*, moving the plot in a specific direction, according to John Eperjesi.[39] For Norris, that direction is literally to Asia, where the wheat is sent on a famine relief mission. Symbolically, though, it travels a more circuitous path.[40] The wheat actually kills, feeds, and brings to life, meting out justice as the world force Norris wants it to be. Meanwhile, the reader is meant to sympathize with the farmers who suffer most, the Hoovens, as they starve to death in the same city where the surplus of the novel's wheat is being prepared to ship to India for famine relief. In other words, people are starving in a land of bonanza production.[41] Indeed, Norris draws a parallel between the names of the girl, Hilda Hooven, and the *Swanhilda*, the ship being sent to India. To Norris, the wheat wants to feed people, and it attempts to cure some of this degree of exploitation.

Norris uses his description of wheat as a challenge against agri-expansion that threatens the farmers who most directly work within its natural environment. This larger commentary complicates Norris's apologia for U.S. globalization at the turn of the twentieth century, and the wheat is more than just a symbol of U.S. agri-expansion, but rather it becomes a symbol of a universally available food source, once it successfully counters capitalistic exploitation.

In *The Octopus* Norris describes a food source that can grow exuberantly and is able to both feed large numbers of people and produce a surplus profit for farmers, connecting nature and human industry in the novel. The two actors cannot be entirely separated in Norris's nature-based naturalism; the wheat field is no wilderness—perhaps nothing truly is. Moreover, Norris equates the railroad with the original ranchers. Neither occupation is ultimately noble in its attitude toward the natural world. Norris does not intend for his original ranchers to be agrarian representations of small-scale farmers. It is acceptable for farmers in Norris's work to be driven by a desire for profit. This is often considered admirable in U.S. society, and Norris maintains this attitude in the figures of the Derricks. On the other hand, Norris also includes the farmer Annixter as an example of a more sustainable western farmer. He seeks to make a profit from the land, yet he also represents the new era of agriculture that does not treat land as a soil mine. Thus, though he dies tragically in the novel's climax as a fulfillment of the naturalist tone, he is not made to suffer in the way that Behrman does. These ranchers—specifically Annixter—work with the wheat for the profit of both. The wheat allows for human industry, even capitalism, until it reaches a level of exploitative agriculture and finds itself compelled to act. By this point the wheat has dominated all of the human characters that have struggled over it. It proves itself ultimately more resilient than either the railroad or the ranchers as they try to take advantage of it.[42] In other words, humans are related in their drive to exploit the wheat— and the natural forces represented by the wheat—beyond a logical level of basic demand met by adequate supply. It is the manipulation of the wheat that leads the majority of the characters of the novel to destruction, while the wheat continues to grow—even into the final images of the text. Norris continues this theme into the second novel in his epic of the wheat, *The Pit*. This strength of ecological purpose is reiterated in his novel as the speculator, Curtis Jadwin, attempts to corner the global wheat market in the Chicago Board of Trade. In *The Pit* the wheat again becomes a significant actor as a natural world force attempting to cure a large-scale manipulation of the wheat trade during the early twentieth century.

WHEAT CORNERED

Norris continues his theme of the wheat acting as a potentially corrective world force in *The Pit*. While wheat remains a motif for him in the later novel, it is as less of a physical and more a psychological presence than it was in *The Octopus*. When wheat does appear in *The Pit*, it is simultaneously relegated to the periphery and recognizable in its significance. Birds feast on samples of wheat off the floor of the Board of Trade after a day of heavy speculation, and Laura Jadwin watches cargo ships filled with grain pass her window at a pivotal moment in the text. The wheat's most crucial action in the novel, though, is to bring about the ruin of Curtis Jadwin, the novel's hero, after he attempts to exploit the grain through an elaborate corner of the market. *The Pit* describes the downfall of Laura and Curtis Jadwin, in both their professional and personal capacities, via speculation in the wheat market for their own gain. The ultimate failure of the Jadwins to successfully manipulate the wheat market, combined with their subsequent punishment—being banished from Chicago at the novel's conclusion—gives Norris the opportunity to keep the novel's focus on the consequences involved when humans try to manipulate the natural world, once again represented by wheat. The main characters in Norris's second novel make their fortunes based on crops they have never seen grown by people they have never met, without any consideration for these producers or their corresponding consumers. In *The Pit* Norris makes wheat act as a corrective force against a figure trying to exploit it. This theme becomes, if anything, more intense as *The Pit* focuses more directly on the economic component of the U.S. wheat market as opposed to the agriculture in *The Octopus*.

Norris brings his discussion of wheat and global agri-expansion to Chicago as the necessary representative of the West and business at the turn of the century. Like Upton Sinclair's *The Jungle* (1906), *The Pit* focuses on Chicago and its connection to the food production industry. Norris shows the global network of wheat that runs across the United States and through Chicago before redistribution around the world. While wheat was distributed primarily to Europe, farmers and Chicago speculators also took into account global wheat producers in nations across Eastern Europe, Russia, Asia, and South America, in addition to the U.S. West. Wheat, in particular, was part of the global market. When the United States went through a depression in the 1890s, wheat hit a low of "an average of 53 1/8¢ a bushel."[43] Later, shortages in the wheat crops in other nations would directly affect the production in western states like California and Kansas. Meanwhile, during the early years of the twentieth century, wheat reached an all-time high. With the inducement of high prices, farmers produced as much of the grain as possible, and incredible fortunes were made in Chicago's Board of Trade. Agriculture became big business because of the centralization of the U.S. wheat industry through Chicago. Therefore, setting the novel in Chicago is significant for a discussion of agri-expansion at the end of the nineteenth century.

The economic world of the Chicago Board of Trade, one of the nation's earliest stock markets, was particularly influential in trading in futures of foodstuffs: pork, beef, oats, and most significantly for Norris, wheat. Speculators could gamble on abstract future estimations of the price of wheat, as opposed to the physical food crop. These contracts were binding for the production of the wheat at a prearranged future date and price.[44] In the world of the eponymous "pit," the speculator was several times removed from the material products being traded. This was an industry based on the manipulation of markets—often to extreme measures. When a group of "bull" speculators "cornered" a market, they sought to command a controlling amount of the city's supply of one particular item, like wheat; they then might set the price of that commodity and potentially make an immense profit. When these future contracts in wheat came due, anyone responsible for distributing the grain would have nowhere to obtain it but through the bull holding the corner.[45] The true danger in a corner, though, was in its potential economic backlash. Bull investors could be held responsible for prices well beyond those on which they had speculated, and they might lose everything in one crash. The results for farmers were more disastrous; they could lose their livelihoods based on the gambling of distant speculators in cities as far away as Chicago. One of the most famous of such bull speculators during the nineteenth century was Joseph Leitner. He attempted the largest wheat corner in the nation's history at that time. However, he eventually came up against a "bear" investor named Philip Armour, of the Armour Grain Elevator Company of Chicago. He was able to break the Leitner corner in 1898. Ultimately, Leitner failed to complete his corner of the wheat market; instead, he reached the extremes of amassing great wealth and losing it all in the same series of events. Indeed, Armour gained control of Leitner's stocks after the breaking of the corner and his subsequent financial loss.[46] Leitner's story was sensationalized as it occurred, and Norris uses much from these events to guide the plot of *The Pit*.

The wheat-related plot of *The Pit* therefore revolves around a Leitner-esque figure, Curtis Jadwin, and his personal speculation project. Norris describes the effects Jadwin's economic actions have on the speculator, his wife, and the people most directly connected to him. In a similar manner as in *The Octopus*, Norris again establishes the significance of wheat over the course of the novel. *The Pit* is based in economics more directly than *The Octopus*, though, so Norris intersperses scenes of the physical form of wheat into the plot so his main characters—and the reader—remember its material significance. In scenes in which wheat is discussed, its power is appreciable. Even the physical board at the Board of Trade demonstrates the significance of wheat: "the young man chalked up cabalistic, and almost illegible figures under columns headed by initials of certain stocks and bonds, or by the words 'Pork,' 'Oats,' or, larger than all the others, 'May Wheat'" (*Pi*, 82). Wheat is described as "a primeval energy, blood-brother of the earthquake and glacier, raging and wrathful that its power should be braved by some pinch of human spawn that dared raise barriers across its courses" (*Pi*, 80). There is a tone of foreboding in Norris's language, as Curtis Jadwin is recognizable as the "human spawn" daring to challenge wheat's natural courses; wheat is already given a degree of agency. When Curtis attempts to manipulate it for his own purposes, the wheat moves, controls aspects of its own fate, and accomplishes its mission while crushing those attempting to subvert it—like Curtis himself.[47]

Norris presents his novel's theme—that the exploitation of the global wheat trade is dangerous—through the character of a reformed speculator named Charles Cressler, who explains one potential consequence of Jadwin's acts. Cressler warns Laura Jadwin of the dangers in treating wheat like a speculative commodity as opposed to the material foodstuff in its most basic form, presenting an element of foreshadowing in the early part of the novel:

> Those fellows in the Pit don't own the wheat; never even see it. Wouldn't know what to do with it if they had it. They don't care in the least about the grain. But there are thousands upon thousands of farmers out here in Iowa and Kansas or Dakota who do, and hundreds of thousands of poor devils in Europe who care even more than the farmer. I mean the fellows who raise the grain, and the other fellows who eat it. It's life or death for either of them. And right between those two comes the Chicago speculator, who raises or lowers the price out of all reason, for the benefit of his pocket. . . . Think of it, the food of hundreds and hundreds of thousands of people just at the mercy of a few men down there on the Board of Trade. (*Pi*, 129)

In this speech Cressler puts a voice to the injustice inherent in speculating in national and global wheat markets and in economic expansion in general. Farmers are exploited for the benefit of the speculator's wealth, wheat is manipulated "out of all reason" to the detriment of the masses, and the farmers as well as the "fellows who eat" alike are fighting "life or death" for their wheat-based livelihood. This lack of concern for the wheat and for the people concerned with its production demonstrates an aspect of the market that angers Cressler. Laura understands his valuation of the market and names it "gambling," a morally suspect activity (*Pi*, 128). Through Cressler, Norris explains both his hopes for the ideal use of wheat to feed the hungry, and the dangers behind a form of market speculation that would exploit such a need. Again, if wheat represents Norris's hopes for a sustainable form of U.S. expansion, then the market—and the people trying to maneuver within it—endangers wheat producers both nationally and internationally vis-à-vis an unsustainable agri-expansion.

Laura Jadwin also faces her connection to her husband's wheat corner as she becomes disillusioned with her life and with her husband's obsession with the wheat market. Wheat appears peripherally in a scene in which Laura meditates upon her life while watching ships laden with the grain pass by the windows of her palatial home: "She could see far out over Lake Michigan, and watch the procession of great lake steamers, from Milwaukee, far-distant Duluth, and the Sault Sainte Marie—the famous 'Soo'—defiling majestically past, making for the mouth of the river, laden to the water's edge with whole harvests of wheat" (*Pi*, 210). In this scene Norris sketches his entire epic: wheat streams in from farms all over the nation, to be traded in Chicago and then to journey to globally expanding markets. It fills the ships "to the water's edge," almost overflowing in abundance. Meanwhile, this scene also demonstrates wheat's importance to the secondary plot of the novel, Laura's trajectory as a heroic character. Wheat plays a prominent role in her personal drama, so much so that it invades the landscape of her otherwise luxurious life. Also, the wheat is being transported to the Chicago grain elevators from the wheat fields of California and the Midwest. This move connects *The Pit* to the end of *The Octopus*, and Laura to the "Relief Committee" women of San Francisco, who send ships filled with wheat to India; the domestic once more combines with the national project.[48] Laura has cooperated with her husband's drive for economic domination and must presumably share in his foreshadowed downfall. In passages like this one, the physicality of the wheat hints at the agency it will gain as it moves and influences characters throughout the novel.[49]

At the pit the physicality of the wheat is emphasized further as pigeons feed on discarded samples of the grain on the floor. The wheat enters the primary stage of the novel's drama as pigeons eat what would normally be considered the detritus of the human actors above. At the end of one scene, Norris depicts, "immediately in front of the entrance to the Board of Trade, a group of pigeons, garnet-eyed, trim, with coral-coloured feet and iridescent breasts, strutted and fluttered, pecking at the handfuls of wheat that a porter threw them from the windows of the floor of the Board" (*Pi*, 264–65). These pigeons are unconcerned that people have made and lost millions of dollars on that site. They alternately represent the natural world amorally distanced from the human drama and the lives of the characters themselves with their narrow focus thrown into relief. Yet, in another scene a group of pigeons become a foreboding plot device. After Cressler feeds the birds at the window with samples of wheat, he notes, "Hullo, hullo—yes, they know me all right. Especially that red and white hen. She's got a lame wing since yesterday, and if I don't watch, the others would drive her off. The pouter brute yonder, for instance. He's a regular pirate. Wants all the wheat himself" (*Pi*, 270). By this point the pigeons have become symbolic of the human drama in the tale, and this is particularly significant as Cressler dies because of his own part concerning the Jadwin corner. The pigeons are shown throughout the novel as liminally related to the U.S. wheat trade. If these pigeons are representations of an aspect of the natural world in a similar way as the wheat, then this scene has an ominous tone regarding their wheat-based relationships with each other.[50]

Norris reminds his readers that as these events are taking place in Chicago, wheat grows in fields across the United States: "It was the Wheat, the Wheat! It was on the move again. From the farms of Illinois and Iowa, from the ranches of Kansas and Nebraska . . . that gigantic world-force, that colossal billow, Nourisher of the Nations, was swelling and advancing" (*Pi*, 373). A scene like this is reminiscent of Norris's lyric passages throughout *The Octopus*, in which the physical grain is seen growing in the fields. This continues Norris's ongoing efforts to make wheat a truly physical character in the text, one that is a "gigantic world-force." Eventually, the wheat defends itself against the speculators who attempt to exploit it. Curtis Jadwin makes his corner, even though he knows that "demand and supply, these were the two great laws the Wheat obeyed," and that he is artificially disturbing that balance (*Pi*, 374). He tries to create a greater demand than supply in order to drive up the price of wheat because he owns controlling shares. At a certain point, though, that elevated price is no longer economically viable. Though wheat, empire-like, desires to grow for its own sake, it remains somewhat aware of a dangerous possibility for an overextension that could ultimately crash the market and any figure directly involved with its manipulation. In this intricate balance of domestic and global wheat markets, a drastic shift can have disastrous consequences.

Curtis Jadwin becomes obsessed with wheat because of his focus on cornering the market. He repeats the refrain "wheat—wheat—wheat, wheat—wheat—wheat" throughout the novel, with more frequency as his physical and mental health deteriorates. Curtis declines into the "human spawn" attempting to dominate this new economic frontier of the "primeval energy" of wheat markets to make his wealth from it. The wrath of the wheat becomes inevitable, then, as Curtis comes to a realization: "For an instant came clear vision. What were these shouting, gesticulating men of the Board of Trade, these brokers, traders, and speculators? It was not these he fought, it was that fatal New Harvest; it was the Wheat; it was—as Gretry had said—the very Earth itself" (*Pi*, 374). In this "clear vision," Curtis realizes that if it comes to a battle against these natural forces, he will not be able to win; instead, he will be beaten and broken by the wheat. Not only does he struggle to manipulate economics and the natural world "out of reason," as Cressler would say, he sees himself as fighting the entire natural world, the "Earth itself." This moment of realization supposes an element of modesty that ultimately allows the wheat to spare his life—contrasted against Behrman's assertion of his masterhood over the wheat that seals his fate in *The Octopus*.

Along the way, however, Curtis manages to ruin his friend, Cressler, and drive him to suicide, before he finally realizes this lesson. Cressler loses a fortune through Curtis's corner, and in his final scene declares, "It looks as though I were busted. I suppose, though, we must all expect to get the knife once in a while—musn't we?" (*Pi*, 331). Cressler admits that he has failed as a speculator, that he is "busted," and he compares himself to the wheat crops themselves that fall under the blade. His life has now been harvested, and his deathblow comes upon realizing that he has been ruined by "Jadwin! You mean J.—Curtis—my friend?" (*Pi*, 331). The next time Laura goes to visit Cressler, she finds him dead by a self-inflicted gunshot wound. Cressler becomes the victim of the force of the market, in this instance, and Curtis is the market's representative who thinks only of his desires while ignoring the farmers and consumers—or even his friends in Chicago. This scene ironically shows Curtis in his moment of victory: "There was no wheat on the Chicago market. He, the great man, the 'Napoleon of La Salle Street,' had it all. He sold it or hoarded it, as suited his pleasure. He dictated the price to those men who must buy it of him to fill their contracts" (*Pi*, 332). Norris's choice in language, describing Curtis as a hoarder, even as a dictator who harms others for his own gain, though, is a severe one. This tone is emphasized by the placement of the scene closely following Cressler's suicide. Cressler has become a victim of Curtis's excessive manipulation, and this action sets in motion the wheat's awakening, creating a situation in which the wheat must retaliate against Curtis to restore balance between economics and nature.

Therefore, in the climax of the novel, Curtis is symbolically drowned in an excess of wheat as Behrman is literally drowned in *The Octopus*. Curtis, a likable person who manages to challenge the forces of nature for the sake of wealth accumulation, if ultimately futilely, survives his final battle against the wheat, unlike the loathsome Behrman. Nevertheless, he must be punished for his exploitation of the natural world. Curtis realizes, "The Wheat had broken from his control" (*Pi*, 392). He is buffeted by a series of natural disaster descriptors: "The avalanche, the undiked Ocean of the Wheat, leaping to the lash of the hurricane, struck him fairly in the face. . . . Blind and insensate, Jadwin strove against the torrent of the Wheat" (*Pi*, 392). He is knocked "insensate" and "blind," the clear loser against the "Ocean of the Wheat." However, he remains a "him" throughout this scene, never becoming an "it" as Behrman does, because Curtis is ultimately a sympathetic character and tragic hero of the novel. Thus, the wheat allows Curtis to live. Though the actual events in this scene involve nothing more physical than a busy day on the trading floor, Norris's language makes wheat a more direct presence in the room.

Beaten by the world force of wheat, Laura and Curtis Jadwin are forced to leave Chicago. In the final scene of the novel, Laura looks up once more at the gothic building that houses the Chicago Board of Trade. Like the menacing railroad in *The Octopus*, this physical representation of agri-expansion in the form of the U.S. wheat market is rich with negative imagery: "the pile of the Board of Trade building, black, monolithic, crouching on its foundations like a monstrous sphinx with blind eyes, silent, grave" (*Pi*, 421). At the story's resolution, Laura returns to her role as the novel's moral center; she judges the market to be a sign of immoral speculation on basic foodstuffs. She goes further as she considers that the true purpose of wheat is simply to feed people. She wonders at the immorality of interfering with something as vital as access to basic foodstuffs and comes to understand the corrective force of the wheat in the novel's climax. She asks, "This huge resistless Nourisher of the Nations—why was it that it could not reach the People, could not fulfil its destiny, unmarred by all this suffering, unattended by all this misery?" (*Pi*, 420). Laura has firsthand experience with the "suffering" that comes from attempting to manipulate a human necessity out of greed. Having gained this wisdom, she is able to voice one of Norris's ultimate themes. It is wrong for people to keep the wheat from its place of providing food for the hungry, and attempts to do so eventually bring about a corrective action from the wheat itself. Wheat, as a part of the larger cycle of nature, is greater than human institutions like economics or agri-expansion and effectively counters them.

Though capitalism may appear inevitable, it does not excuse the exploitation that can occur, and in fact does occur, within its system. Curtis becomes enmeshed within the institution of the Board of Trade and fails to recognize the natural laws of wheat instead of the speculation of his corner. Curtis is thus responsible for his actions in the name of the Chicago Board of Trade and capitalism in general. At some point he must consider the land, the wheat, and the people most directly involved in its production; that he fails to do so causes his own destruction. In *The Pit* the wheat trade ultimately depends on the natural world, the creative force itself.[51] Norris privileges nature in his novel of markets and corners. While he never argues against capitalism or economic imperialism outright, he shows explicitly the dangers of the excessive manipulation of economic laws. Economics and nature vie for legitimacy throughout the novel. In this way the reader can understand how *The Pit* is part of Norris's epic, even though the grain does not appear as frequently in this text as it did in the earlier work. The fact that "nature" defeats the agent of economics shows Norris's text to be an early eco-criticism of the agri-expansion of the twentieth century, and wheat remains the world force with the ability to correct an exploitative system.

CONCLUSION: A WOLFISH FORCE

At the time of his death in 1902, Norris was in the process of buying a ranch north of the Santa Anita Ranch, where he had conducted his research for *The Octopus*. He named his vacation property Quien Sabe, after Annixter's ranch in that novel. Though he had been looking forward to spending time there, Norris died before he had a chance to really get to know his new home. In a letter to a friend, he wrote, "I can shoot deer from my front windows. The quails are a pest. There's a trout stream just around the corner. We have the Stevensons for near neighbors [referring to Robert Louis Stevenson's widow, Fanny]. This beats a New York apartment."[52] The vision of an outdoorsy, farming lifestyle appealed to Norris enough that he tried to create a life for himself along the lines of what he had experienced at Santa Anita Ranch. In this way he follows in the gentleman farmer footsteps of Herman Melville from half a century earlier in his home at Arrowhead, discussed in chapter 1. Norris too had become enamored with a rural farming lifestyle.

In his preface to *The Pit*, Norris describes his idea for a third volume, *The Wolf*, to "probably have for its pivotal episode the relieving of a famine in an Old World community" (*Pi*, ii). For Norris the arc of wheat was to turn ultimately east toward Europe. Presumably, this novel would once again have involved a naturalist system of control (the eponymous "wolf") that would have stood in the way of wheat being properly distributed. In both *The Octopus* and *The Pit*, several characters remark upon the incongruity of an overabundance of wheat and people starving locally and globally. Perhaps this would have also been the focus of *The Wolf*. Though merely speculation, it is possible that the later work would have once again shown the natural world force of wheat as it confronted exploitative human forces.[53] Many of Norris's themes and structures in his epic of the wheat are explainable through the genre of literary naturalism. His naturalism, though, is ultimately centered in nature itself—and the wheat becomes his master symbol, one aspect of the fortune of U.S. agricultural dominance in the aftermath of the Spanish-American War. While Norris has been described as an apologist for U.S. imperialism, his descriptions of the curative force of wheat against unbridled greed show an ambiguity to his feelings about U.S. agri-expansion. Wheat becomes "a concrete symbol of man's relationship to nature," according to Donald Pizer.[54] Norris has managed to effectively connect the lives of wheat growers and consumers globally through the first two volumes of his epic— making his unfinished trilogy itself a powerful statement about U.S. agri-expansion and the natural world.[55] As a symbol of this relationship, wheat restores balance once U.S. capitalism becomes unsustainable. People like S. Behrman and Curtis Jadwin degenerate when they lose respect for important aspects of nature, and Norris wants his readers to take note of their fate.[56]

Fruits of Globalization

In *Beyond the Fruited Plain*, I focus on agriculture through the crops of wheat, sugar, oranges, apples, and beans and through the husbandry of cattle. I argue that the choices made by farmers and reformers during the nineteenth century have had a direct impact on the monoculture, agribusiness, and destructive models of farming seen in the twenty-first century. Bill McKibben observes that in the 1820s the average U.S. farmer worked eighty-hour weeks and subsisted on a diet of bread and milk, earning an average of $1,500 (in current U.S. dollars) per year, "the current African average."[1] The expansion of agriculture relieved many burdens in the lives of U.S. families, but it also created a wave of concern and calls for reform as early as the mid-nineteenth century. Expansion has prevailed, and by the twenty-first century, the crops discussed have become globally dominant. Wheat fed 35 percent of the world's population in the year 2000; in 2001 the United States produced 2.6 billion bushels of the grain, 1.1 billion of which were exported. The nation dominates in wheat production, with Kansas being the greatest producer. Sugar is currently the world's primary sweetener, having displaced fruit juices, honey, and maple sugar. In the year 2000, the United States produced 60 percent of its sugar domestically, relying on imported sugar to make up the difference. Planting and harvesting of sugar remains labor intensive and largely manual. At the same time, oranges, and citrus in general, received an enormous boost in the twentieth century after the discovery of vitamin C; California and Florida orange growers heavily advertised orange juice as a health drink, with immediate and lasting success. In 2002 the United States was second only to Brazil in terms of overall citrus production, around two-thirds of which came from Florida. U.S. Americans drank 4.7 gallons of orange juice per capita in 2003. Apple growers also took advantage of medicinal claims to promote consumption, with a successful "apple a day" advertising campaign. The Red Delicious became the most popular apple in the world by the mid-twentieth century. By the twenty-first century, tastes have changed, and the Red Delicious is being challenged by varieties like Granny Smith, Fuji, Yellow Delicious, and Gala. An adaptable species, thirty-five U.S. states grow apples, the greatest quantities being grown in Washington, New York, Michigan, California, Pennsylvania, and Virginia. Other regional staples, like baked beans and huckleberries from the north-eastern United States, have remained steady, if not dominant, crops. Finally, the dairy industry experienced a massive expansion through the twentieth century following the scientific discovery of calcium and reports of its healthfulness. Europe is the world's leading producer of dairy; in the United States, California became the leading state in 1993, besting Wisconsin. These representative crops, as well as the authors whose work focuses on them, continue to be significant in discussions of twenty-first-century agriculture.[2]

In 1901 John D. Rockefeller founded the Rockefeller Institute of Medical Research to focus specifically on "scientific agriculture," following in the tradition of the land-grant college system, the Grange movement, and other nineteenth-century agricultural reform programs. The Rockefeller Institute helped fund research for maize experiments in Mexico in 1941.[3] This led to the 1957 Rockefeller Foundation "maize improvement scheme" in India, which expanded to the Inter-Asian Corn Program in 1967.[4] These experiments led to what became known as the "green revolution" of the twentieth century. Organizations like the Rockefeller Foundation, the U.S. Agency for International Development (USAID), and the World Bank turned to agricultural developments in science and technology to provide higher yield crops throughout the world, particularly cereal crops like corn, rice, and wheat. They succeeded in vastly increasing the overall world food supply. However, there have been complications in such agricultural ventures, such as in global food aid. Politics, based to a large extent on Cold War competition, played a large part in determining what kinds of food aid were given to certain countries. By 1971 the director of the Ford Foundation's agricultural program, Lowell Harding, noticed, "The green revolution is exerting a destabilizing influence on traditional social and political institutions. . . . Increased output is not necessarily associated with positive social change."[5] Further, by the 1990s reformers like Vandana Shiva were calling the green revolution a categorical failure in areas like the Punjab region of India, where instead of giving people cheap food, it cost the poor disproportionally by creating an increased need for agricultural inputs like pesticides, excessive irrigation, and the repeated purchase of so-called miracle seeds.[6] The green revolution managed to produce a greater quantity but not quality of food, and the globally hungry largely have remained underfed. Many of the issues written about during the revolution in agriculture during the nineteenth century remain in the twenty-first century—the two eras are connected through their agri-expansion.

Agri-expansion has also bridged critical writings from both periods. Discussions about food production exploded in the late twentieth and early twenty-first centuries. John McPhee's *Oranges* (1967) focuses on Florida, and he discusses Harriet Beecher Stowe's orange grove there. Michael Pollan references Henry David Thoreau's famous *Walden* experiment in *Second Nature* (1991) and his work with apples in *Botany of Desire* (2001). In 2010 Andrew Beahrs wrote about Mark Twain's diet in *Twain's Feast*, following his culinary trail across the country. Moreover, muckrakers continue to challenge abuses in food production, looking specifically at the production and consumption of large-scale cereal crops and animal products. I want to conclude my study of nineteenth-century literary agri-reformers, therefore, with a few examples of food production and consumption experiments in the twenty-first century, as writers continue to challenge the ongoing development of agri-expansion. Anna Lowenhaupt Tsing discusses small-scale harvesting in Borneo, Bill McKibben looks at sustainable agriculture in Bangladesh, and Ruth

Ozeki imagines a radical agricultural movement in her novel, *All Over Creation* (2003). In the twenty-first century, we must learn from the earlier eras, hopefully applying their lessons to our own experience with agri-globalization; meanwhile, we must use our current moment to further understand the cultural movements from the nineteenth century.

In the late twentieth century, Anna Lowenhaupt Tsing described the Meratus Dayaks of the "small swidden fields" and mountain regions of Borneo.[7] These farmers demonstrate a relationship with the forest at once cultural, agricultural, and sustainable. Apparent "hillbillies," the Meratus are in fact part of the legacy of imperialism; they struggle to maintain their way of life in the midst of agricultural globalization. In their inhabitation of the Meratus Mountains, they demonstrate a relationship with the forest more functional than the artificial preservation of land promoted by conservationists or the abuses of land used in modern agriculture (*F*, 174). The Agrarian Law of 1871 divided Borneo into "native land and land for European exploitation," placing the Meratus in a liminal "gap" between native use and imperialism (*F*, 195). Anything deemed European-usable land was exploited for mining, plantation farming, and other economic projects. Only lands deemed unfit for such exploitation were left to the native population. There was an organizational assumption that these wild lands were completely uninhabited—even uninhabitable—by humans; however, these forest spaces were far from being either wild or empty. Even the environmentalists of the present fail to account for communities like the Meratus, who in fact make their homes in these forests and swidden fields and have been living in such a gap since the nineteenth century. Tsing shows that the Meratus harvest their plants communally, live simply off that harvest, and manage to supplement their income by trading surplus crops. This localized knowledge of the plants and animals in one particular bioregion gives the Meratus community a market niche unavailable to multinational agribusinesses, and in this way they have managed to survive encroaching globalization. The Meratus work to maintain their hybrid, seemingly deviant, lifestyle against the forces of both agribusinesses focused on expansion, as well as the conservation organizations attempting to entirely remove the human element from the space.

Instead of considering certain forests as cordoned off, the people of the Meratus region engage with the species around them as part of a sustainable economy. The connection between the Meratus people and the nonhuman species living in the same forest is shown in the pyramid of relationships between the honeybees, the Mangaris trees that house the bees, and the human harvesters of these species (*F*, 181). The Meratus have an economic connection to the honeybees and correspondingly to the Mangaris trees through the harvesting and selling of the honey produced. They cultivate the Mangaris trees so honeybees will choose this particular forest as opposed to elsewhere. This allows the Meratus to find an additional dietary and economic resource. Thus, the ownership of a Mangaris tree and cultivation of the honey grown within it is seen as both a responsibility and an investment in a sustainable form of harvesting: "Most commonly, a man claims a tree by being the first to clean it, or if the tree has been abandoned by other claimants, by reviving its cleaning. He passes this claim to his children as long as they are active in maintaining the tree as a honey tree" (*F*, 181). For the Meratus, ownership is based upon a relationship of engagement; it must be earned and maintained. For their economic and dietary benefit, they protect the habitat of these honeybees from other exploiters who view the taller Mangaris trees as single-use investments, to be cut down and replaced with smaller, faster-growing brush that can grow to logging height more quickly. In this scenario the honeybees would be forced to leave the forest. To prevent that, the Meratus protect the trees from loggers and thereby maintain the habitat for the productive honeybees, and "each species comes to depend on it [the arrangement]" (*F*, 182). The relationship between farmer, honeybee, and Mangaris tree, then, benefits the trees and the honeybees as well as the harvesters themselves.

In addition, the Meratus have their own "cash crop" industry in Borneo. The durian fruit is the most popular fruit of that region, as well as a symbolic crop of a localization effort, much like Thoreau's beans—and opposed to Norris's global wheat. Through the harvesting of the durian fruit, Tsing shows another instance in which the Meratus work with other species inhabiting the same forest, as opposed to the Western model of agriculture that would involve clearing the forest for cultivated fields (*F*, 178). The Meratus tend and harvest their trees, keep away only the harmful weeds, and allow beneficial animals to graze there and to fertilize the trees. Tsing writes, "Through a combination of distributing, planting, tending, and saving trees, Meratus increase the durian population of the forest" (*F*, 179). This method, by increasing the numbers of the cultivated fruit, therefore works. Furthermore, the Meratus logic of ownership of the durian trees, along with any of the trees' descendants, is passed down through families based on maintenance. If onetime owners "leave the area and stop paying enough attention to the tree to know its uneven fruiting schedule," another member of the community can take over the rights to that tree and its harvest (*F*, 179). In this case legal ownership transfers to the new steward of the tree. Ownership requires an undeviating connection with the tree—failing in that relationship voids possession in a way that would not exist in the capitalist structure of the global agriculture that threatens the Meratus.

To be sure, Tsing also shows the flaws in the Meratus dietary and economic plan; they are not an overly romanticized society. At times they have overharvested, drawn by the higher returns from foods labeled "organic," for example; they have sold inferior plants to buyers who lack the local knowledge required to appreciate the difference; and they have come to rely on global market fluctuations in their harvesting. On the whole, though, Tsing shows that the Meratus are an example of a viable community that has managed to survive agri-expansion in Borneo. The Meratus culture has succeeded in the way the reformists from *Beyond the Fruited Plain* hoped for, if perhaps not in a manner equivalent to the average Western consumer's concept of success. Tsing, an outsider studying their culture but never quite within it, carefully expresses her respect for the ability of the Meratus to withstand encroaching globalization. In the end, according to Tsing, "the forest, whether young or old, is never a homogenous 'wild' place; it is a finely differentiated set of simultaneously social and natural locations" (*F*, 193). Perhaps the most important aspect of the adaptation of the Meratus to agricultural globalization is the fact that they are not truly "wild" but rather a part of Borneo's society. Neither the businesses nor the conservation organizations know what to do with them. Tsing, however, has an idea; she believes that the Meratus are a useful example of a sustainable agricultural community.

In another example of a viable local agricultural movement competing against globalization, Bill McKibben cites the revitalizing economy in rural Bangladesh. The farming village of Gorasin has joined the nation's "Nayakrishi Andolon (or New Farming) movement" (DE, 200). Even in this rural village, global issues of pollution and agri-expansion had become an unwanted presence. Locals noted that cows had been dying from eating the grass, people were getting into conflicts over reduced resources, and the women were getting rashes and "gastric trouble" from drawing water from the well (DE, 200). The people of Gorasin decided to become part of the Nayakrishi movement coordinated by "the Center for Development Alternatives (known by its Bengali acronym, UBINIG), a Dhaka-based organization" (DE, 201). Now, Gorasin is "one of several organic oases" in the farming regions of Bangladesh (DE, 200). The Nayakrishi component of UBINIG is designed to help rural farming communities support themselves through organics without having to participate in the more destructive aspects of global agribusiness. One of UBINIG's goals is in the protection of local species through an elaborate—locally maintained—seed bank. McKibben describes the warehouse, where "25 varieties of papaya were growing, along with 112 varieties of jackfruit, all catalogued by the farmers by taste, size, color, season, habitat. Wicker baskets and clay pots in a darkened shed contained 300 varieties of local rice, 20 kinds of bitter gourd, 84 varieties of local beans" (DE, 201). The harvesting and cataloguing of local seeds has become a communal effort as opposed to a commodity-based import controlled by corporations. In addition, the organization returns the duty of cataloguing and distributing seeds to the women of the community, as opposed to corporate seed distributers. This move makes a strong feminist statement by returning to women of rural farming communities like Gorasin the status that they had lost through agri-expansion, a loss that had in many cases made the women feel redundant and like "a burden" on their villages (*DE*, 202). McKibben uses economics to view the Nayakrishi as an organic movement that is trying to find its own "gap" in global agri-expansion.

McKibben begins his description of the people of Gorasin by introducing their local agriculture: "sesame seed plants, loofah sponge gourds, eggplants, sugarcane, bamboo. Onions, pulses, all manner of local leafy greens. All grown without pesticides, without fertilizer, and without seed imported from the laboratories of the West" (*DE*, 200). The list of foods grown is placed directly against its severed connection to large-scale Western agriculture. McKibben introduces the villagers' concept of their identity—both before and since the adoption of Nayakrishi. One villager says, "We Bengalis are made of rice and fish. . . . Since we've started organic farming, the fish are now healthier and more plentiful" (*DE*, 200–201). For the villagers the threat to their local identity from global agri-expansion was a rallying point. The farmers of Gorasin communicate a sense of pride about their choice in organic agriculture through the New Farming Movement: "The minute you say 'Nayakrishi' . . . people will pay more, because they know they're saving on health care" (*DE*, 201). The quality of the food and the quality of health, then, are intimately connected, and the Gorasin have adapted their identity to include the Nayakrishi movement. As identity is linked to culture, McKibben concludes his discussion of the Gorasin villagers with a description of such a cultural moment. In an idyllic evening scene in which people are talking and laughing as children play nearby and everyone eats locally harvested bananas, a villager begins to sing. Translated, he sings, "Food from Nayakrishi is so much better. No longer do I eat the poisons. Why should I eat that life-destroying stuff? Bangladesh will come to an end, unless you turn to Nayakrishi. If you use organic fertilizer, the Almighty will be behind you, and you'll be having no more gastric problems" (*DE*, 202). McKibben carefully notes the rhetorical question in the song, the ultimatums issued, and the appeal to "the Almighty" on behalf of organic agriculture. This is not a light song, designed for humorous purposes, yet the mood of the evening is decidedly fun. This song is clearly a familiar one for the rest of the community, and they clap rhythmically to the "reedy" tune. Furthermore, the song places "the Almighty" in the same sentence as "gastric problems," a move that suggests an element of levity within the work. As this moment shows, then, the people of Gorasin are forming a positive new cultural identity involving shared songs around their organic food production.

This organic "New Farming" community-involved experiment in rural Bangladesh would clearly not appeal to everyone in the West, as the people of Gorasin live decidedly below the poverty level for Western standards. McKibben concludes, "It's easy to romanticize happy village life. (Just as it's easy to romanticize 'modern agriculture' . . .) What's important is simply to realize that places like Gorasin represent another data point, one well outside a conventional view of the world" (*DE*, 202). McKibben uses the Gorasin as an example of a viable alternative to the Western paradigm. While he returns to his U.S. home and capitalist economy after his visit to Gorasin, demonstrating his ultimate loyalty to the Western lifestyle, his point is that such examples of functioning alternatives to global agri-expansion are necessary models to examine even in the United States. Perhaps there is something in the Nayakrishi model that the West—especially the United States—can apply in its own agriculture, where there is a similar desire for healthy foods, a reduction in the use of pesticides, and a more sustainable living wage for farmers.

Ruth Ozeki looks for such alternative agricultural communities in the United States in her satiric novel on genetically modified (GM) crops and radical organic activists, *All Over Creation*. She follows in the muck-raking tradition of Upton Sinclair, doing work that hits U.S. citizens in their stomachs and that can hopefully change U.S. agri-expansion through regulation and greater consumer involvement. Ozeki's thinly veiled satire follows the history of Monsanto's NewLeaf potato, "the first bioengineered Bt crop plant to be marketed."[8] Indeed, the actual story of "NewLeaf" potatoes containing the Bt gene marketed and distributed by Monsanto to some extent was decided in 2001, when Frito-Lay and McDonald's refused to invest in Monsanto's potatoes out of fear of consumer reaction.⁹ In her fictionalized account, Ozeki renames the potato NuLife and the company Cynaco, and she locates her story in the small town of Liberty Falls, Idaho. Most interestingly, she introduces the Seeds of Resistance, an anti-GM organic activist group that educates people about the dangers of GM foods, performing "Guerrilla gardening. Defiance farming. Radical acts of cultivation."¹⁰ Indeed, at one point a member holds a banner that reads, "RESISTANCE IS FERTILE" (AC, 416). Through these colorfully imagined examples, Ozeki is able to imagine an extreme U.S.-based activist group that educates consumers. Her Seeds are a necessary step in her own reform work against agri-expansion.

Ozeki's eco-warriors wander the Idaho landscape in a Winnebago named "Spudnick" that runs on biodiesel fuel. Going beyond the relatively safe consumer activity of "buying organic," the Seeds cause a disturbance in small-town grocery stores where they hand out fliers about the dangers of GM potatoes, they apply their own biohazard stickers to packaged potato goods in refrigerator aisles (their labels read: "DANGER! BIOHAZARD! THESE POTATOES MAY CONTAIN A GENETICALLY ENGINEERED PESTICIDE!" underneath an image of a potato overlaid with skull and crossbones [AC, 150]), and they address the public—specifically mothers and children—about the dangers of GM foods while dressed in homemade Mr. Potato Head or dairy cow costumes. In one case they are detained but ultimately not charged for disrupting the peace because their fellow shoppers refuse to press charges, and ultimately, even the store manager refrains from going against public opinion. Meanwhile, in one of their "network of cells" in a house in Oakland, California, the Seeds and their associates run a different series of radical actions. They have "bicycle posses" that trespass into neighborhood yards to plant vegetable gardens unbeknownst to the owners of those yards, they "reclaim"—that is, steal—straw bales from a nearby racetrack for their mulch, and they throw "seed bombs" of native plants over the fences of the well-manicured lawns of government and corporate headquarters—technically vandalism but they call it "vegetative anarchy" (AC, 257). Ozeki describes a nighttime planting operation in which members pull up sod in the medians of busy streets and replace it with trees: peach, pear, persimmon, nut, and fig. As Ozeki writes, "In a few years, they'd be bearing fruit. Food for the people, the leader explained. They were liberating traffic strips and other public land sites across the city. As long as they were neat, the city workers never noticed. Mostly they just mowed right around the trees" (*AC*, 256). These actions are extreme, but harmless, even hopeful and potentially necessary in an environment where a multinational agricultural corporation like Monsanto is the primary enemy and the food itself becomes the symbolic battlefield.

In one of their more dramatic actions, the Seeds throw a tofu cream pie (made from genetically modified soybeans) in the face of the CEO of Cynaco Corporation. A member of the "Pastry Platoon," who is part of the larger "Dessert Storm," dresses once again in a Mr. Potato Head costume in order to give this CEO the ultimate slapstick judgment. This operation, though, is more elaborate than a boy throwing a pie in someone's face. In addition to the pie-throwing event itself, connected protesters hand out pamphlets of "a recent exposé on Cynaco" and heckle the CEO with questions about the company's relationship with lobbyists and lack of evidence about the healthfulness of GM crops, asking ultimately, "Is it Cynaco's long-term policy to mine Third World genetic resources, engage in globalized biopiracy, and rob developing countries of their ability to produce food independently and sustainably" (*AC*, 258–59). These are some of the issues facing contemporary farmers like the Meratus Dayaks of Borneo and the Nayakrishi farmers of Bangladesh. Furthermore, employing a network of committed activists in "sympathizer copy shops and Internet cafés throughout the city," the Seeds manage a sophisticated publicity campaign following this action (*AC*, 259). In the hours and days following this seemingly insignificant, frankly silly, feat against the CEO of Cynaco, the group receives e-mails telling of press coverage in local papers, as well as international coverage from Britain and India. The Seeds are described as a successful global community of guerrilla activists working against multinational agricultural corporations.

After showing the hardships Idaho farmers are enduring for the profit of a very few corporations—in this case, Cynaco—Ozeki gives voice to an instance of hopeful farming praxis in the form of her Seeds. At the same time, she keeps her characters human, and therefore flawed. Her descriptions of a pornography site run by the group, multiple arrests, and the inevitable tragedy that occurs at the climax of the novel show that the radical actions of the Seeds may not be viable to emulate in their fullest extent. However, Ozeki also describes practical actions that the average U.S. consumer could apply in her or his own life. In a large measure, her Seeds are ultimately successful in their guerrilla warfare against Cynaco's introduction of the GM potato, and fiction follows fact as Cynaco stops distributing their NuLife potatoes by the end of the novel. Ozeki's final image regarding the Seeds shows, however, that their story cannot end there. Though Cynaco "terminates" its line of NuLife potatoes in the United States, it decides instead to target "Asia and the Third World" with the same GM potato, in a scene that recalls Norris's final image of the ship filled with U.S. surplus wheat being sent on a famine relief mission to India (*AC*, 344). Thus, the actions of Ozeki's Seeds of Resistance cannot stop at the national level; they must continue to be a global presence against multinational agricultural corporations. At the end of the novel, Ozeki shows the activists leaving for Seattle to engage in a World Trade Organization–like global economic conference; their battle against agri-expansion continues.

These examples of small-scale agricultural communities like the Meratus Dayaks, the Nayakrishi organic farmers of Bangladesh, and even the fictional U.S.-based Seeds of Resistance show how it is possible to survive and fight against increasing agri-globalization represented by corporations like Monsanto. To do so, farmers must live almost entirely without the products of capitalism; however, once they have made that sacrifice, they can maintain their lives on remarkably little. In Bourdieu's terms of diet as class marker, cultures like the Meratus and the Gorasin are on the opposite side of the spectrum from the Seeds and their audience in the United States—or of the agricultural reformers discussed elsewhere in *Beyond the Fruited Plain*. However, they are a useful example of an alternative farming life that is ultimately more sustainable than current Western—especially U.S.—practices. As Northrup Frye says, "Literature does not reflect life, but it doesn't escape or withdraw from life either: it swallows it."[11] Literature is a productive tool in its ability to engage in social circumstances, even in terms of policy itself. The authors I examine throughout *Beyond the Fruited Plain* were already responding to a world growing globally capitalistic in the nineteenth century. This has continued to be the subject of heated debates and calls for reform into the twenty-first century. The two periods, it stands to reason, are intimately connected through the revolutionary industrialization of major goods—specifically foodstuffs. Ideally, if we can recognize common themes in the agri-expansion of the nineteenth and twenty-first centuries, this process may not have to be repeated into the future.

NOTES

ABBREVIATIONS

A: *The Autobiography of Mark Twain* (Mark Twain)

AC: *All Over Creation* (Ruth Ozeki)

C: *Correspondence* (Herman Melville)

D: "A Deal in Wheat" (Frank Norris)

DE: *Deep Economy: The Wealth of Communities and the Durable Future* (Bill McKibben)

Ex: *Excursions* (Henry David Thoreau)

F: *Friction* (Anna Lowenhaupt Tsing)

FE: *Following the Equator and Anti-Imperialist Essays* (Mark Twain)

HHP: *House and Home Papers* (Harriet Beecher Stowe)

LH: *Mark Twain's Letters from Hawaii* (Mark Twain)

LM: *Life on the Mississippi* (Mark Twain)

O: *Omoo: A Narrative of Adventures in the South Seas* (Herman Melville)

Oc: *The Octopus: A Story of California* (Frank Norris)

OF: *Oldtown Folks* (Harriet Beecher Stowe)

P: *Pierre; or, The Ambiguities* (Herman Melville)

Pi: *The Pit: A Story of Chicago* (Frank Norris)

PL: *Palmetto Leaves* (Harriet Beecher Stowe)

PT: *The Piazza Tales and Other Prose Pieces 1839–1860* (Herman Melville)

T: *Typee: A Peep at Polynesian Life* (Herman Melville)

UTC: *The Annotated Uncle Tom's Cabin* (Harriet Beecher Stowe)

W: *Walden* (Henry David Thoreau)

WF: *Wild Fruits* (Henry David Thoreau)

INTRODUCTION

1. Washington, "National Board of Agriculture," 35.

2. Washington, "National Board of Agriculture," 35.

3. Jefferson, *Memoirs, Correspondence, and Miscellanies,* 21.

4. While Washington and Jefferson owned plantations in Virginia, other founding fathers worked northern farms. John Adams, as well as his son, John Quincy Adams, owned a smaller farm in Massachusetts and documented the management of their land in personal diaries. For more information about the connection between food and the founding fathers, see DeWitt, *Founding Foodies.*

5. See also Gigante, *Taste*; Korsmeyer, *Making Sense of Taste*; and Morton, *Poetics of Spice.*

6. For example, William Conlogue reads agricultural literature of the nineteenth century as a series of questions: "How have we been at work in the world? How have we enacted on the ground what we think in our heads? What world do we want to create or maintain? How can we do it responsibly?" (*Working the Garden,* 9).

7. Donna R. Gabaccia adds to this discussion by focusing on agricultural industrialization during this period: "For better or worse, American foods have more often been products of American industry than of American kitchens" ("As American as Budweiser?" 175). Janet Flammang adds that this culminated around the turn of the twentieth century as food entered into "a national food marketplace," with U.S. goods like "Gold Medal Flour, Coca-Cola, Van Camp's canned beans" becoming representative of the national cuisine (*Taste of Civilization,* 64).

8. In addition, Malcolm Waters presents his explanatory theorem involving three key aspects of society that are directly involved in globalization—economy, politics, and culture: *"material exchanges localize; political exchanges internationalize; and symbolic exchanges globalize"* (*Globalization,* 9, Waters's italics).

9. Michael Hardt and Antonio Negri write, "When the flesh of the multitude is imprisoned and transformed into the body of global capital, it finds itself both within and against the processes of capitalist globalization" (*Multitude,* 101).

10. Hardt and Negri, *Empire,* 170. In the Constitution itself, Native Americans were elided, African Americans were incorporated physically into the national body under the well-known "three-fifths" rule (171).

11. Steger, *Globalism,* 14.

12. Buell, *Future of Environmental Criticism,* 84–85.

13. Buell, *Writing for an Endangered World,* 3. Also, Buell cites Ulrich Beck's "techno-determinist holism" that "industrial modernization has permanently

destabilized life on earth because technology can no longer control the damage wrought by its own unintended consequences" (*Future of Environmental Criticism*, 90).

14. Expanding this to a global context, Jürgen Osterhammel and Niels P. Peterson describe a European "timber famine" that occurred around the turn of the twentieth century as an event that introduced people to the ideas of limited resources and *Raubwirtschaft*, or the "exploitative and destructive economy" of extractive industries, such as the global sugar or wheat trade (*Globalization*, 83).

15. Goodrich, *Recollections of a Lifetime*, 60.

16. Goodrich, *Recollections of a Lifetime*, 78.

17. Kirkland, *A New Home*, 36.

18. Kirkland, *A New Home*, 36 (Kirkland's italics).

19. Joseph Schafer observes that these theories of agriculture and expansion are interrelated: "The military, political, and diplomatic history of America's territorial development makes a very general framework for her agricultural expansion" (*Social History of American Agriculture*, 2).

20. Osterhammel and Peterson, *Globalization*, 78–79.

21. Root and de Rochemont, *Eating in America*, 154.

22. Osterhammel and Peterson, *Globalization*, 88. They also note that the Philippines became the United States' "first colonial possession outside the Western Hemisphere" (94).

23. Wayne D. Rasmussen's edited collection of agricultural documents highlights some of the advances most noteworthy both during the period he calls the "First American Agricultural Revolution, 1861–1914," as well as in the midst of the U.S. green revolution, the period in which he wrote (*History of American Agriculture*, 103–96).

24. Rasmussen uses the example of the fertilizer industry to show parallel innovations in the nineteenth century and the twentieth: "While it was not until much later that fertilizer changed the entire picture of American agricultural production, the foundations were laid in this early period" (*History of American Agriculture*, 86).

25. Tom Standage discusses the nineteenth-century development of the telegraph as directly comparable to and as revolutionary as the Internet in the twentieth century. Even Samuel Morse's first two telegraphed messages on May 24, 1844, demonstrate the cultural significance of this technological advance. After his Biblical "WHAT HATH GOD WROUGHT," Morse asked the question that would fuel communications from that point on: "HAVE YOU ANY NEWS?" (*Victorian Internet*, 148).

26. Osterhammel and Peterson, *Globalization*, 69–80.

27. Phillips, "Antebellum Agricultural Reform," 802–3.

28. Watson, *Address of Elkanah Watson*, 8.

29. Watson, *Address of Elkanah Watson*, 9.

30. Colman, *Fourth Report*, 14.

31. See Hurt, *American Agriculture*, 117, 216.

32. Emerson, "Farming," in *Essential Writings*, 673.

33. See Sarver, *Uneven Land*, 20–45.

34. Compare this to Emerson's description of farmers in "The American Scholar": "Man is thus metamorphosed into a thing, into many things. The planter, who is Man sent out into the field to gather food, is seldom cheered by any idea of the true dignity of his ministry. He sees his bushel and his cart, and nothing beyond, and sinks into the farmer, instead of Man on the farm" (44).

35. Emerson, *Essential Writings*, 676.

36. Lincoln, "Address before the Wisconsin State Agricultural Society," 143.

37. Fite, *American Farmers*, 1–8.

38. Kelley, *Origin and Progress*, 30–31.

39. See Williams, *Origins of Federal Support*, 1–13.

40. Rasmussen, *History of American Agriculture*, 109. He adds that the Department of Agriculture was "raised to cabinet status in 1889" and traces "the beginnings of the modern science of nutrition" to an 1869 Yale thesis written on the nutritive breakdown of four types of corn: "*Early Dutton Corn . . . The common Yellow Corn . . . King Phillip Corn . . . Stowell's Evergreen Sweet Corn*" (106, 122–23, Rasmussen's italics).

41. See Kiple and Ornelas, *Cambridge World History of Food*, 2:1314.

42. Kathryn Kish Sklar notes that Beecher's domestic manual was "was reprinted nearly every year from 1841 to 1856" (*Catharine Beecher*, 151).

43. William E. Cain writes that of these "the most common were the thirty or more across the country that subscribed to the tenets of the French socialist Charles Fourier" who was also influential with the Brook Farm members ("Henry David Thoreau 1817–1862: A Brief Biography," 26).

44. Smith, *Oxford Companion*, 608.

45. Hawthorne, *Blithedale Romance*, 47.

46. Alcott, "Transcendental Wild Oats," 88.

47. Alcott, "Transcendental Wild Oats," 88.

48. Maura D'Amore notes, "The narrative certainly satirizes the formation of Brook Farm and its eventual dissolution as the product of what we might identify today as bourgeois liberalism, but it also lingers on the initial impulse that led to its formation as a complex desire for intimacy with other humans" ("Hawthorne and the Suburban Romance," 157).

49. Twain is now the author of new best-selling works in three different centuries. Not even Shakespeare has achieved this feat.

50. See Denning, *Mechanic Accents*, and Streeby, *American Sensations*, for more on popular writing of the nineteenth and early twentieth century. Harriet Beecher Stowe has been read as corresponding in the domestic side of U.S. imperialism, though my reading looks at her writing as more of a work of reforming U.S. politics from within that domestic realm.

51. The narrator's reference to the Carolinas can be seen as connecting the "industrial" North with the "agricultural" South well before the result of the Civil War.

1. EXPANDING AGRICULTURE

1. In *Writing for an Endangered World*, Lawrence Buell notes that *Moby-Dick* is based "in and about the moment when the world was coming under the regime of global capitalism" (205). This assessment applies to Melville's land-based writings as well.

2. Williams, *Country and the City*, 2.

3. Marx, *Machine in the Garden*, 10.

4. Marx, *Machine in the Garden*, 284.

5. Because of this need for U.S. goods, national exports ballooned from "$20.2 million in 1790 to $108.3 million in 1807" while even "domestically produced exports more than doubled from $19.9 million to $48.7 million" (Sellers, *Market Revolution*, 22). Charles Sellers adds that "American shipowners' share of American trade climbed from 59 percent to 92 percent, and their earnings from $5.9 million to $42.1 million. These enormous increases financed an almost four-fold jump in imports for domestic consumption" (22).

6. Robertson-Lorant, *Melville*, 44.

7. Sellers, *Market Revolution*, 20–21.

8. Bidwell, "Pioneer Agriculture," 193–96.

9. Robertson-Lorant continues, "Herman liked seeing the horses, cattle, oxen, sheep, swine, and other barnyard animals that filled the village green" (*Melville*, 58).

10. Watson, *Mr. Watson's Address*, 4.

11. Watson, *Mr. Watson's Address*, 9.

12. Melvill, *Address of Thomas Melvill*, 11.

13. Melvill, *Address of Thomas Melvill*, 11.

14. Leyda, *Melville Log*, 63.

15. Leyda, *Melville Log*, 63–64.

16. Leyda, *Melville Log*, 63.

17. Robertson-Lorant writes, "The Panic ruined those heavily in debt, as banks tightened credit drastically, plunging the country into a severe depression that lasted for five years. Numerous banks went under, nine-tenths of the nation's factories closed, and cities could not build almshouses and poorhouses fast enough to house the working-class families who found themselves jobless and out on the street" (*Melville*, 61–62).

18. Quoted in Parker, *Herman Melville*, 1:733 (italics in the original).

19. As their tour was of an official capacity, Melville and Robert had their itinerary published in the local paper, moreover, describing their July 18, 1850, departure. Hershel Parker notes, "On the wagon Herman had improved odd moments by reminding himself of the names of grasses, or learning names of newly introduced varieties, for he listed these on the back flyleaf: Redtop, Ribbon Grass, Finger Grass, Orchard Grass, Hair Grass" (*Herman Melville*, 737).

20. Parker, *Herman Melville*, 737.

21. Melville, *Piazza Tales*, 450 (hereafter cited parenthetically as *PT*).

22. According to Parker, "Published in the Pittsfield *Culturist and Gazette* on 9 October 1850, the report passed for what it was. On 23 October the editor, Stephen Reed, published a lampoon from the 'Bunkum Agricultural Society' signed by 'Z.Q. Factminus, Esq. *Chairman*" (*Herman Melville*, 738).

23. Parker, *Herman Melville*, 736.

24. Melville, *Correspondence*, 173 (hereafter cited parenthetically as *C*).

25. Robertson-Lorant, *Melville*, xvi.

26. Furthermore, Gavin Jones credits Melville with being perhaps unique in his "sustained development of a dynamic, balanced, yet critical response to the contentious cultural questions that always seem to inform debates over socio-economic inequality" (*American Hungers*, 22).

27. Robertson-Lorant, *Melville*, 114. Robertson-Lorant adds, "People in the Typee Valley needed only to reach into the trees or turn over the fertile soil to find ample food" (*Melville*, 109).

28. Melville, *Typee*, 116 (hereafter cited parenthetically as *T*).

29. Melville, *Omoo*, 202 (hereafter cited parenthetically as *O*).

30. John Bryant notes that Melville would call this industry "The Wall Street Spirit" in *The Confidence-Man* (1857) (introduction to *Typee*, xviii).

31. Gollin, "Quondam Sailor and Melville's *Omoo*," 77.

32. Howard Faulkner lists some of the genres into which *Pierre* has been placed: "Gothic, city-romance, domestic, journey of self-discovery, *ekphrastic* (portraits and pillars for statues are relevant symbols), epistolary (letters are sent, though often burned), philosophical, autobiographical" ("Ambiguousnesses," 43).

33. Robertson-Lorant, *Melville*, 304.

34. Howard and Parker, "Historical Note," 366.

35. Summerhill, *Harvest of Dissent*, 32. For an additional history on the anti-rent movement, see Otter, *Melville's Anatomies*, 197.

36. Summerhill, *Harvest of Dissent*, 34.

37. Otter, *Melville's Anatomies*, 197.

38. Melville, *Pierre*, 11 (hereafter cited parenthetically as *P*).

39. Otter, *Melville's Anatomies*, 197. Otter adds, "Melville associates the possession of land with the exploitation of poor whites and Native Americans" (200).

40. Meanwhile, Delly observes that the city "feels not so soft as the green sward," to which Pierre bitterly replies that may be because "the buried hearts of some dead citizens have perhaps come to the surface" (*P*, 230).

41. Kelley, "*Pierre's* Domestic Ambiguities," 96.

42. Melville's fun with names continues. A nineteenth-century "Teamster" was a person who drove a team of horses, etc. So he plays off the title of "Squire" with the labor of being a "teamster" in this name. Moreover, a "colter" was a blade attached to a plow—the Coulters are specifically part of the advancing agricultural field.

43. There have been several explanations as to why Melville would have chosen that year to set his story. Gavin Jones notes that this is the date of Thomas Robert Malthus's publication of *Observations on the Effects of the Corn Laws* (*American Hungers*, 49). David H. Evans observes as well that 1814 is the date of the foundation of the Lowell textile mill, "the first completely integrated textile mill on the continent" ("That Great Leviathan," 322). Both of these events highlight factory and agriculture industrialization and expansion during the period well before the agricultural revolution or the time of the Industrial Revolution in the United States.

44. Schmidt, "Growth of Home and Foreign Markets," 197–209.

45. This history will be useful as well in chapter 5, which examines the representation of the globalization of the U.S. wheat trade at the turn of the twentieth century in Frank Norris's work.

46. The Coulters are figures like those that will eventually lead to U.S. Naturalism in another half century, in the post–Industrial Revolution era. For a more detailed discussion of the issue of food and imperialism during the turn of the twentieth century, see chapter 5.

47. Several critics have seen Blandmour as a satire of a Thoreauvian form of self-reliant, or voluntary, poverty. However, in chapter 2 I show Thoreau's harsh critique of this system through his various attempts to reform food production at the agricultural level.

48. This comparison works for his maple sugar–like wife as well.

49. After witnessing the Coulters' lives, his "normative discourse is rendered speechless," according to Gavin Jones (*American Hungers*, 50).

50. Weinstein, *Literature of Labor*, 87; and Robertson-Lorant, *Melville*, 343.

51. In his study of the seedsman narrator, Graham Thompson writes, "Fine paper is also vital for the protection of an important business interest whose expansion and profitability are enhanced by the coordination of paper and postal technologies" ("'Plain Facts' of Fine Paper," 517).

52. For a discussion of the distribution of seeds through the mail in the nineteenth century, see Henkin, *Postal Age*, 60–61.

53. Winter, "Seeds of Discontent," 17–35.

54. Weinstein, "Melville, Labor, and the Discourses of Reception," 203–23.

55. Jones writes, "Industrialism can, in certain cases, impoverish workers by trapping them in a social position with deleterious consequences for both body and mind" (*American Hungers*, 51).

56. Weinstein, *Literature of Labor*, 87.

57. Earlier in the story, the foreman must bring the narrator's cheeks back to life after he experiences minor frostbite. Like the mythic Actaeon, the narrator feels like he is being torn apart by dogs after seeing something feminine and forbidden.

58. Weinstein, *Literature of Labor*, 103.

59. Melville, *Moby-Dick*, 206.

60. Melville, "Rose Farmer," 78.

61. Melville, "Rose Farmer," 81 (Melville's italics).

2. LOCAL BEANS, APPLES, AND BERRIES

1. Thoreau, *Wild Fruits*, 243 (hereafter cited parenthetically as *WF*). Though both selections in *Wild Fruits* have been previously published, I look at them as framed within Thoreau's larger writing project on edible and nonedible plants.

2. Bourdieu, *Distinction*, 185.

3. Robinson, "Unchronicled Nations," 335.

4. Smith, *Oxford Companion*, 284. Robert A. Gross observes, "To cut transportation costs and improve access to the Boston market, John Thoreau participated in a statewide petition campaign in 1835 for the elimination of all tolls on bridges into the capital. Energetic entrepreneurs, the pencil-makers 'John Thoreau & Son' were as fully engaged in the market revolution as any other business in Concord" ("Terrible Thoreau," 197).

5. Colman, *Fourth Report*, 198.

6. Gross, "Terrible Thoreau," 192.

7. Colman, *Fourth Report*, 208.

8. See Gross, "Culture and Cultivation," 53–60.

9. Colman, *Fourth Report*, 355.

10. Thoreau, *Correspondence*, 123 (Thoreau's italics).

11. Thoreau, *Journal of Henry David Thoreau*, 10:168 (Thoreau's italics).

12. Harding, *Days*, 455.

13. Thoreau, *Journal of Henry David Thoreau*, 8:25.

14. Harding, *Days*, 89–90. Thoreau ran a short-lived school in Concord with John in 1838 (79–88).

15. Harding, *Days*, 86.

16. Robinson, *Thoreau and the Wild Appetite*, 19.

17. Robinson humorously concludes, "Thoreau does not tell us too much about his ordinary daily fare. He is saving up for the feasts" (*Thoreau and the Wild Appetite*, 18).

18. Thoreau, *Excursions*, 206 (hereafter cited parenthetically as *Ex*).

19. Stuart, *Bloodless Revolution*, 418.

20. Kiple and Ornelas, *Cambridge World History of Food*, 1316.

21. Emerson, "Thoreau," in *Essential Writings*, 815. Emerson's eulogy of Thoreau was originally published in the August 1862 edition of the *Atlantic Monthly*.

22. Thoreau, *Walden*, 214 (hereafter cited parenthetically as *W*).

23. Stuart, *Bloodless Revolution*, xxi.

24. Levenstein, *Revolution at the Table*, 4–5.

25. Tichi, "Domesticity on Walden Pond," 96.

26. Brown, *Domestic Individualism*, 104–9.

27. Emerson, "Thoreau," 823.

28. Lawrence Buell maintains, "Thoreau's allegiances, when it came to choosing between options, were all against upscale commercialized farming and on the side of what is now called sustainable agriculture" (*Environmental Imagination*, 129).

29. *Walden* was written over the course of nine years; Thoreau began his Walden experiment on the Fourth of July, 1845. Its presentation represents the persona "Thoreau" at various stages in his moral evolution over that time. "Thoreau," the persona developed in *Walden*, is not completely representative of historical Thoreau, who often ate in town and relied on dietary alternatives not detailed within the text.

30. Gross, "Great Bean Field Hoax," 488–91.

31. In "Culture and Cultivation," Robert A. Gross notes that hay had increased in average bushels between the years 1840 and 1850 from 15.1 to 27.7 while the producers had dropped from 171 to 108; likewise, corn production in bushels had risen from 70.9 to 82.7 while the producers had dropped from 150 to 105 (60).

32. Gross, "Great Bean Field Hoax," 493.

33. Actually, Thoreau also grew other crops in his plot, but beans were his focus.

34. In some ways this disregard of convention is reminiscent of the failures of Brook Farm and Fruitlands, even though Thoreau's experience in nature would have made him a far more capable farmer than his fellow philosophers.

35. Leo Marx adds that *Walden* is Thoreau's "bitter comment on the methods of capitalist 'husband-men'" (*Machine in the Garden*, 258).

36. Robinson, "Unchronicled Nations," 329.

37. Other significant wild animals for Thoreau are the owl, muskrat, hare, fox, partridge, loon, ant, and squirrel. Key domestic animals are the horse, ox, cat, and dog. Neill Matheson contrasts Thoreau's descriptions of "interspecies neighborliness" with other instances of "an animal intelligence that looks back and responds to human attempts to construe or confront it" ("Thoreau's Inner Animal," 19). Though Matheson does not discuss the woodchuck directly, it exemplifies this relationship.

38. For additional treatments of diet in *Walden*, see Wagner, "Dining Out with Henry Thoreau," 1–4; Adams and Adams, "Thoreau's Diet at Walden," 247–64; and Garren, "Food for Thought," 340–47.

39. According to Ryan Patrick Hanley, Thoreau "meant, at least in part, to have us rethink that artificial distinction which Thoreau believes we have drawn between the savage and the noble" ("Thoreau among His Heroes," 62).

40. Thoreau also gives an alternative example of consumption practices in the figure of Alek Therien, the woodchopper in "Visitors," an "animal man" who lives almost entirely on meat (*W*, 146). Though not Thoreau's ideal consumer, Therien engages in a simplified lifestyle and sustainable diet that Thoreau appreciates as well.

41. Harding, *Days*, 185.

42. Harding, *Days*, 185.

43. Harding, *Days*, 185.

44. Thoreau, *Journal 4*, 454–55.

45. Joan Burbick notes, "If diet were based on indigenous plants, clearly the social and economic order of the Yankee settler would be undone" (*Healing the Republic*, 65).

46. Wagenknecht, *John Greenleaf Whittier*, 112.

47. Joan Burbick writes, "Proper diet and vegetarianism are central issues, even though [Thoreau] freely admits to his moral lapses in regard to his principles" (*Healing the Republic*, 64).

48. Thoreau chooses a familiar local folk story for this message—Frank Davidson traces the history of the bugs in the apple-tree table in his essay, "Melville, Thoreau, and 'The Apple-Tree Table'" (479–480).

49. For an earlier version of the essays "Wild Apples" and "Huckleberries," see *Henry David Thoreau: Collected Essays*, 444–501. For a useful reading of Thoreau's critique of contemporary technology in *Wild Fruits*, see Hiltner, "Ripeness," 323–38.

50. This social focus in Thoreau's later work is discussed in Newman, *Our Common Dwelling*, 101–5.

51. There is a similar application of mythic allusions to fruits in Harriet Beecher Stowe's discussion of oranges, covered in chapter 3.

52. In "Walking," Thoreau's most involved discussion of the preservation of wilderness, he describes a similar market road: "If you would go to the political world, follow the great road,—follow that market man, keep his dust in your eyes, and it will lead you straight to it—for it too has its place merely, and does not occupy all space. I pass from it as from a bean field into the forest, and it is forgotten" (*Ex*, 192).

53. Harding, *Days*, 205.

54. According to Newman, "*Wild Fruits* clearly confirms the trajectory of Thoreau's traverse from idealism and individualism to materialism and communalism," where he hopes that the "sacramental consumption of wild fruits, should it be taken up by the hundred instead of just the one, might well redeem a New England society that has modernized itself into an almost total ignorance of nature" (*Our Common Dwelling*, 171, 175).

55. See Gilmore, "Indian in the Museum," 25–63; Rose, "Following the Trail of Footsteps," 77–99; and Sayre, *Thoreau and the American Indians*.

56. Newman, *Our Common Dwelling*, 179.

57. Derrida, "Eating Well," 282 (Derrida's italics).

3. FRUITS OF REGIONALISM

1. Stowe gives an example of a minstrel show for her audience, putting such a show in the context of slavery; this piece becomes both an implicit criticism of the dehumanizing tendencies of slavery through Haley's character as well as an implicit sanction of such shows through their presumed familiarity among her intended audience. For discussions of the original "Jump Jim Crow" figure and minstrelsy, in the context of the history of African Americans after the failure of Reconstruction, see Woodward, *Strange Career of Jim Crow*.

2. Indeed, oranges came to be associated with Eva to the extent that the publisher of *Uncle Tom's Cabin* paid John Greenleaf Whittier fifty dollars to commission a poem about "Little Eva" as part of the legacy of the novel in which he writes, "For the golden locks of Eva / Let the sunny south land give her / Flowery

pillow of repose, / Orange bloom and budding rose" (quoted in Hedrick, *Harriet Beecher Stowe*, 224).

3. In *Reconstruction*, Eric Foner discusses the period of Radical Reconstruction, when military rule was established in the South (228–80).

4. See Tompkins, *Sensational Designs*, especially 122–46.

5. Bourdieu, *Distinction*, 2.

6. Bourdieu, *Distinction*, 185.

7. For a discussion of race and U.S. expansion, see Horsman, *Race and Manifest Destiny*.

8. The Lowell Mills are also referenced in Herman Melville's work on U.S. labor; see chapter 1.

9. R. Douglas Hurt writes, "When the antebellum period began, the ax and the plow served as the most common farm tools, but by 1860 horse-powered seed drills, cultivators, and reapers had replaced hand-powered tools" (*American Agriculture*, 117–18).

10. Hedrick, *Harriet Beecher Stowe*, 1.

11. Hedrick, *Harriet Beecher Stowe*, 32.

12. Hedrick, *Harriet Beecher Stowe*, 102.

13. Quoted in Hedrick, *Harriet Beecher Stowe*, 64. For more on the work of women abolitionist writers leading up to and following the Civil War, including Harriet Beecher Stowe, see Sizer, *Political Work*.

14. Quoted in Applegate, *Most Famous Man*, 150.

15. Beecher, *Plain and Pleasant Talk*, 20–21.

16. Kelley, *Origin and Progress*, 73.

17. Thulesius, *Harriet Beecher Stowe in Florida*, 54.

18. John McPhee adds, "The Florida Citrus Commission likes to promote him as a man who was trying to find the Fountain of Youth but actually brought it with him" (*Oranges*, 89).

19. Thulesius, *Harriet Beecher Stowe in Florida*, 39.

20. For a discussion of New England apples and their purpose in agricultural reform during the antebellum period in the work of Henry David Thoreau, see chapter 2.

21. McPhee, *Oranges*, 66. Ironically, McPhee notes that the term "citrus," from the Roman *citreum*, is in fact a misnomer: "In the eighteenth century, the Swedish botanist Carolus Linnaeus nonetheless made the name 'citrus' official for the genus. So lemons, limes, citrons, oranges, grapefruit, and tangerines are now grouped under a name that means cedar"; meanwhile, "orange" is itself derived from Sanskrit (*Oranges*, 64).

22. Stowe, *Palmetto Leaves*, 17 (hereafter cited parenthetically as PL).

23. According to Hedrick, "Stowe was careful in her outward behavior . . . for it allowed her to move back and forth between the private and public realms and to have an influence in both" (*Harriet Beecher Stowe*, 238).

24. Stowe, *Uncle Tom's Cabin*, 307 (hereafter cited parenthetically as *UTC*).

25. Stowe and Stowe, *Harriet Beecher Stowe*, 217.

26. Carolyn Karcher observes that this practice in the novel demonstrates that "all human beings are interconnected" ("Stowe and the Literature," 206). Henry Louis Gates Jr. and Hollis Robbins add, "Stowe asks her readers to recognize that external markers such as name, race, or dress do not define a man—only his inner characteristics matter" (*UTC*, 11n).

27. Gates and Robbins note, "Augustine, like Mr. Shelby, appreciates food while discoursing on slavery" (*UTC*, 232n).

28. Root and de Rochemont, *Eating in America*, 125. Reginald Horsman responds to this attitude: "Well-off European travelers scoffed at westerners who seemed to have salt pork on the table at every meal, but ordinary Europeans regarded any meat as a luxury" (*Feast or Famine*, 3).

29. Stowe, *House and Home Papers*, 228–29 (hereafter cited parenthetically as *HHP*).

30. Noelle Gallagher observes that the Halliday kitchen is not merely a "domestic" space; Rachel has gone beyond the purely domestic in her production of food: "The model in use is thus not, as Tompkins would suggest, one of agricultural self-sufficiency, but one of systematized, although modest, manufacture" ("Bagging Factory," 179).

31. Buell, "Harriet Beecher Stowe," 193.

32. Thulesius, *Harriet Beecher Stowe in Florida*, 33–34; Diane Roberts calls Kingsley "a strange hybrid of Simon Legree and Augustine St. Clare" ("Harriet Beecher Stowe," 200).

33. According to Thulesius, Frederick was perpetually traveling to Jacksonville on "secret pub crawls"; eventually, he went to San Francisco, where he vanished completely, "and although the Stowes made inquiries for years, he was never found" (*Harriet Beecher Stowe in Florida*, 76, 77). As the instigator of Frederick's alcoholism was pain management owing to an injury suffered during the Civil War, his eventual loss is one more casualty of the war.

34. Stowe, "Our Florida Plantation," 649. Stowe's family and biographers, Charles and Lyman, agree, noting that Stowe "apparently felt little or no regret for the pecuniary loss" (Stowe and Stowe, *Harriet Beecher Stowe*, 218).

35. Hedrick, *Harriet Beecher Stowe*, 330.

36. Rachel Naomi Klein comments that Stowe, like many idealistic reformers from the North, is "chronically incapable" of truly perceiving "the aspirations and outlook of the former slaves" ("Harriet Beecher Stowe," 141).

37. Thulesius observes, "Reed's term was a difficult period during which he faced black suffrage conflicts, a lack of civil government and an unstable budget" (*Harriet Beecher Stowe in Florida*, 44).

38. John Foster Jr. and Sarah Whitmer Foster discuss the Reconstruction history during the period of Stowe's tenure in Florida. Furthermore, they note the fame of Stowe's letters upon first publication in the *Christian Union*, which had a circulation of greater than eighty thousand. In these letters Stowe specifically recommends Florida to health seekers, wildlife adventurers, and "industrious young men . . . willing to plant citrus trees or other experimental crops" (*Beechers, Stowes, and Yankee Strangers*, 89).

39. Quoted in Thulesius, *Harriet Beecher Stowe in Florida*, 69.

40. Quoted in Hedrick, *Harriet Beecher Stowe*, 329–30.

41. Quoted in Thulesius, *Harriet Beecher Stowe in Florida*, 83–84.

42. McPhee, *Oranges*, 96.

43. Doris Van Kampen and Carol Ann Moon note, "She also tried many other cash crops, including sugar cane and garden vegetables; she reported on four years' worth of yield for a variety of crops, and was most satisfied with sugar cane, cucumbers, and Irish potatoes" ("Power of the Pen," 61).

44. Maria I. Diedrich writes, "Like most Euro Americans, Stowe was intimidated at the visible presences of millions of free African Americans in Reconstruction America and unable to accept them as American citizens" ("Kitchen Hierarchies," 111). However, Stowe spends her time in Florida with the intention of forming integrated schools and churches—working to overcome her own prejudices.

45. Her chapter continues with the neighboring white community rallying in support of "Old Cudjo" against a land agent, helping him be "re-instated in his rights" (*PL*, 277).

46. Kennedy, *Southern Exposure*, 22.

47. Range, "Freedmen's Bureau," 12–14. In *A Right to the Land*, Edward Magdol adds, "In sum, the freedmen were refused permanent title to the lands they occupied and on which they had constructed schools, churches, homes, and organized villages and communities" (159).

48. Range, "Freedmen's Bureau," 3.

49. Magdol, *Right to the Land*, 212.

50. McPhee, *Oranges*, 95–96.

51. Van Kampen and Moon, "Power of the Pen," 55. Furthermore, Thulesius quotes a contemporary visitor describing "the gothic cottage of Mrs. Harriet Beecher Stowe at the edge of a great grove of oaks and in the middle of a luxuriant orange grove. We found the two daughters of Mrs. Stowe upon the dock, to

whom Mr. Dennis gave messages of remembrance to their mother" (*Harriet Beecher Stowe in Florida*, 95).

52. Buell, "Harriet Beecher Stowe," 193.

53. John McPhee notes, "For seventeen years she ran a successful orange grove—apparently with very little help from her husband" (*Oranges*, 96). Thulesius adds that a tourist encountered Calvin Stowe, stating, "I thought this was Harriet Beecher Stowe's place," and was brusquely answered by Calvin, "So it is . . . and I'll have you know that I am the proprietor of Harriet Beecher Stowe and of this place—now git!" (*Harriet Beecher Stowe in Florida*, 96).

54. Klein notes that Stowe believed "that the female 'heart' might have a salutary impact on public life" ("Harriet Beecher Stowe," 147).

55. The other work is *Dred* (Hedrick, *Harriet Beecher Stowe*, 344).

56. Though the novel is set in a post–Revolutionary War setting, Hedrick continues, "*Oldtown Folks* was directly influenced by Reconstructionist politics" (*Harriet Beecher Stowe*, 342). Edward Tang also observes the connection between the two periods in Stowe's work: "Both advance the moral promise and offer the opportunity to reorder society in the wake of revolutionary events" ("Making Declarations of Her Own," 85).

57. Hedrick, *Harriet Beecher Stowe*, 415.

58. Carwardine, "Lincoln's Religion," 245–46.

59. Hedrick, *Harriet Beecher Stowe*, 81.

60. Stowe, *Oldtown Folks*, 282 (hereafter cited parenthetically as *OF*).

61. Amy Kaplan observes that Sarah Josepha Hale, editor of the influential *Godey's Lady's Book*, started the campaign for a national Thanksgiving holiday in 1847. Hale attempted to "create a common history by nationalizing a regional myth of origins and transposing it to the territories most recently wrested away from Indians and Mexicans" (*Anarchy of Empire*, 35).

62. Stowe does, however, make a detailed list of the kinds of pies made for the holiday feast: "Pumpkin pies, cranberry pies, huckleberry pies, cherry pies, green-currant pies, peach, pear, and plum pies, custard pies, apple pies, Marlborough-pudding pies,—pies with top crusts, and pies without,—pies adorned with all sorts of fanciful flutings and architectural strips laid across and around, and otherwise varied" (*OF*, 286).

63. The *Oldtown Folks* Thanksgiving feast can be compared to the rough picnic of *Palmetto Leaves*: "An impromptu picnic was proclaimed through the house. Every one dropped the work in hand, and flew to spreading sandwiches. Oranges were gathered, luncheon-baskets packed; and the train filed out from the two houses. The breeze was fresh and fair; and away we flew" (*PL*, 165–66).

64. Naranjo-Huebl, "Take, Eat," 598.

65. Pryse argues that Stowe's regionalism paved the way for the voices of Kate Chopin, Alice Dunbar-Nelson, Sui Sin Far, Zitkala-Sa, Mary Austin, and Charles Chesnutt, among others ("Harriet Beecher Stowe and Regionalism," 149).

66. Herman Melville meditates on charity and domestic agriculture in his writings as well; see chapter 1.

67. Foster and Foster write that the Stowes "gave lovingly to the state, enriching its schools, churches, and political life, even as their projects were largely unsuccessful in the long-term" (*Beechers, Stowes, and Yankee Strangers*, 127–28).

68. Thulesius, *Harriet Beecher Stowe in Florida*, 91; Hedrick, *Harriet Beecher Stowe*, 397.

69. Foster and Foster, *Beechers, Stowes, and Yankee Strangers*, 96–97.

70. For a discussion of Twain's agriculturally based commentary on U.S. imperialism during the late nineteenth century, see chapter 4.

4. SWEET EMPIRES OF LABOR

1. In his recap of the Tom Sawyer story, Huck says, "When I couldn't stand it no longer, I lit out. I got into my old rags, and my sugar-hogshead again, and was free and satisfied" (Twain, *Adventures of Huckleberry Finn*, 17). The reader can almost imagine the author being jealous of Huck Finn's bed as opposed to his own normal bed.

2. Mark Twain's speech from the *New York Herald*. Quoted in Twain, *Mark Twain's Weapons of Satire*, 5.

3. See Inglis and Gimlin, *Globalization of Food*, 3–5.

4. Twain also discusses Hawaiian oranges—predating Stowe's work with the crop. In his case, though, oranges would have been more of an imported, rather than a regional, good (*Letters from Hawaii*, 206–7).

5. According to Philip H. Herbst in *The Color of Words*, "coolie" is defined as "an unskilled Asian laborer" who often "had been kidnapped or pressed into labor by force and shipped to foreign countries such as Peru and Cuba." He adds "the term was applied by Europeans in India and China to a native laborer hired at subsistence wages. In California since the 1860s, Chinese immigrants or sojourners were viewed as a 'race of coolies' who threatened white California labor" (58).

6. Mintz, *Sweetness and Power*, 29, 53.

7. Mintz, *Sweetness and Power*, 38.

8. Mintz, *Sweetness and Power*, 70.

9. Mintz, *Sweetness and Power*, 71.

10. Mintz, *Sweetness and Power*, 61.

11. Mintz, *Sweetness and Power*, 188.
12. Twain, *Life on the Mississippi*, 476–79 (hereafter cited parenthetically as *LM*).
13. Mintz, *Sweetness and Power*, xviii (Mintz's italics).
14. The official dates of the Philippine-American War are 1899 to 1902, but guerrilla action lasted until 1913.
15. Zwick, "Mark Twain and Imperialism," 228.
16. Crapol, *James Blaine*, 46.
17. LaFeber, *New Empire*, 119.
18. His tour of the nations of the British Empire furnished him with opportunities to perform in English. The Philippines was at this time still a Spanish colony.
19. In the notes to Twain's *Autobiography*, the Philippine tariff bill is "proposed to permit Philippine sugar to enter the United States for three years at one-fourth of current duties, and subsequently to establish free trade between the islands and the United States. Vigorously opposed by the domestic sugar industry, the bill nevertheless passed by a wide margin in the House of Representatives on 16 January 1906, only to be buried in committee in the Senate on 2 March. Attempts to revive it later in 1906 and 1907 failed" (*Autobiography*, 562, hereafter cited parenthetically as *A*).
20. Quoted in Jung, *Coolies and Cane*, 23.
21. Du Bois, *Writings*, 592. He also connects the political power of the corporations involved in "sugar, coal and oil" as being parallel in their exploitation of labor and extensive political power (582).
22. For discussions of Twain's anger at U.S. racism, domestic and international, see Fishkin, *Was Huck Black?* and Zwick, introduction to *Mark Twain's Weapons of Satire*.
23. Fishkin, *Lighting Out for the Territory*, 14, 20, 21.
24. Fishkin, "Mark Twain and Race," 154.
25. According to Rob Wilson, Twain "promoted the linkage of Hawai'i to capitalist designs upon the Pacific" ("Exporting Christian Transcendentalism," 525). Wilson further observes that "the first sugar plantation in the islands was set up on Kauai by William Hooper from Boston in 1835" (533). At this time the labor would have been primarily performed by the native Hawaiians.
26. Root and de Rochemont, *Eating in America*, 267.
27. Jung, *Coolies and Cane*, 63.
28. Wilson, "Exporting Christian Transcendentalism," 523. For a contemporary version of the Hawaiian culture from the Hawaiian perspective, see Liliuokalani, *Hawaii's Story*.
29. Twain, *Letters from Hawaii*, 12 (hereafter cited parenthetically as *LH*).
30. Root and de Rochemont, *Eating in America*, 267.

31. Zwick, "Mark Twain and Imperialism," 230. He also notes that Twain's writings succeed because of his "mixture of humor, vivid descriptions of people and scenery, and geographic and economic facts and projections" (230).

32. This tone is comparable to Frank Norris's early writings around the time leading up to the Spanish-American War, discussed in chapter 5.

33. Jung names sugar and slavery "the twin forces that enriched western Europe, enslaved western Africa, and colonized the Americas for centuries" (*Coolies and Cane*, 40).

34. While Jung's work about coolie labor on sugar plantations focuses on Louisiana, it can be applied to Hawaiian plantations as well. "The close association between slavery and coolieism, in turn, incorporated coolies in the domestic struggle over slavery," and this becomes part of the debate leading up to the Civil War. In this way the struggle with human rights that was part of the antislavery platform is seen in a broader context (*Coolies and Cane*, 222).

35. Jung, *Coolies and Cane*, 11, 224.

36. Twain represents this subjugation, in the words of Amy Kaplan, "as a replacement for the loss of slave labor at home," and "the 'free' labor of 'Kanaka men and women' was much cheaper" than even the original purchase of slaves pre-emancipation would have been (*Anarchy of Empire*, 77).

37. During Twain's time in Hawaii, Kaplan observes, he "learned a lesson in the transnational dimensions of whiteness that emerged from the movement of labor, capital, and racial discourses across the globe" (*Anarchy of Empire*, 81). Upon visiting the islands, Twain finds "men and women of mixed races and multiple nationalities" whose "modern and cosmopolitan qualities" reminded him of his childhood (64–65). He is not the most surprised by Hawaiian savagery, but by its civilization, by the inversion of many of his preconceptions.

38. Yunte Huang writes that the Chinese in California worked in "California mines, manufacturing businesses, and public improvement corporations (railroad building)" (*Transpacific Imaginations*, 14).

39. Though Kaplan observes Twain's ability to romanticize native Hawaiians through a connection to the African Americans he remembers from his youth, Wilson maintains that Twain still urges "the adoption of a new Asian Pacific form of slavery through the exploitation of contract labor" ("Exporting Christian Transcendentalism," 531).

40. Quoted in Wilson, "Exporting Christian Transcendentalism," 523.

41. Cooper, *Around the World*, 1–3. In his introduction to *Following the Equator*, Fred Kaplan notes that Henry Huttleston Rogers—vice president of Standard

Oil—convinced Twain that the lecture tour was the best way to fully repay his creditors (1).

42. Melton, *Mark Twain, Travel Books, and Tourism*, 138.

43. Kaplan, introduction, 4.

44. Melton notes that this travel narrative is "like a sad, if cynical, acknowledgment of what is to come" (*Mark Twain, Travel Books, and Tourism*, 139).

45. Twain, *Following the Equator*, 352 (Twain's italics; hereafter cited parenthetically as *FE*). Melton adds, "The German was, in effect, punishing the Indian on Twain's behalf, since both the supervisor and the servant were, after all, serving him" (*Mark Twain, Travel Books, and Tourism*, 350).

46. As discussed in chapter 3, Harriet Beecher Stowe introduces the Thanksgiving feast as, indeed, a unifying national holiday with only positive implications.

47. Quoted in Cooper, *Around the World*, 260. Cooper adds, "If no countries are remote, Mauritius ... is the next best thing, at least to Europeans and Americans for whom the place is little more than a name" (260).

48. Twain, "Hawaiian Story."

49. Cooper adds, "When slavery was abolished in the 1830s, the British imported Indian indentured laborers, mainly Hindus, to work the sugar plantations. They remain the majority, and because Mauritius is a democracy, Hindus dominate the government" (*Around the World*, 261).

50. Rowe, "Mark Twain's Critique," 122.

51. Robinson, "Dreaming Better Dreams," 450–51.

52. Zwick notes that Twain's late anti-imperialist and other writings are not "merely part of an optimistic public persona (Mark Twain) that was put forward by a deeply pessimistic author (Samuel Clemens)" ("Mark Twain and Imperialism," 245).

53. Catherine Carlstroem and Forrest G. Robinson note striking similarities between the works of Mark Twain and Karl Marx. Discussing *Following the Equator*, they write, "Both deploy surface/depth and microcosm/macrocosm models in treating socioeconomic problems; but while Marx proceeds in a rationally ordered way, taking one logical and clearly defined step at a time, Twain is a literary stylist whose stories, when closely examined, reveal insights and emergent positions bearing on American and international economics that closely parallel those of his European counterpart" ("Twain and Marx," 118).

54. Twain, *Mark Twain's Weapons of Satire*, 89.

55. Zwick observes, "Although most of Twain's anti-imperialist writings have now been published in full, Paine's vision of 'the traditional Mark Twain' has endured" ("Mark Twain and Imperialism," 247).

56. Zwick, "Mark Twain and Imperialism," 247–48.

1. In *Future of Environmental Criticism*, Buell adds that this is itself an "omnibus term" for "tales that frame environmental ethics in varied ways" (1–2).

2. As an example of the lack of critical attention given to Norris's work in eco-criticism, Bill McKibben's anthology, *American Earth*, includes the work of Theodore Dreiser but not Frank Norris.

3. Norris, "Frontier Gone at Last," 1185.

4. Benn Michaels, *Gold Standard*, 185.

5. Conlogue, *Working the Garden*, 15–16.

6. For more on the early development of the bonanza farm in the U.S. Midwest, see Drache, *Day of the Bonanza*, 25–33.

7. Crapol, *James Blaine*, 46.

8. LaFeber, *New Empire*, 9–10, 18.

9. Conlogue, *Working the Garden*, 38–39.

10. Conlogue, *Working the Garden*, 40.

11. Williams, *Origins of Federal Support*, 12.

12. Howells, "Frank Norris," 772.

13. Norris, "Comida," 344. While Norris traveled to Cuba as a correspondent for *McClure's Magazine*, he never published anything about his time in Cuba in that periodical.

14. In an interview about his time in Cuba, Norris romanticizes U.S. soldiers: "I don't believe the idea of falling back even entered their heads.... You can't whip such men, you know. You can kill them, you can starve them in Andersonville or you can blow them up in Havana harbor but you can't whip them. That's how and why we won this war." (Crisler, "Frank Norris in Cuba," 2).

15. Norris, "Frontier Gone at Last," 1184.

16. Felipe Fernandez-Armesto writes that wheat "has diversified more dramatically, invaded more new habitats, multiplied faster and evolved more rapidly without extinction than any other known organism. It now covers more than 600 million acres of the surface of the planet" (*Near a Thousand Tables*, 94).

17. According to Joseph R. McElrath Jr. and Jesse S. Crisler, both Emile Zola, the father of naturalism, and Norris share a vision of "Nature" that is expressed "in a lugubrious minor key" (*Frank Norris*, 211).

18. Donald Pizer credits LeConte with influence over Norris that appears in his depiction of wheat in *The Octopus*. He also describes the influence of a divine nature in *The Octopus* that is an "evolutionary theism which attributes to nature the power and qualities usually assigned to a personal, supernatural deity" ("Concept of Nature," 73). Michael Lundblad also discusses LeConte's influence on *The Octopus* in *Birth of a Jungle*, especially p. 99.

19. Harold Kaplan adds, "One can say that a study of literary naturalism leads to a series of paradoxes" ("Naturalist Fiction and Political Allegory," 150).

20. Pizer, *Novels of Frank Norris*, 116.

21. Norris, "Deal in Wheat," 5 (Norris's italics; hereafter cited parenthetically as D).

22. See Marut, "Sam Lewiston's Bad Timing," 76–79.

23. Dawson, "Transforming History," 120–21.

24. Norris, *The Octopus*, 2:14 (hereafter cited parenthetically as *Oc*).

25. Norris, *The Pit*, 269 (hereafter cited parenthetically as *Pi*).

26. In *Future of Environmental Criticism*, Buell observes that Cicero's is the earliest usage of that term (1).

27. Quoted in McElrath and Crisler, *Frank Norris*, 350.

28. Quoted in McElrath and Crisler, *Frank Norris*, 354.

29. See Starr, introduction to *The Octopus*, xv.

30. From 1895 to 1898, Norris wrote as a correspondent for several periodicals. He traveled to South Africa, where he witnessed the Jameson Raid on an assignment for the *San Francisco Chronicle*, and covered the Cuban portion of the Spanish-American War for *McClure's Magazine*.

31. Norris has often been criticized for his depiction of Presley, who is regarded as an avatar for Norris himself. However, when the reader first meets Presley, he is talking to Mr. Hooven, a poor tenant farmer on the Derrick property. Presley has an obvious dislike for Hooven, which makes Presley seem classist. So, although the novel is told in Presley's voice, he is an unreliable narrator. For more on Norris's depiction of Presley, see Lewis, *Unsettling the Literary West*, 143–44.

32. Norris's post-Spanish-American-War novel is about wheat, and not about another natural substance. He could not write and epic of pine or stone. This move shows the intertwined paths of the natural and human worlds.

33. See Lye, *America's Asia*, specifically 72–86.

34. For more on Annixter's role as a new farmer, see Sarver, *Uneven Land*, 96–99.

35. Florian Frietag writes, "In paragraphs that grow shorter and shorter, Norris contrasts extremely detailed descriptions of the various dishes served at the dinner party with an almost pathological analysis of Mrs. Hooven's slow starvation" that ends with the conclusion of the elaborate meal and Mrs. Hooven's death ("Naturalism in Its Natural Environment?" 105).

36. Norris inserts the figure of the president of the Pacific and Southwestern Railroad, Shelgrim, to give a complementary voice to the force of the railroad. Shelgrim states, "Wheat must grow. Can any one stop the Wheat? Well, then, no more can I stop the Road" (*Oc*, 2:286). While at first this argument sways Presley, ultimately he finds Vanamee's argument more convincing.

37. Newspaper clipping, "Sinks to Death in a Grain Pit."

38. Norris's issues with race and ethnicity in his works have received much critical attention. See Pizer, *American Naturalism and the Jews*; and Lye, *America's Asia*.

39. Eperjesi, *Imperialist Imaginary*, 72.

40. Colleen Lye describes this as the "U.S.-to-Asia export" of wheat and adds, "The shipping of Behrman's corpse across the Pacific forms an integral part of the narrative movement toward the realization of market inevitability, the recognition that wheat is all-powerful, and, moreover, that its power is good" (*America's Asia*, 77).

41. Pizer adds, "The cycle of growth and the fulfillment of demand by supply are completed regardless of whatever harm and destruction men bring upon themselves in their attempts to hinder or manipulate these natural processes for their own profit" ("Concept of Nature," 79).

42. Stephanie Sarver adds that "Norris's attention to the rise of agriculture in California speaks to a larger awareness of the changing shape of agriculture nationwide" and that Norris draws "parallels between the ranchers and the railroad magnates; as businessmen none is more guilty than another. Indeed, they are similarly motivated by profit and, toward that end, are exercising force on the environment through the manipulation of the wheat. Moreover, both groups are simultaneously subject to larger forces: the ranchers are subject to the force of the railroads, and the railroads are subject to the larger and amorphous universal force" (*Uneven Land*, 81).

43. Marut, "Sam Lewiston's Bad Timing," 75.

44. For a useful general breakdown of trading futures of wheat and other grains, see Cronon, *Nature's Metropolis*, 120–32.

45. In trading, "bears" are more conservative, whereas "bulls" are willing to take greater risks to turn a profit. Interestingly, the names of two of Chicago's national sports teams are the Bears of the National Football League and the Bulls of the National Basketball League.

46. Dawson, "Transforming History," 120.

47. Norris had originally planned for *The Pit* to be focused exclusively on the character of Laura Jadwin, her story being the nonwheat element of the novel. However, the Leitner-influenced Curtis Jadwin story, an epic of wheat in itself, took over. Joseph R. McElrath Jr. and Gwendolyn Jones explain that for Norris, even in a literary form, wheat cannot be ultimately contained (introduction to *The Pit*, xvi–xix).

48. For a larger discussion about the significance of the domestic project in terms of the national, see the agricultural and dietary reform in Harriet Beecher Stowe's work in chapter 3.

49. In a later scene, Laura's sister, Page, confronts her on her lack of connection to the wheat market and therefore to her husband's work. She argues, "If you did care a little more about wheat—about your husband's business . . . Just think; he may be fighting the battle of his life down there in La Salle Street, and you don't know anything about it—no, nor want to know" (*Pi*, 399–400). In this comment Page gives the domestic argument to the agri-expansionist project of the Jadwins.

50. This scene, in which the human characters are paralleled with animals, is reminiscent of earlier discussions of animals being related to humans in Thoreau's writing, discussed in chapter 2.

51. Richard Lehan compares the limits of social institutions, that wheat speculation is "governed by laws that ultimately come back to nature—the land, the wheat, and the forces out of which life germinates" ("European Background," 63).

52. Quoted in McElrath and Crisler, *Frank Norris*, 424.

53. Malcolm Cowley adds, "In his novels wheat was not a grain improved by man from various wild grasses and grown by men to meet human needs; it was an abstract and elemental force like gravity" ("Naturalism in American Literature," 64–65).

54. Pizer, *Novels of Frank Norris*, 117.

55. Richard Lehan adds that ultimately "a third volume was unnecessary"; he continues, "Norris had already shown how the growing and selling of wheat touches the lives of everyone worldwide, and he had clearly documented the biological basis of economics and the process of degeneration that can occur when one is no longer in touch with the rhythms of the land" ("European Background," 64).

56. For discussions of the global importance of corn, see Fussel, *Story of Corn*; Pollan, *Omnivore's Dilemma*; and Warman, *Corn and Capitalism*.

EPILOGUE

1. McKibben, *Deep Economy*, 42–43 (hereafter cited parenthetically as *DE*).

2. For wheat, see "Wheat" in Kiple and Ornelas, *Cambridge World History of Food*, 2000 II.A.10, and Smith, *Oxford Companion* (619–20); for sugar, see "Sugar" in *Cambridge* II.F.2 and *Oxford Companion* (570–71); for oranges, see *Oxford Companion* (130–31, 425–26); for apples, see *Oxford Companion* (21–22); for beans, see *Oxford Companion* (39); for dairy products, see "Milk and Dairy Products," *Cambridge*, III.9 and *Oxford Companion* (182–83).

3. Dowie, *American Foundations*, 106–11; also see Jain, *Green Revolution*; and "History," Ford Foundation, http://www.fordfoundation.org/about-us/history.

4. Ellen Messer, "Maize," in *Cambridge World History of Food*, II.A.4.
5. Quoted in Dowie, *American Foundations*, 114.
6. Shiva, "Green Revolution in the Punjab," 57.
7. Tsing, *Friction*, 174 (hereafter cited parenthetically as *F*).
8. McHugh, "Flora, Not Fauna," 27.
9. According to McHugh, "So far, NewLeaf is the only GM crop plant to be taken off the market" ("Flora, Not Fauna," 27).
10. Ozeki, *All Over Creation*, 257 (hereafter cited parenthetically as *AC*).
11. Quoted in Kilgour, *From Communion to Cannibalism*, 234.

BIBLIOGRAPHY

Adams, Stephen J., and Barbara Adams. "Thoreau's Diet at Walden." In *Studies in the American Renaissance, 1990*, edited by Joel Myerson, 247–64. Charlottesville: University Press of Virginia, 1990.

Alcott, Louisa May. "Transcendental Wild Oats." In *Silver Pitchers, and Independence: A Centennial Love Story*, 79–101. Boston: Roberts Brothers, 1876.

Applegate, Dabby. *The Most Famous Man in America: The Biography of Henry Ward Beecher*. New York: Doubleday, 2006.

Beecher, Henry Ward. *Plain and Pleasant Talk about Fruits, Flowers, and Farming*. New York: Derby and Jackson, 1859. http://name.umdl.umich.edu/agk 7246.0001.001.

Benn Michaels, Walter. *The Gold Standard and the Logic of Naturalism: American Literature at the Turn of the Century*. Berkeley: University of California Press, 1998.

Bidwell, Percy W. "Pioneer Agriculture." *Readings in the Economic History of American Agriculture*, edited by Louis Bernard Schmidt and Earle Dudley Ross. New York: Macmillan, 1925.

Bourdieu, Pierre. *Distinction: A Social Critique of the Judgement of Taste*. Translated by Richard Nice. Cambridge MA: Harvard University Press, 1984.

Brown, Gillian. *Domestic Individualism: Imagining Self in Nineteenth-Century America*. Berkeley: University of California Press, 1990.

Bryant, John. Introduction to *Typee: A Peep at Polynesian Life*, by Herman Melville. Edited by John Bryant. New York: Penguin Classics, 1996.

Buell, Lawrence. *The Environmental Imagination: Thoreau, Nature Writing, and the Formation of American Culture*. Cambridge MA: Harvard University Press, 1995.

———. *The Future of Environmental Criticism: Environmental Crisis and Literary Imagination*. Malden MA: Blackwell, 2005.

———. "Harriet Beecher Stowe and the Dream of the Great American Novel." In *The Cambridge Companion to Harriet Beecher Stowe*, edited by Cindy Weinstein, 190–202. Cambridge: Cambridge University Press, 2004.

———. *Writing for an Endangered World: Literature, Culture, and Environment in the United States and Beyond*. Cambridge MA: Harvard University Press, 2001.

Burbick, Joan. *Healing the Republic: The Language of Health and Culture of Nationalism in Nineteenth Century America*. New York: Cambridge University Press, 1994.

Cain, William E. "Henry David Thoreau 1817–1862: A Brief Biography." In *A Historical Guide to Henry David Thoreau*, edited by William E. Cain, 11–57. New York: Oxford University Press, 2000.

Carlstroem, Catherine, and Forrest G. Robinson. "Twain and Marx." In *The Jester and the Sages: Mark Twain in Conversation with Nietzsche, Freud, and Marx*, edited by Forrest G. Robinson, Gabriel Noah Brahm Jr., and Catherine Carlstroem, 89–134. Columbia: University of Missouri Press, 2011.

Carwardine, Richard. "Lincoln's Religion." In *Our Lincoln*, edited by Eric Foner, 223–48. New York: W. W. Norton, 2008.

Colman, Henry. *Fourth Report on the Agriculture of Massachusetts: Counties of Franklin and Middlesex*. Boston: Dutton and Wentworth, 1841.

Conlogue, William. *Working the Garden: American Writers and the Industrialization of Agriculture*. Chapel Hill: University of North Carolina Press, 2001.

Cooper, Robert. *Around the World with Mark Twain*. New York: Arcade Publishing, 2000.

Cowley, Malcolm. "Naturalism in American Literature." In *American Naturalism*, edited by Harold Bloom, 49–80. Philadelphia: Chelsea House, 2004.

Crapol, Edward P. *James Blaine: Architect of Empire*. Wilmington DE: Scholarly Resources, 2000.

Crisler, Jesse S. "Frank Norris in Cuba during the Spanish-American War: A Previously Unnoted Interview." *Frank Norris Studies* 3 (2003): 1–3.

Cronon, William. *Nature's Metropolis: Chicago and the Great West*. New York: W. W. Norton, 1991.

D'Amore, Maura. "Hawthorne and the Suburban Romance." *Studies in American Fiction* 37, no. 2 (Fall 2010): 155–80.

Davidson, Frank. "Melville, Thoreau, and 'The Apple-Tree Table.'" *American Literature* 25, no. 4 (January 1954): 479–88.

Dawson, Jon Falsarella. "Transforming History: The Economic Context of Frank Norris's 'A Deal in Wheat.'" *Studies in American Naturalism* 4, no. 2 (Winter 2009): 119–31.

Denning, Michael. *Mechanic Accents: Dime Novels and Working-Class Culture in America*. New York: Verso, 1987.

Derrida, Jacques. "Eating Well, of the Calculation of the Subject." In *Points . . . : Interviews, 1974–1994*, edited by Elisabeth Weber, translated by Peggy Kamuf. Stanford CA: Stanford University Press, 1995.

DeWitt, Dave. *The Founding Foodies: How Washington, Jefferson, and Franklin Revolutionized American Cuisine*. Naperville IL: Sourcebooks, 2010.

Diedrich, Maria I. "Kitchen Hierarchies." In *Beyond Uncle Tom's Cabin: Essays on the Writing of Harriet Beecher Stowe*, edited by Sylvia Mayer and Monika Mueller, 109–24. Lanham MD: Rowman & Littlefield, 2011.

Dowie, Mark. *American Foundations: An Investigative History*. Cambridge MA: MIT Press, 2001.

Drache, Hiram M. *The Day of the Bonanza: A History of Bonanza Farming in the Red River Valley of the North*. Minneapolis: Lund Press, 1964.

Du Bois, W. E. B. *Writings*. Edited by Nathan Huggins. New York: Library of America, 1986.

Emerson, Ralph Waldo. *The Essential Writings of Ralph Waldo Emerson*. Edited by Brooks Atkinson. New York: Modern Library, 2000.

Eperjesi, John R. *The Imperialist Imaginary: Visions of Asia and the Pacific in American Culture*. Hanover NH: University Press of New England, 2005.

Evans, David H. "'That Great Leviathan . . . Which Is but an Artificial Man': Moby-Dick and the Lowell Factory System." *ESQ: A Journal of the American Renaissance* 50, no. 4 (2004): 315–50.

Faulkner, Howard. "The Ambiguousnesses: Linguistic Invention in *Pierre*." *Leviathan: A Journal of Melville Studies* 12, no. 2 (June 2010): 41–50.

Fernandez-Armesto, Felipe. *Near a Thousand Tables*. New York: Free Press, 2004.

Fishkin, Shelley Fisher. *Lighting Out for the Territory: Reflections on Mark Twain and American Culture*. New York: Oxford University Press, 1997.

———. "Mark Twain and Race." In *A Historical Guide to Mark Twain*, edited by Shelley Fisher Fishkin, 127–62. New York: Oxford University Press, 2002.

———. *Was Huck Black? Mark Twain and African-American Voices*. New York: Oxford University Press, 1994.

Fite, Gilbert C. *American Farmers: The New Minority*. Bloomington: Indiana University Press, 1981.

Flammang, Janet A. *The Taste of Civilization: Food, Politics, and Civil Society*. Urbana: University of Illinois Press, 2009.

Foner, Eric. *Reconstruction: America's Unfinished Revolution, 1863–1877*. New York: Harper Perennial, 2002.

Foster, John T., Jr., and Sarah Whitmer Foster. *Beechers, Stowes, and Yankee Strangers: The Transformation of Florida.* Gainesville: University of Florida Press, 1999.

Frietag, Florian. "Naturalism in Its Natural Environment? American Naturalism and the Farm Novel." *Studies in American Naturalism* 4, no. 2 (Winter 2009): 97–118.

Fussel, Betty. *The Story of Corn.* New York: Knopf, 1994.

Gabaccia, Donna R. "As American as Budweiser and Pickles? Nation-Building in American Food Industries." In *Food Nations: Selling Taste in Consumer Societies,* edited by Warren Belasco and Philip Scranton, 175–93. New York: Routledge, 2002.

Gallagher, Noelle. "The Bagging Factory and the Breakfast Factory: Industrial Labor and Sentimentality in Harriet Beecher Stowe's *Uncle Tom's Cabin.*" *Nineteenth-Century Contexts* 27, no. 2 (June 2005): 167–87.

Garren, Samuel B. "Food for Thought: Bread and Cultural Critique in Thoreau's *Walden* and Orwell's *The Road to Wigan Pier.*" CLA *Journal* 50 (March 2007): 340–47.

Gigante, Denise. *Taste: A Literary History.* New Haven: Yale University Press, 2005.

Gilmore, Paul. "The Indian in the Museum: Henry David Thoreau, Okah Tubbee, and Authentic Manhood." *Arizona Quarterly* 54 (Summer 1998): 25–63.

Gollin, Rita K. "The Quondam Sailor and Melville's *Omoo.*" *American Literature* 48, no. 1 (March 1976): 75–79.

Goodrich, Samuel Griswold. *Recollections of a Lifetime, or Men and Things I Have Seen.* Vol. 1. New York: Miller, Orton and Mulligan, 1856.

Gross, Robert A. "Culture and Cultivation: Agriculture and Society in Thoreau's Concord." *Journal of American History* 69, no. 1 (June 1982): 42–61.

———. "The Great Bean Field Hoax: Thoreau and the Agricultural Reformers." *Virginia Quarterly Review* 61, no. 3 (Summer 1985): 483–97.

———. "'That Terrible Thoreau': Concord and Its Hermit." In *A Historical Guide to Henry David Thoreau,* edited by William E. Cain, 181–241. New York: Oxford University Press, 2000.

Hanley, Ryan Patrick. "Thoreau among His Heroes." *Philosophy and Literature* 25 (Spring 2001): 59–74.

Harding, Walter. *The Days of Henry Thoreau: A Biography.* Princeton NJ: Princeton University Press, 1962.

Hardt, Michael, and Antonio Negri. *Empire.* Cambridge MA: Harvard University Press, 2000.

———. *Multitude: War and Democracy in the Age of Empire.* New York: Penguin, 2004.

Hawthorne, Nathaniel. *The Blithedale Romance*. 1852. Reprinted with introduction by Arlin Turner. New York: W. W. Norton, 1958.

Hedrick, Joan. *Harriet Beecher Stowe: A Life*. New York: Oxford University Press, 1994.

Henkin, David M. *The Postal Age: The Emergence of Modern Communication in Nineteenth-Century America*. Chicago: University of Chicago Press, 2006.

Herbst, Philip H. *The Color of Words: An Encyclopaedic Dictionary of Ethnic Bias in the United States*. Yarmouth ME: Intercultural Press, 1997.

Hiltner, Ken. "Ripeness: Thoreau's Critique of Technological Modernity." *Concord Saunterer, Special Walden Sesquicentennial Issue* (2004): 323–38.

Horsman, Reginald. *Feast or Famine: Food and Drink in American Westward Expansion*. Columbia: University of Missouri Press, 2008.

———. *Race and Manifest Destiny: Origins of American Racial Anglo-Saxonism*. Cambridge MA: Harvard University Press, 1981.

Howard, Leon, and Hershel Parker. "Historical Note." In *Pierre, or The Ambiguities*, by Herman Melville. Edited by Harrison Hayford, Hershel Parker, and G. Thomas Tanselle. Evanston IL: Northwestern University Press, 1971.

Howells, William Dean. "Frank Norris." *North American Review* 175 (December 1902): 769–78.

Huang, Yunte. *Transpacific Imaginations: History, Literature, Counterpoetics*. Cambridge MA: Harvard University Press, 2008.

Hurt, R. Douglas. *American Agriculture: A Brief History*. Rev. ed. West Lafayette IN: Purdue University Press, 2002.

Inglis, David, and Debra Gimlin. *The Globalization of Food*. New York: Berg, 2009.

Jain, H. K. *The Green Revolution*. New Delhi: Studium Press, 2010.

Jefferson, Thomas. *Memoirs, Correspondence, and Miscellanies, from the Papers of Thomas Jefferson*, edited by Thomas Jefferson Randolph. Vol. 4, *The Writings of Thomas Jefferson*. 2nd ed. Boston: Gray and Bowen, 1830.

Jones, Gavin. *American Hungers: The Problem of Poverty in U.S. Literature, 1840–1945*. Princeton NJ: Princeton University Press, 2008.

Jung, Moon-Ho. *Coolies and Cane: Race, Labor, and Sugar in the Age of Emancipation*. Baltimore: Johns Hopkins University Press, 2006.

Kaplan, Amy. *The Anarchy of Empire in the Making of U.S. Culture*. Cambridge MA: Harvard University Press, 2002.

Kaplan, Fred. Introduction to *Following the Equator and Anti-Imperialist Essays*, by Mark Twain. New York: Oxford University Press, 1996.

Kaplan, Harold. "Naturalist Fiction and Political Allegory." In *American Naturalism*, edited by Harold Bloom. Philadelphia: Chelsea House, 2004.

Karcher, Carolyn N. "Stowe and the Literature of Social Change." In *The Cambridge Companion to Harriet Beecher Stowe,* edited by Cindy Weinstein, 203–18. Cambridge: Cambridge University Press, 2004.

Kelley, Oliver Hudson. *Origin and Progress of the Order of the Patrons of Husbandry in the United States: A History from 1866 to 1873.* Philadelphia: J. A. Wagenseller, 1875.

Kelley, Wyn. "*Pierre's* Domestic Ambiguities." In *The Cambridge Companion to Herman Melville,* edited by Robert S. Levine, 91–113. Cambridge: Cambridge University Press, 1998.

Kennedy, Stetson. *Southern Exposure: Making the South Safe for Democracy.* Tuscaloosa: University of Alabama Press, 1991.

Kilgour, Maggie. *From Communion to Cannibalism: An Anatomy of Metaphors of Incorporation.* Princeton NJ: Princeton University Press, 1990.

Kiple, Kenneth F., and Kriemhild Coneè Ornelas, eds. *Cambridge World History of Food.* 2 vols. New York: Cambridge University Press, 2000.

Kirkland, Caroline. *A New Home—Who'll Follow; or, Glimpses of Western Life.* 4th ed. New York: C. S. Francis, 1850.

Klein, Rachel Naomi. "Harriet Beecher Stowe and the Domestication of Free Labor Ideology." *Legacy: A Journal of American Women Writers* 18, no. 2 (2001): 135–52.

Korsmeyer, Carolyn. *Making Sense of Taste: Food and Philosophy.* Ithaca NY: Cornell University Press, 1999.

LaFeber, Walter. *The New Empire: An Interpretation of American Expansion 1860–1898.* Ithaca NY: Cornell University Press, 1963.

Lehan, Richard. "The European Background." In *The Cambridge Companion to American Realism and Naturalism: From Howells to London,* edited by Donald Pizer, 47–75. Cambridge: Cambridge University Press, 1995.

Levenstein, Harvey. *Revolution at the Table: The Transformation of the American Diet.* Berkeley: University of California Press, 2003.

Lewis, Nathaniel. *Unsettling the Literary West: Authenticity and Authorship.* Lincoln: University of Nebraska Press, 2003.

Leyda, Jay. *The Melville Log: A Documentary Life of Herman Melville 1819–1891.* Vol. 1. New York: Gordian Press, 1969.

Liliuokalani. *Hawaii's Story by Hawaii's Queen.* Rutland VT: Charles E. Tuttle, 1964.

Lincoln, Abraham. "Address before the Wisconsin State Agricultural Society." In *Harvest: An Anthology of Farm Writing,* edited by Wheeler McMillen. New York: Appleton-Century, 1964.

Lundblad, Michael. *The Birth of a Jungle: Animality in Progressive Era U.S. Literature and Culture.* New York: Oxford University Press, 2013.

Lye, Colleen. *America's Asia: Racial Forms and American Literature, 1893–1945*. Princeton NJ: Princeton University Press, 2004.

Magdol, Edward. *A Right to the Land: Essays on the Freedmen's Community*. Westport CT: Greenwood Press, 1977.

Marut, David. "Sam Lewiston's Bad Timing: A Note on the Economic Context of 'A Deal in Wheat.'" *American Literary Realism, 1870–1910* 27, no. 1 (Fall 1994): 74–80.

Marx, Leo. *The Machine in the Garden: Technology and the Pastoral Ideal in America*. New York: Oxford University Press, 1964.

Matheson, Neill. "Thoreau's Inner Animal." *Arizona Quarterly: A Journal of American Literature, Culture, and Theory* 67, no. 4 (Winter 2011): 1–26.

McElrath, Joseph R., Jr., and Gwendolyn Jones. Introduction to *The Pit: A Story of Chicago*, by Frank Norris. New York: Penguin Classics, 1994.

McElrath, Joseph R., Jr., and Jesse S. Crisler. *Frank Norris: A Life*. Urbana: University of Illinois Press, 2006.

McHugh, Susan. "Flora, Not Fauna: G M Culture and Agriculture." *Literature and Medicine* 26, no. 1 (Spring 2007): 25–54.

McKibben, Bill. *Deep Economy: The Wealth of Communities and the Durable Future*. Oxford: Oneworld, 2007.

McPhee, John. *Oranges*. New York: Farrar, Straus and Giroux, 1967.

Melton, Jeffrey Alan. *Mark Twain, Travel Books, and Tourism: The Tide of a Great Popular Movement*. Tuscaloosa: University of Alabama Press, 2002.

Melvill, Jr., Thomas. *Address of Thomas Melvill, Jun. Esq. Delivered before the Berkshire Society for the Promotion of Agriculture and Manufactures*. Pittsfield MA: Phineas Allen, 1815.

Melville, Herman. *Correspondence*. Edited by Harrison Hayford, Hershel Parker, and G. Thomas Tanselle. Evanston IL: Northwestern University Press and Newberry Library, 1993.

———. *Moby-Dick, or The White Whale*. 1851. Reprint edited by Harrison Hayford, Hershel Parker, and G. Thomas Tanselle. Evanston IL: Northwestern University Press and Newberry Library, 1988.

———. *Omoo: A Narrative of Adventures in the South Seas*. 1847. Reprint edited by Harrison Hayford, Hershel Parker, and G. Thomas Tanselle. Evanston IL: Northwestern University Press and Newberry Library, 1968.

———. *The Piazza Tales and Other Prose Pieces 1839–1860*. Edited by Harrison Hayford, Alma A. MacDougal, and G. Thomas Tanselle. Evanston IL: Northwestern University Press and Newberry Library, 1987.

———. *Pierre; or, The Ambiguities*. 1852. Reprint edited by Harrison Hayford, Hershel Parker, and G. Thomas Tanselle. Evanston IL: Northwestern University Press and Newberry Library, 1971.

———. "The Rose Farmer." In *American Poetry: The Nineteenth Century*. Vol. 2, *Herman Melville to Stickney; American Indian Poetry; Folk Songs and Spirituals*, edited by John Hollander. New York: Library of America, 1993.

———. *Typee: A Peep at Polynesian Life*. 1845. Reprint edited by Harrison Hayford, Hershel Parker, and G. Thomas Tanselle. Evanston IL: Northwestern University Press, 1968.

Mintz, Sidney. *Sweetness and Power: The Place of Sugar in Modern History*. New York: Penguin, 1985.

Morton, Timothy. *The Poetics of Spice: Romantic Consumerism and the Exotic*. New York: Cambridge University Press, 2000.

Naranjo-Huebl, Linda. "'Take, Eat': Food Imagery, the Nurturing Ethic, and Christian Identity in *The Wide, Wide World, Uncle Tom's Cabin*, and *Incidents in the Life of a Slave Girl*." *Christianity and Literature* 56, no. 4 (Summer 2007): 597–631.

Newman, Lance. *Our Common Dwelling: Henry Thoreau, Transcendentalism, and the Class Politics of Nature*. New York: Palgrave Macmillan, 2005.

Newspaper clipping, "Sinks to Death in a Grain Pit." November 6, [1899]. Frank Norris Collection. Bancroft Library. University of California–Berkeley.

Norris, Frank. "Comida: An Experience in Famine." *Atlantic Monthly* 83 (March 1899): 343–48.

———. "A Deal in Wheat." In *A Deal in Wheat and Other Stories of the New and Old West*. New York: Doubleday, Page, 1903.

———. "The Frontier Gone at Last." In *Novels and Essays*, 1183–90. New York: Library of America, 1986.

———. *The Octopus: A Story of California*. 2 vols. Garden City NY: Doubleday, 1901.

———. *The Pit: A Story of Chicago*. New York: Doubleday, Page, 1903.

Osterhammel, Jürgen, and Neils P. Peterson. *Globalization: A Short History*. Translated by Dona Geyer. Princeton NJ: Princeton University Press, 2005.

Otter, Samuel. *Melville's Anatomies*. Berkeley: University of California Press, 1999.

Ozeki, Ruth. *All Over Creation*. New York: Viking, 2003.

Parker, Hershel. *Herman Melville: A Biography. Vol. 1, 1819–1851*. Baltimore: Johns Hopkins University Press, 1996.

Phillips, Sarah T. "Antebellum Agricultural Reform, Republican Ideology, and Sectional Tension." *Agricultural History* 74, no. 4 (Autumn 2000): 799–822.

Pizer, Donald. *American Naturalism and the Jews: Garland, Norris, Dreiser, Wharton, and Cather*. Urbana: University of Illinois Press, 2008.

———. "The Concept of Nature in Frank Norris' 'The Octopus.'" *American Quarterly* 14, no. 1 (Spring 1962): 73–80.

———. *The Novels of Frank Norris*. Bloomington: Indiana University Press, 1966.

Pollan, Michael. *Omnivore's Dilemma*. New York: Penguin, 2006.

Pryse, Marjorie. "Harriet Beecher Stowe and Regionalism." In *The Cambridge Companion to Harriet Beecher Stowe*, edited by Cindy Weinstein, 131–53. Cambridge: Cambridge University Press, 2004.

Range, Henry B., Jr. "The Freedmen's Bureau in Florida during the Early Reconstruction Period 1865–1870." Dissertation, Union Institute and University, 2002.

Rasmussen, Wayne D., ed. *Readings in the History of American Agriculture*. Urbana: University of Illinois Press, 1960.

Roberts, Diane. "Harriet Beecher Stowe and Florida Tourism." In *Literary Tourism and Nineteenth Century Culture*, edited by Nicola J. Watson, 196–209. New York: Palgrave Macmillan, 2009.

Robertson-Lorant, Laurie. *Melville: A Biography*. New York: Clarkson Potter, 1996.

Robinson, David M. "'Unchronicled Nations': Agrarian Purpose and Thoreau's Ecological Knowing." *Nineteenth-Century Literature* 48, no. 3 (December 1993): 326–40.

Robinson, Forrest. "Dreaming Better Dreams: The Late Writing of Mark Twain." In *A Companion to Mark Twain*, edited by Peter Messent and Louis J. Budd, 449–66. Malden MA: Blackwell Publishing, 2005.

Robinson, Kenneth Allen. *Thoreau and the Wild Appetite*. New York: AMS Press, 1985.

Root, Waverly Lewis, and Richard de Rochemont. *Eating in America: A History*. New York: William Morrow, 1976.

Rose, Suzanne D. "Following the Trail of Footsteps: From the Indian Notebooks to *Walden*." *New England Quarterly* 67 (March 1994): 77–99.

Rowe, John Carlos. "Mark Twain's Critique of Globalization (Old and New) in *Following the Equator, A Journey around the World* (1897)." *Arizona Quarterly* 61, no. 1 (Spring 2005), 109–135.

Sarver, Stephanie. *Uneven Land: Nature and Agriculture in American Writing*. Lincoln: University of Nebraska Press, 1999.

Sayre, Robert F. *Thoreau and the American Indians*. Princeton, NJ: Princeton University Press, 1977.

Schafer, Joseph. *The Social History of American Agriculture*. New York: Macmillan, 1936.

Schmidt, Louis Bernard. "Growth of Home and Foreign Markets." In *Readings in the Economic History of American Agriculture*, edited by Louis Bernard Schmidt and Earle Dudley Ross, 197–234. New York: Macmillan, 1925.

Sellers, Charles. *The Market Revolution: Jacksonian America 1815–1846*. New York: Oxford University Press, 1991.

Shiva, Vandana. "The Green Revolution in the Punjab." *Ecologist* 21, no. 2 (March/April 1991): 57–60.

Sizer, Lyde Cullen. *The Political Work of Northern Women Writers and the Civil War, 1850–1872.* Chapel Hill: University of North Carolina Press, 2000.

Sklar, Kathryn Kish. *Catharine Beecher: A Study in American Domesticity.* New Haven CT: Yale University Press, 1973.

Smith, Andrew F., ed. *Oxford Companion to American Food and Drink.* New York: Oxford University Press, 2007.

Standage, Tom. *The Victorian Internet: The Remarkable Story of the Telegraph and the Nineteenth Century's On-line Pioneers.* New York: Walker, 1998.

Starr, Kevin. Introduction to *The Octopus: A Story of California,* by Frank Norris. New York: Penguin Classics, 1994.

Steger, Manfred B. *Globalism: Market Ideology Meets Terrorism.* 2nd ed. Lanham MD: Rowman & Littlefield, 2005.

Stowe, Charles Edward, and Lyman Beecher Stowe. *Harriet Beecher Stowe: The Story of Her Life.* Boston: Houghton Mifflin, 1911.

Stowe, Harriet Beecher. *The Annotated Uncle Tom's Cabin.* 1852. Reprint edited by Henry Louis Gates Jr. and Hollis Robbins. New York: W. W. Norton, 2007.

—— [Christopher Crowfield, pseud.]. *House and Home Papers.* Boston: Ticknor and Fields, 1865.

——. *Oldtown Folks.* 1869. Reprint, New Brunswick NJ: Rutgers University Press, 1987.

——. "Our Florida Plantation." *Atlantic Monthly* 43, no. 259 (May 1879): 641–49.

——. *Palmetto Leaves.* 1873. Reprinted with introduction by Mary B. Graff and Edith Cowles. Gainesville: University of Florida Press, 1999.

Streeby, Shelley. *American Sensations: Class, Empire, and the Production of Popular Culture.* Berkeley: University of California Press, 2002.

Stuart, Tristram. *The Bloodless Revolution.* New York: W. W. Norton, 2007.

Summerhill, Thomas. *Harvest of Dissent: Agrarianism in Nineteenth-Century New York.* Urbana: University of Illinois Press, 2005.

Tang, Edward. "Making Declarations of Her Own: Harriet Beecher Stowe as New England Historian." *New England Quarterly* 71, no. 1 (March 1998): 77–96.

Thompson, Graham. "The 'Plain Facts' of Fine Paper in 'The Paradise of Bachelors and the Tartarus of Maids.'" *American Literature* 84, no. 3 (September 2012): 505–32.

Thoreau, Henry D. *The Correspondence of Henry David Thoreau.* Edited by Walter Harding and Carl Bode. New York: New York University Press, 1958.

——. *Excursions.* Edited by Joseph J. Moldenhauer. Princeton NJ: Princeton University Press, 2007.

———. *Henry David Thoreau: Collected Essays and Poems*. Compiled by Elizabeth Hall Witherell. New York: Library of America, 2001.

———. *Journal 4: 1851–1852*. Edited by Leonard N. Neufeldt and Nancy Craig Simmons. Princeton, NJ: Princeton University Press, 1992.

———. *The Journal of Henry David Thoreau*. Vol. 8, *November 1, 1855–August 15, 1856*. Edited by Bradford Torrey. Boston: Houghton Mifflin, 1906.

———. *The Journal of Henry David Thoreau*. Vol. 10, *August 8, 1857–June 29, 1858*. Edited by Bradford Torrey. Boston: Houghton Mifflin, 1906.

———. *Walden*. 1854. Reprint edited by J. Lyndon Shanley. Princeton NJ: Princeton University Press, 1971.

———. *Wild Fruits*. Edited by Bradley Dean. New York: W. W. Norton, 2000.

Thulesius, Olav. *Harriet Beecher Stowe in Florida, 1867 to 1884*. Jefferson NC: McFarland, 2001.

Tichi, Cecilia. "Domesticity on Walden Pond." In *A Historical Guide to Henry David Thoreau*, edited by William E. Cain, 95–121. New York: Oxford University Press, 2000.

Tompkins, Jane P. *Sensational Designs: The Cultural Work of American Fiction, 1790–1860*. New York: Oxford University Press, 1986.

Tsing, Anna Lowenhaupt. *Friction*. Princeton NJ: Princeton University Press, 2005.

Twain, Mark. *Adventures of Huckleberry Finn*. 1884. Reprinted with introduction by Toni Morrison. New York: Oxford University Press, 1996.

———. *The Adventures of Tom Sawyer*. 1876. Reprinted with introduction by E. L. Doctorow. New York: Oxford University Press, 1996.

———. *The Autobiography of Mark Twain*. Vol. 1. Edited by Harriet Elinor Smith. Berkeley: University of California Press, 2010.

———. *Following the Equator and Anti-Imperialist Essays*. 1897. Reprinted with introduction by Gore Vidal. New York: Oxford University Press, 1996.

———. "Hawaiian Story." January 1884. Mark Twain Papers. Bancroft Library. University of California–Berkeley.

———. *Life on the Mississippi*. 1883. Reprinted with introduction by Willie Morris. New York: Oxford University Press, 1996.

———. *Mark Twain's Letters from Hawaii*. Edited by A. Grove Day. Honolulu: University Press of Hawaii, 1966.

———. *Mark Twain's Weapons of Satire: Anti-Imperialist Writings on the Philippine-American War*. Edited by Jim Zwick. Syracuse NY: Syracuse University Press, 1992.

Van Kampen, Doris, and Carol Ann Moon. "The Power of the Pen: The 'Invitation Letters' to Florida and Their Writers." In *Florida Studies: Proceedings of the 2008*

Annual Meeting of the Florida College English Association, edited by Claudia Slate and April Van Camp. Newcastle upon Tyne: Cambridge Scholars, 2009.

Wagenknecht, Edward. *John Greenleaf Whittier: A Portrait in Paradox*. New York: Oxford University Press, 1967.

Wagner, Frederick. "Dining Out with Henry Thoreau: A Field Guide to Food Wild, Cultivated, and Transcendental." *Thoreau Society Bulletin* 175 (April 1986): 1–4.

Warman, Arturo. *Corn and Capitalism: How a Botanical Bastard Grew to Global Domination*. Chapel Hill: University of North Carolina Press, 2003.

Washington, George. "The President Recommends Creation of a National Board of Agriculture." In McMillen, *Harvest: An Anthology of Farm Writing*, 41–42.

Waters, Malcolm. *Globalization*. London: Routledge, 1995.

Watson, Elkanah. *Address of Elkanah Watson, Esq. Delivered before the Berkshire Agricultural Society . . .* Pittsfield MA: Phineas Allen, 1814.

———. *Mr. Watson's Address, Delivered to the Members of the Berkshire Agricultural Society . . .* Pittsfield MA: Phineas Allen, 1811.

Weinstein, Cindy. *The Literature of Labor and the Labors of Literature: Allegory in Nineteenth-Century American Fiction*. New York: Cambridge University Press, 1995.

———. "Melville, Labor, and the Discourses of Reception." In *The Cambridge Companion to Herman Melville*, edited by Robert S. Levine, 202–23. Cambridge: Cambridge University Press, 1998.

Williams, Raymond. *The Country and the City*. New York: Oxford University Press, 1973.

Williams, Roger L. *The Origins of Federal Support for Higher Education: George W. Atherton and the Land-Grant College Movement*. University Park: Pennsylvania State University Press, 1991.

Wilson, Rob. "Exporting Christian Transcendentalism, Importing Hawaiian Sugar: The Trans-Americanization of Hawai'i." *American Literature* 72, no. 3 (September 2000): 521–52.

Winter, Aaron. "Seeds of Discontent: The Expanding Satiric Range of Melville's Transatlantic Diptychs." *Leviathan: A Journal of Melville Studies* 8, no. 2 (2006): 17–35.

Woodward, C. Vann. *The Strange Career of Jim Crow*. New York: Oxford University Press, 1974.

Zwick, Jim. Introduction to *Mark Twain's Weapons of Satire: Anti-Imperialist Writings on the Philippine-American War*, by Mark Twain. Edited by Jim Zwick. Syracuse NY: Syracuse University Press, 1992.

———. "Mark Twain and Imperialism." In *A Historical Guide to Mark Twain*, edited by Shirley Fisher Fishkin, 227–55. New York: Oxford University Press, 2002.

INDEX

abolitionism, 105; Stowe and, 106, 108, 136; in *Uncle Tom's Cabin*, 111, 113, 115, 137–38

Adams, John, 226n4

Adams, John Quincy, 226n4

The Adventures of Huckleberry Finn (Twain), 19, 140, 240n1

The Adventures of Tom Sawyer (Twain), 139–40

African Americans, 226n10; and orange growing, 103, 121–22; and Radical Reconstruction, 122, 128, 238n47; Stowe and, 126–28, 136, 238n44; and sugar plantations, 145. *See also* slavery

agricultural reform, 3; Melville and, 30, 31–35; nineteenth-century movements for, 14–19; Stowe efforts for, 105, 109, 119; Thoreau efforts for, 79–80, 83–84, 92; Watson and Colman efforts for, 10–12

agricultural societies, 34–35, 71; Berkshire, 30–31, 33; Otsego County, 47

agricultural technology, 10, 82–83, 105, 110, 236n9

agriculture: communal, 38–39, 92–93, 100, 216; cultural significance of, 3; education and, 181–82; Emerson on, 13, 228n34; and exploitation of farmers, 8, 28, 202–3; idealized representations of, 7–8; and industrialization, 4, 8, 14, 83; Lincoln on, 14; and literature, 4, 18, 25, 35–36; livestock husbandry, 11, 42; modern expansion of, 211–12; nineteenth-century revolutionizing of, 15, 69–70; as Norris motif, 183, 189, 198, 246n42; organic farming, 3, 218–19; in Polynesia, 40–41; scientific, 212; tenant farming, 36, 46, 49, 52; as term, 4; Thoreau view of, 68, 69, 82, 83–84; and U.S. global expansion, 9–10, 41, 65, 147, 151–52; Washington on, 1; and westward expansion, 9, 69–70, 227n19; women and, 49. *See also* oranges; sugar; wheat

agri-expansion: beginnings of, 12; and diet, 68, 89; global, 5, 146, 173, 177–78, 217–18; Hawaii as example of, 151; imperialism's

186, 187, 191, 198, 207–8, 209;
Thoreau on, 83, 100, 234n35
Carlstroem, Catherine, 243n53
cattle, 33–34, 42–43, 49, 80
"The Celebrated Jumping Frog of
Calaveras County" (Twain), 157
Center for Development Alternatives
(UBINIG), 217
Channing, William Ellery, 72
Chicago IL, 200, 201
Child, Lydia Maria, 16–17
Chinese: in California, 160, 242n38;
as "coolies," 24, 147–48, 151,
153–61, 240n5, 241n25; and immi-
gration, 155–56
Chinese exclusion laws, 156
Christian Union, 107, 238n38
citrus fruit, 108, 236n21. *See also*
oranges
Civil War, 12, 15, 30, 150
Clemens, Samuel. *See* Twain, Mark
Colman, Henry, 10–12, 69, 70;
*Fourth Report on the Agriculture
of Massachusetts*, 70–71; Thoreau
debate with, 79, 80, 83, 84
communal ownership and harvesting, 92–93, 100, 216
Concord grape, 71
Concord MA, 80, 93
Conlogue, William, 181, 226n6
conspicuous consumption, 93–94
"coolie" labor: British employment of,
148; brutality toward, 163, 243n45;
definition of, 240n5; in Hawaii,
154–55; recruitment of, 162,
164–65, 166, 167; and slavery, 142,
148–49, 155, 156, 158–59, 164–65,
242n34, 242n36; sugar industry
use of, 142, 143, 146, 148–49,

164–66; trade in, 24, 164–65;
Twain call for importation of,
147–48, 151, 154–55, 241n25;
Twain opposition to, 162, 163–64
Cooper, Robert, 243n47, 243n49
corn, 80; as cash crop, 81, 233n31;
Melville on production of, 34–35
Crisler, Jesse S., 244n17
Cuba: monument to Twain in, 174;
Norris on, 182, 244nn13–14; and
sugar, 149, 170
cuisines. *See* diet and cuisines

dairy industry, 49, 212
D'Amore, Maura, 228n48
"A Deal in Wheat" (Norris), 24,
184–85
Department of Agriculture, 228n40
de Rochemont, Richard, 9, 151
Derrida, Jacques, 101
Dickens, Charles, 116
Diedrich, Maria I., 238n44
diet and cuisines: agri-expansion and,
68, 89; of Borneo Meratus, 216;
Bourdieu on, 105; economy and,
82; European, 112, 117–18, 133–34;
meat-based, 77, 80, 89; regional
foods, 23, 103–4, 108, 110, 111, 131,
132–33; Stowe on, 111–12, 116–19,
133–34, 138; Thoreau project to
reform, 22, 68, 70, 76, 78, 85–86,
91, 92; Thoreau's diet, 74–77, 88;
U.S., 111–12, 116–19, 133–34, 138,
234n45, 237n28
Dolan, Patrick, 195
Du Bois, W. E. B., 149, 155, 175,
241n21
durian fruit, 215–16
Duyckinck, Evert, 27, 36

Minott, George, 72–73
Mintz, Sidney, 142, 143, 145
missionaries, 165
Missouri Compromise of 1820, 105
Moby-Dick (Melville), 65, 66, 229n1
Moon, Carol Ann, 238n43
Morrill Acts, 15–16, 181
Morse, Samuel, 227n25
Mussel Slough Tragedy, 188–89

National Grange of the Order of
    Patrons of Husbandry. *See* Grange
    movement
Native Americans, 26n10, 75; foods
    of, 81, 98; Melville depiction of,
    48, 231n39
naturalism, 231n46; literary, 183,
    245n19; Norris and, 189–90, 191,
    209
Negri, Antonio, 6, 226n9
New Farming Movement, 217–19
New Home—Who'll Follow (Kirk-
    land), 8
Newman, Lance, 235n54
New York Herald, 140
Nickerson, Margaret, 128
Norris, Frank, 19, 24–25, 176–209;
    agriculture as motif in, 183, 189,
    198, 246n42; on agri-expansion,
    177–78, 187, 191–92, 198, 209;
    background and career of, 182;
    on capitalism, 24, 178, 186, 187,
    191, 198, 207–8, 209; on Cuba,
    182, 244nn13–14; depiction
    of railroads by, 187–90, 192,
    198, 245n36; on globalization,
    25, 177–78, 182, 186–87, 191;
    on imperialism, 208, 209; and
    naturalism, 189–90, 191, 209; as

news correspondent, 182, 245n30;
    ranch purchased by, 208–9; on
    speculation in wheat, 185, 186,
    199–208; on sustainability, 191,
    198; works: "A Deal in Wheat,"
    24, 184–85; "The Frontier Gone
    at Last," 182; *The Octopus*, 24–25,
    176, 177, 183, 186, 187–99, 209,
    245n31, 245nn33–34, 246n40; *The
    Pit*, 25, 176, 177, 185, 186, 199–208,
    209, 246n47, 247n49; *The Wolf*
    (uncompleted), 177, 209, 247n55
Notes on the State of Virginia (Jef-
    ferson), 2

The Octopus (Norris), 24–25, 176,
    177, 183, 186, 187–99, 209, 245n31,
    246n40; railroads in, 187–90,
    192, 198, 245n36; starvation of
    workers in, 193, 245n35; wheat as
    character in, 195–96, 197
Oldtown Folks (Stowe), 23, 103, 106,
    130–37, 138, 239n56, 239n62; on
    regional foods, 134–35; on sharing
    of food, 136–37; Thanksgiving
    Day scene in, 104, 119–20, 239n63
Omoo (Melville), 36–37, 40–43, 159
oranges, 111–14, 240n4; African Amer-
    icans and, 103, 121–22; and apples,
    109; Greeks and, 108–9; in modern
    day, 211–12; in *Palmetto Leaves*, 23,
    103, 104, 106, 119, 120, 121–22; and
    slavery, 103, 113–14; South associa-
    tion with, 103, 108; Stowe growing
    of, 113, 120–21, 123, 125, 129–30,
    237n34, 238n43, 239n53; in *Uncle
    Tom's Cabin*, 23, 102–3, 106, 110–11,
    112–15, 119, 235–36n2
Oranges (McPhee), 213

Stowe, Harriet Beecher (*cont.*)
104, 106, 119–20, 130–37, 138,
239n56, 239nn62–63; *Palmetto
Leaves*, 23, 103, 104, 106, 107,
109, 119, 120–30, 138; *Uncle Tom's
Cabin*, 19, 23, 102–3, 104, 106,
110–16, 119, 137, 235–36nn1–2,
237n26
Stowe, Lyman, 111, 237n34
sugar: "coolie" labor used in, 142, 143,
146, 148–49, 164–66; Cuba and,
149, 170; *Following the Equator*
on, 161–73; and globalization,
147, 151–52, 153–61, 171; global
trade in, 141, 142–43, 147–48, 152,
164, 167, 170; growth in production of, 142–43, 211; Hawaii
production of, 150, 151–52, 153,
154, 170; imperialism and, 141–
42; labor used in production of,
144–46; "Letter 23" of Twain on,
153–61; in Louisiana, 140, 153, 155;
maple, 139–40, 144; Mauritius
and, 171; and slavery, 142, 150,
242n33; as Twain theme, 23–24,
139–41
sustainability, 213–14, 215, 217, 221;
Melville on, 35, 56, 230n26; Norris
on, 191, 198; Thoreau on, 68, 69,
78, 79, 83, 93, 94, 99, 233n28

Tang, Edward, 239n56
telegraph, 10, 181, 227n25
tenant farmers, 36, 46, 49, 52
La Terre (Zola), 183
Thanksgiving: as national holiday,
131, 239n61; Stowe idealization of,
119, 131–33, 135–36, 239nn62–63
Therien, Alek, 234n40

Thompson, Graham, 232n51
Thoreau, Henry David, 67–101;
agrarian goals of, 22, 69, 83, 101;
agricultural experiments of, 22,
72, 75–76, 78, 79; on agricultural
implements, 82–83; on agricultural reform, 79–80, 83–84, 92;
agri-expansion challenged by, 22,
69, 75, 80, 81, 83, 84, 91, 92–93,
98–99, 100, 110; on alternative consumption practices, 86,
234n40; asceticism of, 68–69; on
commercialization and capitalism, 83, 96–97, 99–100, 234n35;
communalist perspective of, 92–
93, 235n54; dietary reform project
of, 22, 68, 70, 76, 78, 85–86, 91,
92; diet of, 74–77, 88; family of,
73–74; influence of, 19, 77; local
foods privileged by, 22, 68, 69,
70, 74, 78, 84, 85, 94, 97; Minott
as mentor and guide for, 72–73;
simplicity privileged by, 68, 69,
79–80, 83, 85, 90–91; on sustainability, 68, 69, 78, 79, 83, 93, 94,
99, 233n28; vegetarianism of, 68,
70, 75–77, 87, 234n47; works:
"Resistance to Civil Government," 90; *Walden*, 22, 68, 76, 78,
79–92, 233n29, 234n35; "Walking," 75, 235n52; *A Week on the
Concord and Merrimack Rivers*,
35, 78; *Wild Fruits*, 22, 67–68, 78,
91–100, 235n54
Thoreau, John, 73, 232n4
Thulesius, Olav, 237n33, 238–39n51,
238n37
Tichi, Cecilia, 77
Tolstoy, Leo, 19